# THE RICHEST MAN IN THE WORLD

## THE STORY OF ADNAN KHASHOGGI

## RONALD KESSLER

WARNER BOOKS

A Warner Communications Company

Ⓦ  Warner Books, Inc., 666 Fifth Avenue, New York, NY 10103


Printed in the United States of America
First Printing: June 1986
10  9  8  7  6  5  4  3  2  1

**Library of Congress Cataloging-in-Publication Data**

Kessler, Ronald.
    The richest man in the world.


    Bibliography: p.
    Includes index.
    1. Khashoggi, Adnan.    2. Millionaires—Saudi Arabia—
Biography.    I. Title.
HG172.K48K47    1986        332′.092′4        85-41002
ISBN 0-446-51339-3

Book design: H. Roberts

# THE RICHEST MAN IN THE WORLD

## THE STORY OF ADNAN KHASHOGGI

### RONALD KESSLER

*For my mother and father*

# ACKNOWLEDGMENTS

Bernard Shir-Cliff, editor in chief of Warner Books, provided brilliant direction throughout the preparation of this book. His is a singular example of how an editor can enhance writing and reporting without being intrusive.

Julian Bach, my agent, provided encouragement and helpful pointers from the preparation of the book proposal to the final manuscript.

Many people offered to help during my projected travels with Khashoggi by critiquing the food, taking photographs, or carrying my baggage. In the end, my wife, Pamela Kessler, got to attend his fiftieth birthday party in Spain and added her observations and insights to mine, as she did throughout the reporting and writing of the book.

She and my children, Greg and Rachel Kessler, and my stepson, Mike Whitehead, provided emotional support without which I could not have written this book.

To them, to my editor and agent, and to the people who gave of their time in interviews, I give my thanks.

The events and dialogue presented in this book are based on the recollections of one or more of the participants, or on contemporaneous memos, letters, telexes, or transcripts of tape recordings. The reader is encouraged to refer to the Author's Note beginning on page 259 for a more detailed description of the sources for this book.

# CONTENTS

# THE RICHEST MAN IN THE WORLD

## THE STORY OF ADNAN KHASHOGGI

### RONALD KESSLER

# Fiesta at "La Baraka"

"Slave of the lamp," Aladdin said. "I am hungry. Bring me some good things to eat."

The jinni vanished and reappeared in a twinkling, carrying upon his head a priceless tray of virgin silver which held 12 dishes of the choicest meats, together with a pair of silver goblets, two flasks of clear old wine, and bread whiter than snow.

—*Aladdin and the Enchanted Lamp*

FOR five days, the guests had been landing at the small airport on Spain's Costa del Sol. Brooke Shields, Sean Connery, Shirley Bassey, Philippe Junot of Monaco—four hundred guests in all, coming for the fiftieth birthday party of the richest man in the world.

Assigned full-time to the airport, Alex Sardon and his assistant whisked them into limousines or taxis to hotels in Marbella, a sun-drenched Mediterranean beach town that provides an alternative to Nice and Cannes for the very wealthy.

There, they waited for the evening of July 24, 1985—by the pool, refreshing their tans alongside topless girls from Sweden and France, or on the hotel terrace, stuffing themselves with buffet lunches of smoked Scottish salmon, chilled lobsters, grilled prawns, shrimp-filled avocados, fried squid, paella, and chocolate éclairs laced with chocolate cream.

Soon, the streets and phone system in the tiny resort became paralyzed as guests visited among themselves and called home to let everyone know they had received the most coveted invitation since the coronation of Louis XIV. Their host was Adnan Mohamed Khashoggi, a Saudi Arabian middleman who had made more money more quickly than anyone in history—a man whose wealth was rivaled only by his genius at dealing with people and his obsessive need to spend.

Two months before, 1,472 newspapers ran stories saying the party would take place at a New York restaurant and would cost $750,000. Doug Henning, the magician, was to produce a cake out of thin air and float it to Khashoggi's table.

But Robert A. Shaheen, Khashoggi's executive assistant, decided New York could not hold four hundred guests at the best hotels on such short notice. So he chose instead Marbella, where Khashoggi has a sprawling ranch high on a hill overlooking the sea.

It's just one of his twelve homes: Khashoggi also maintains residences in Paris, Cannes, Kenya, the Canary Islands, Madrid, Rome, Jeddah, Riyadh, Beirut, Monte Carlo, and New York.

Each of the homes is fully staffed at all times in case "AK," as he is known to friends and associates, should drop by. Each home has a ten-foot-wide bed for him. And each has a swimming pool, even the Manhattan apartment that consists of two floors of the Olympic Tower and is valued at $25 million.

But the Marbella home, situated on five thousand rolling acres, is the biggest, with its own discotheque, bowling alley, rifle range, and dry cleaner, not to mention twenty Arabian stallions and two hundred African animals, including a puma. And the villa is only a two-minute ride on Khashoggi's helicopter to the *Nabila*, one of his two yachts.

In Puerto Banus, the Marbella port where Khashoggi had a special berth built for the boat, the 282-foot *Nabila* is a dazzling sight. A third the size of the luxury liner *United States*, the boat is considered by Time-Life Books to be the "most opulent modern yacht afloat." Borrowed by Hollywood for the James Bond movie *Never Say Never Again*, it was designed and built in Italy and came complete with its own speedboats and helicopter at a cost of $70 million.

With chamois-leather ceilings and walls, the *Nabila* has the requisite swimming pool, surrounded by lounges that rise into the air for better tanning, plus a discotheque, a sauna, a fully equipped operating room, a movie theater, a helipad, a communications room for placing calls to anywhere in the world, and a forty-member crew.

Frequently, it is bedecked with stunning young women as well, their favors sometimes paid for like the Dom Pérignon champagne and beluga caviar constantly ferried to the boat by helicopter.

It is an afternoon's preoccupation for local tourists to come down to the port and there to walk past the shops and Americanized bars, past the ice-cream stands and luxury apartments, and then to trudge along the seawall, like lemmings drawn to the sea, for a closer look at the yacht, moored handsomely broadside to the harbor.

Those who come to Marbella not knowing who owns the gleaming white yacht soon find out. They stop and ask at any sailboat that looks like its deckhands might speak their language. And so one hears in every tongue, "Whose boat?"

But tourists who get too close encounter one of ten security guards stationed around the yacht, augmented by men monitoring video cameras inside and out and boats patrolling the nearby waters—all linked by walkie-talkies. While their language may sound strange, their tense tone of voice conveys the message, so tourists stay clear of the red carpet that leads to the yacht.

Occasionally, the tourists' vigilance is rewarded when Khashoggi rides by. While they swelter under the hot sun, he is cool in a tan suit as he sits regally behind the parted curtains in the backseat of his silver Mercedes 600 limousine.

Day and night, limousines drop chiefs of state and heads of Fortune 500 companies and movie stars at the boat, and there is the chop-chop-chop of the helicopter shuttling them to and from one of Khashoggi's three commercial-size airplanes.

Each of the planes is fully staffed at all times with American pilots, ready to take off on less than an hour's notice to anywhere in the world. Each plane is custom-fitted with gold-plated faucets and gold-plated seat belts, a separate bedroom for Khashoggi, and lounges that put *Air Force One* to shame.

Khashoggi's latest, a $31-million DC-8, sat at the Málaga airport near Marbella, the "III" insignia of his company, Triad, visible on the tail. As long as a jumbo jet and as wide as a Boeing 727—which Khashoggi also owns—the DC-8 can cruise for fifteen hours without refueling. It has a complete kitchen, a custom-made $600,000 set of triangular chinaware with silverware trimmed in gold, and meeting rooms that look like a set from *Star Wars.*

Khashoggi delights in showing visitors an electronic map that displays the plane's location as it flies over the globe.

So that Khashoggi never has to bother with luggage, the planes, as well as the homes and yachts, have a complete wardrobe of Cifonelli suits and custom-made Sulka shirts.

In the homes, on the planes, or on the yachts, Khashoggi throws parties attended by movie stars and heads of state: Farrah Fawcett, Raquel Welch, Christopher Reeve, Frank Sinatra, King Juan Carlos of Spain, King Constantine of Greece, Christie Brinkley, Morgan Fairchild, Cheryl Tiegs, Sammy Davis, Jr., Jane Seymour, Roger Moore.

But Khashoggi's hobnobbing with the glamorous and powerful goes beyond entertaining them. In the two months preceding the birthday party, he flew to see eleven chiefs of state as part of secret Middle East peace negotiations. Then, taking along a bearded Moslem holy man for good luck, he flew to Geneva a week after the birthday party on a secret mission for King Fahd of Saudi Arabia.

The way others take the Eastern shuttle to Washington, he flew back to Spain the same day.

The DC-8's log looks like someone had thrown darts at a gazetteer. Two weeks' entries in May 1985 are not untypical. On the 20th, he flew from Jeddah to Madrid; on the 21st, from Madrid to Málaga, Spain; on the 22nd, from Málaga to London and then to Paris; on the 23rd, from Paris to Madrid and on to Cairo; on the 25th, from Cairo to Riyadh and then to Jeddah; on the 27th, from Jeddah to Nice and then to Rome; on the 28th, from Rome to Nice and then to Paris; on the 29th, from Paris to New York and then to Washington, D.C.; on the 30th, from Washington to St. Croix in the Virgin Islands.

If the pace is dizzying, Khashoggi has offices in thirty-eight countries to help with arrangements. Running the entire nation-state of planes, yachts, and homes, and overseeing Khashoggi's other affairs, is Shaheen, his executive assistant and right-hand man for twenty-five years. An American of Syrian descent, he has a high forehead and could pass for a college professor. Even when boarding the *Nabila* from one of its tenders, he always manages to wear a white starched shirt and expensive suit pressed as perfectly as Plexiglas.

Just before the birthday party, he checked into a two-bedroom suite at the Puente Romano Hotel. With Regine's nightclub on a lower level and cannas, roses, and lavender all around, the Spanish-style hotel is Marbella's poshest, its swimming pools tucked into a village of connecting white stucco buildings with clay tile roofs.

When he wasn't reading messages to Khashoggi while his boss jumped on a trampoline, Shaheen was sitting on a white wicker sofa on the white marble floor of his suite at the hotel, a white telephone receiver sprouting from his ear. The hotel operators knew his suite number, L-31, by heart. They had to stack calls from all over the world until he was ready to take them.

"You're a star," Shaheen, dressed tropical in white shirt and white pants, was telling a disappointed man who had not been invited to the party. "The chief loves you."

Shaheen always called his boss "the chief."

Then a call came in from an Arab associate in the United States. He had a proposal for an $800-million project.

"Send me the papers," Shaheen said as the man caught his breath.

"Goofs!" Shaheen shouted at a new assistant who had sent baggage to the wrong city, then kept Shaheen waiting while a secretary got him on the line.

"I thought I could delegate responsibility to you," he said. "Anyway," in a softer tone of voice, "you'll learn."

Mohamed, Khashoggi's oldest son, wanted to use the yacht.

"Better ask your father," Shaheen said.

The hotel operator cut in with a call from the DC-8 flying over Germany.

"I'll take it," he said, reaching for another Opera Pastanesi chocolate-covered Turkish delight from the box on the hammered-copper coffee table.

As evening fell like a pink and blue powder, two-way radios in specially hired buses and limousines crackled with the dispatch: "Fiesta à 'La Baraka.'"

As the birthday guests traveled up the twisting road toward the ancient town of Ronda, the drivers pointed out where Khashoggi's property began. Then they drove on another five minutes. There, a sign at the blue lattice gate to the estate said "La Baraka"—French for "luck."

A guard checked off names from a long list, then waved

the guests past. A man darted from the bushes, a machine gun strapped over his shoulder. With one hundred such guards patrolling the property, similar encounters would be repeated many times during the night.

At the end of a winding road lined with pink and white oleander, the guests got out in front of the Spanish stucco ranch house. The scene they approached was Disneyesque: Khashoggi standing outside, flashbulbs going off on cameras, and a clown on stilts extending a dismembered hand on a stick in greeting. A jester was equally friendly, and knights on horseback stood in file.

Khashoggi, in white dinner jacket, had rosy cheeks and curly black hair that was thinning to baldness above his shiny forehead. He had a neatly trimmed moustache, a short neck, and a double chin. Five feet four inches tall and weighing more than two hundred pounds, he somehow managed to look robust rather than flabby. At times, he seemed to roll rather than to walk.

His most distinguishing characteristic was the eyelashes that framed his glistening brown eyes. They were long and black and very curly, like a child's.

As each guest shook hands with him, a band of musicians in period dress struck up a tune on lutes and recorder, in keeping with a Renaissance era theme. He took in the guests with his deep gaze, a charming mysteriousness to it.

Standing beside him was Lamia, his twenty-eight-year-old Italian wife. Tall, with tan skin that set off striking blue eyes, she was so beautiful and charming that men never failed to suck in their breath when they saw her.

Closer up, she seemed almost childlike, tentative. Wearing a raspberry pink Cardin *haute couture* gown, she looked like a glorious bird of paradise, with large ruffles sticking out like wings at her shoulders over a sheath skirt.

While her ruby and diamond choker and earrings were stunning, what caught the eye about her costume was the illusion of gold peacock feathers sprouting from the chignon of her dark brown hair. It was a creation of her hairdresser, who formed spun gold from Lamia's hair by coating it with a gummy substance, then spraying the "feathers" with gold.

Impelled to see what surprises awaited them, the guests entered the central hall, where they felt rather foolish. How should one react when encountering an archway made of crossed swords held aloft by fifty costumed pages? Dressed in plumed cavalier hats, lion-crested doublets, breeches, and tights, the pages were at once respectful and wry, into the fun of the situation.

Into the main lounge the guests went. A woman in a low-cut blue gown with a ruffled neckline rubbed her fingers across a glass globe that held what seemed like heat-seeking light—a fiber-optics display. The blue flashes from the pink central fire leaped up and attached themselves to the glass beneath the woman's artfully manicured nails.

From the lounge with its low, cushiony white sofas, the guests passed through a wide-open doorway to a portico above a marble terrace. The terrace seemed to drive a wedge between two hills, and the symmetry of the view was breathtaking. Straight ahead were the Mediterranean and Gibraltar, with the shores of Morocco visible in the distance.

Just below the terrace, where the trees were individually illuminated, wild birds called to each other in the perfumed air.

As night fell, the guests munched on caviar-topped tartlets and sipped Moët & Chandon champagne, secure in the knowledge that they had achieved the pinnacle of social success and curious to know who else was in the same enviable position.

There was the *crème de la crème* of European society: the duchess of Seville, wearing a hat of floppy pink and turquoise feathers; Count Jaime de Mora y Aragón, scion of Spanish royalty, sporting a walking stick; Countess Gunila von Bismarck, whose sunburned face was framed with platinum hair; and Prince and Princess Von Thurn Und Taxis, among the continent's richest aristocrats, she wearing a bejeweled collar said to be worth a cool million. And then there were Princess Bridgett of Sweden, Princess Fabiola of Belgium, Robert Mitterrand, brother of the French president, German Prince Alphonso von Hohenlohe, and Philippe Junot, former husband of Princess Caroline.

Not to mention the Archduchess Helene and Archduke Ferdinand von Habsburg, Archduchess Sophie von Habsburg, and Prince Hubertus von Hohenlohe and Prince Heinrich Hanau.

On the marble terrace, Maxwell M. Rabb, the U.S. ambassador to Italy, was describing the consoles that concealed remote controls and telephones behind the beds on Khashoggi's yacht, where he was staying with his wife, Ruth.

Helicoptered to the party from the yacht, the former New York lawyer had become reacquainted with Khashoggi a few months earlier. Both had been at a Paris wedding given for the daughter of Prince Karim Aga Khan, the spiritual leader of the Ismaili Moslems and son of the late playboy Prince Aly Khan.

Describing the conveniences on the yacht, Rabb was saying, "You push a button, and it closes the curtain. You push another button, and it raises or lowers the television."

Brooke Shields, in gold-lamé jacket, diamond necklace, black pants, and high heels, towered majestically over the crowd, with her mane of streaked hair and her million-dollar smile. Excitedly, she lined up Khashoggi and his family for snapshots, unaware of the prohibition on cameras.

Former CIA agent Miles Copeland talked about his son, Stewart, the drummer in the Police rock band. Each does his own thing, then they get together for an album and make a few million, he was saying.

Victoria Sellers, the twenty-year-old daughter of Britt Ekland and Peter Sellers, was an alluring conversation piece herself, wearing a short black lace dress with a wide expanse of sheer nothing down most of her front and back.

The guests talked, too, of their host and his fabulous wealth. Was it all real? Why does he give such spectacular parties? Is he a smart Saudi Arabian middleman or a fixer, an Arab Rockefeller or just lucky?

Before they got the answers to their questions, dinner was served at midnight. Just before the party, a third wing to the mansion had been completed; it held a great green gazebo, where the main festivities would take place. Down a flight of stairs the guests went, where thirty-five tables were arranged around a dance floor, with a stage in the front of the room. Two additional dining rooms were ready to serve dinner, one a formal setting where the duchess of Seville held court at the head of the table.

An easel at each setting displayed Khashoggi's face smiling from the cover of *Leaders* magazine, which goes only to heads of state, chief executives of major international corporations, and the Pope. Inside the magazine was an interview illustrated with pictures of him with Henry A. Kissinger, Turgut Ozal, prime minister of Turkey, Marshal Mobutu Sese Seko, president of Zaire, and Queen Sirikit of Thailand.

Now, as the champagne was poured like soda and a clown joked and leered, the guests helped themselves to a buffet with some fifty items: andouillette of bass with crayfish sauce; flaky pastry filled with scallops, crayfish, and roe au Roquefort;

shrimp pâté; salad of crayfish and *haricots verts*; grilled bass with tarragon; salmon soufflé with basil; roast leg of veal forestière; pheasant terrine in feathers; whole lamb barbecued over wood; Middle Eastern dips; beef filet *en croûte en gelée*; endive; hearts of palm; and white asparagus.

On the stage, madrigal singers performed as the guests ate their fill.

"Parsley, sage, rosemary, and thyme," they sang gently.

Finally, the dishes were cleared for dessert. There were homemade caramel, honey, chocolate, coffee, and mint ice creams; sherbets made of pineapple, kiwi, grapefruit, passion fruit, and tomato; and homemade chocolates and cakes topped with raspberries, strawberries, kiwi, fresh currants, and passion fruit.

At a central table, Khashoggi sat between Brooke Shields and Princess Taxis, of the million-dollar collar. As he smiled and talked animatedly, it was hard to tell which role he enjoyed more: host or birthday boy.

As the birthday crowd waited expectantly, an actor identified himself as Henry VIII and took his place on a throne. Called to the stage, Khashoggi was regaled with a birthday proclamation to the "world's greatest," complete with a greeting from Ron and Nancy Reagan.

Donning an ermine cape, he signaled Ali, his six-year-old son by Lamia, to join him. Khashoggi knelt down by the boy as he listened. Dressed in a gold jacket, Ali was an adored prince.

Then the fifty pages began marching, prancing down the steps and into the party room. Each page held fifty silvery, ellipsoidal balloons aloft, each costing $2.50 and bearing the legend "world's greatest" on a map of the globe in blue, red, purple, green, orange, and yellow.

Soon, the three-story-high center of the room was filled with the balloons, obscuring the light. A bag previously filled with 2,500 balloons had been lodged in the ceiling. Now it was released upon the guests below. There was a hush, then pandemonium, as otherwise dignified celebrants began stomping on the 5,000 balloons, producing the sound and fury of the Fourth of July.

Cowering at a table near the center was Soraya Khashoggi, his first wife and mother of five of Khashoggi's six children. With her flawless English complexion and a low-cut gown of royal blue studded with rhinestones, she looked like a lusty, well-endowed wench from *Tom Jones.*

Her $2.5-billion divorce suit against Khashoggi made sensational headlines and was billed at the time as the largest in history. Orchestrated by lawyer Marvin Mitchelson, it included charges that Khashoggi paid off American executives, provided Saudi princes with call girls, and gave a $60,000 bracelet to a daughter of then President Richard M. Nixon.

Even bigger headlines accompanied her disclosure in a London courtroom in 1979 that she had been having a torrid love affair with "Mr. X," a prominent British politician. Later, Winston Churchill, a member of Parliament and grandson of the wartime prime minister, identified himself as "Mr. X."

But clearly that was history; now she was very much a part of the festivities. At the table, she clutched one of her sons to her, trying to ward off the balloons popping loudly all around her.

Making an entrance on its own table borne by four waiters, the birthday cake was a work of art—literally. On top was a gold crown measuring thirty-two inches by thirty-two inches, made of sugar. It was crafted by René Neou, Khashoggi's chief chef who formerly worked at Elysée Palace, the official residence of the French president. Neou had flown to the Louvre to study Louis XIV's coronation crown, then returned with his plan for the cake.

The crowd joined in as Shirley Bassey, best remembered as the woman who sang "Goldfinger," belted out, "Happy birthday, dear Adnan." Then Dante, a British rock group, took over, followed by Sabah, an acclaimed Middle Eastern belly dancer.

The party ended at nine the following morning, when pasta was served for breakfast.

It was the birthday party to end all birthday parties.

And what does one give the richest man in the world? One of his brothers gave him a lion cub, who played with the guests. A regal gift, appropriate for an astrology buff born under the sign of Leo, it wore a collar studded with diamonds.

Over the next two weeks, there would be a party every night, either at Khashoggi's villa or on his yacht.

On the Sunday evening following the birthday party, the tourists at the boat parted to let the limousines through, dropping off a total of fifty guests at the breakwater where the *Nabila* has its berth.

Out came Count Jaime de Mora y Aragón and his smiling countess, residents of Marbella, where their home is a museum, its walls covered with seventeenth- and eighteenth-century French, Italian, and Spanish paintings, including Goyas and El Grecos.

The countess wore a bright red dress, while the count wore a bright red silk shirt of the same shade under his white suit, with a red scarf at his neck. Carved on the head of his walking stick was his portrait, looking like Salvador Dali, with pointy beard and wolflike face.

Walking over a red-carpeted dock planted with red geraniums, the guests entered the *Nabila* through doors that slid silently open to reveal on the opposite wall a replica of the black stone that forms the cornerstone of the *Ka'bah*, a cube-like monument in Mecca that Moslems face when they pray. The replica was a gift from King Fahd of Saudi Arabia when he was crown prince.

Up the stairs went the guests, to an enormous lounge and bar done in chrome and chamois leather with sofas of puffy cushions piled on cushions.

Wearing a white suit with a blue silk shirt open at the neck, Khashoggi ambled diffidently, swinging his arms slightly as if his upper body were only loosely connected to his lower. Sometimes looking lost and shy, he darted from guest to guest. He was eager for them to enjoy themselves.

Asked about the Légers on the yacht, Khashoggi grabbed a guest's arm and pointedly counted them: one, two, three, four, five.

What about the one in his bedroom? the guest wanted to know.

"That's a Picasso," he said, smiling.

Lamia was dressed in a pink and aquamarine sheath, so besequined she looked like a mermaid covered with scales. As a guest approached, she displayed a charming warmth, taking the guest by the arm and leading her aside for a tête-à-tête, the way ladies walked in the garden at the turn of the century.

Argentine millionaire Carlos Perdomo and his wife, Norma Jessica, were telling how they met AK. They were sailing in the Caribbean on their boat, the *Jessica*, which is said to be the world's largest privately owned sailboat, when the owner of the *Nabila* requested permission to come aboard.

"*He* wanted to see *our* boat?" Norma Perdomo was saying.

Permission to come aboard granted, they became friends.

On a corner of a sofa sat a blonde woman from Nottingham, England. Her husband, a packaging salesman, swore he was the most ordinary person at the party. His wife had done modeling for a Khashoggi company six years earlier.

Some of the guests got a tour of the *Nabila*'s five decks before dinner. There was a three-room medical clinic, staffed at all times while afloat by a medical doctor, who managed to coexist with a chiropractor in pursuit of Khashoggi's good health; the swimming pool with its own whirlpool, surrounded by lounges the size of queen-size beds; Khashoggi's bedroom, done in browns, with its double king-size bed; and a communications room off the bridge, where two mates watched four video screens monitoring the four movies being shown on board.

When dinner was served at midnight, the guests helped themselves to three buffets—French, Italian, and Middle Eastern—while a trio of Spanish musicians visited each table. A Lebanese man joined in the singing in Spanish, one of eight languages in which he is fluent.

Then there was dancing in the disco, presided over by an Italian disc jockey. Overhead in the ceiling, portraits of Khashoggi's smiling face and that of Nabila, his saucy twenty-three-year-old daughter, alternately lit up over the dance floor. Lights throbbed yellow, red, green, and blue in time with the music and reflected in mirrored channels down the walls.

"Celebrate!" Lamia sang along, her arms high above her head, her body undulating with Madonna's voice. "It would be so nice if we took a holiday...."

The trappings of power—the parties, the yachts, the planes, and the homes—are the patina that great wealth gives, the shimmering glow of mist rising from a lake. They give no hint of what lies beneath the surface, nor of what obsessions drove this gleaming-eyed financial giant to acquire wealth of colossal proportions and to spend it at the rate of more than $300,000 a day, every day of the year.

Estimated at $2 billion to $4 billion, Khashoggi's wealth dwarfs the fortunes of America's richest men. In total assets, Khashoggi has surpassed the eccentric and elusive Howard R. Hughes, who had a mere $1.5 billion.

Khashoggi's real estate developments in Salt Lake City alone—Triad Center and Triad International Center—are worth well over $1 billion. In Gabon, he is developing a stretch of land as big as the state of Delaware. In Houston, he is building a $1-billion real estate development with a thousand-room hotel and 2 million square feet of office space. In Pennsylvania, he plans to turn garbage into electricity.

In Turkey, he has started a $100-million joint venture with the Turkish government to develop tourism. In Indonesia, he operates a tanker business for transporting oil. In Brazil, he owns meat-packing facilities and has started a joint shipping venture to export meat and wheat to Saudi Arabia.

In California, Khashoggi and his brother Essam own Oasis Petroleum Corp., a $1-billion gasoline and petroleum marketer operating in twenty-three states, and they are major stockholders in Barrick Resources Corp., which explores for gas and oil in the U.S., Canada, and Alaska. From Spain, Khashoggi exports trucks and buses to Egypt. In South Korea, he owns a bank. In China, he is planning a $1-billion development that will include a bridge in Shantou, a hotel, a motorcycle factory, a fishing operation, and a food processing plant.

All told, he operates in thirty-eight countries.

Unlike Hughes, who inherited a $500-million business from his father, Khashoggi, like John D. Rockefeller and Andrew Carnegie, started with nothing. But Khashoggi had connections. His father was physician to King Abdul-Aziz, the first ruler of modern Saudi Arabia. He parlayed this entrée into a role as an agent on Saudi defense contracts that ballooned as oil money cascaded into the desert kingdom.

There are those who say, as do Peter Collier and David Horowitz in *The Rockefellers*, that great wealth comes as an accident.

"It was as if a door had stood open for a brief moment and Rockefeller, who just happened to be passing by, managed to squeeze in before it closed," they wrote.

Khashoggi himself has ascribed his wealth to "having a desire, with the ambition to achieve certain things," to "being in the right place at the right time," and to "daring to act publicly against the mores of my society."

It's true that the absence of either income taxes or rigorous antitrust enforcement aided Rockefeller in founding the Standard Oil Co. Carnegie happened to begin manufacturing steel when there was a great need for it for railroad bridges, previously made of wood.

One could argue that Khashoggi fell into a similarly fortunate situation, enabling him to make use of the mores of his culture and his boyhood connections at a time when billions of dollars in oil wealth began pouring into Saudi Arabia.

Yet these are simplistic explanations. They fail to account for the fact that there were others who lived in the same place at the same time, with even better connections—people who didn't perceive the opportunities and seize them, reaping the benefits that seem so obvious in retrospect.

Rockefeller saw that refining, rather than strictly oil exploration, held the greatest promise. Khashoggi foresaw the riches that were about to glut Saudi Arabia like swollen rivers overflowing their banks.

Rockefeller was a master at marshaling and using power: taking advantage of the appropriate moment, seeing others' vulnerabilities, forging the appropriate alliance to gain what he wanted.

Khashoggi is a genius at negotiating. He spends twenty minutes deciding which suit to wear to match the sensibilities of the people he will be seeing. He sets up meetings at the same time with three to six competitors, each vying for the same business deal.

Always held on his turf in an environment of splendor rivaling the Sun King's, the meetings melt the resolve of the parties to hold out for better terms, while the heady atmosphere fuels their greed.

His eyes fasten on his listeners, following their eye movements. If he detects disagreement or a lack of understanding, he goes back over a point, winking or slapping his listener's knee. By conceding everything to the other side and frankly describing his own motives, he enhances his credibility, then alternately draws the string tighter and loosens it as he makes his arguments.

With Americans, he does a good imitation of a Brit, drawing up his nose and affecting a stuffy, clipped accent. With Brits, he gets belly laughs with his imitation of an arrogant American.

He talks rapidly but softly in English and uses the jargon of his listeners, calling the Defense Department DOD. But if he forgets a word or name, he pauses to remember it, lingering well beyond the point when most people, out of embarrassment, would have gone on to something else.

The quintessence of the word *engaging*, he is absolutely nonthreatening, with his arm flung over the back of a sofa to include his guest. He genuinely likes people. Yet talking with Khashoggi is like being in the eye of a hurricane.

Sometimes, a trace of sadness clouds his eyes, as if his prodigious wealth has not satisfied the yearnings in his bosom. One comes away thinking of him as a sweet, vulnerable man— a man who needs to be protected from those who feed on his wealth like piglets sucking on their mother's teats.

Yet the impression is one more weapon in his arsenal, a way of diminishing defenses and endearing people to him. Like Rockefeller, he has a sense of whimsy about him, a childlike inquisitiveness and playfulness that engenders trust. He understands what others want out of a transaction, knows what he wants, and sees where the two paths converge.

While both contributed to society by creating jobs and donating money, Khashoggi and Rockefeller developed controversial if not unsavory reputations: for Rockefeller, of trampling on competitors and even his own brother through secret cartel arrangements with railroads; for Khashoggi, of selling arms by manipulating or bribing government officials.

The truth is more complex.

Khashoggi is at once the ultimate capitalist and the ultimate bohemian; the ultimate fixer and the ultimate consumer; a citizen of the world and a diplomat without portfolio; a man who knows the Koran by heart and a gambler who loses millions at the roulette tables; a uniquely complex man and a disarmingly simple person; a playboy and a man obsessed; an underdog and a modern Midas.

He has explored the outer limits of success, power, and all that money can buy.

Khashoggi's story begins in the desert, where he was born, and in a secret commission given to him by his king.

# Baba

Allah hath favored some of you above others in provision.

—*The Koran*

**K**ING Faisal of Saudi Arabia presented an imposing figure as he strode from a limousine at 1600 Pennsylvania Avenue into Washington's blazing sun.

Standing six feet tall and dressed in the flowing robes of a bedouin, the sixty-two-year-old monarch stood an inch shorter than his host, President Lyndon B. Johnson. A hooked nose, grooved face, and unsmiling countenance gave the king an austere appearance.

Stumbling over the Arabic greeting that he had rehearsed, the President told Faisal on the south lawn of the White House: "Your country, under Your Majesty's wise rule, has made great steps forward. Roads, public works, health services, new schools, and new educational opportunities—all these stand as eloquent testimony to your active development efforts."

During the next ten days, the king was the official guest

of the U.S. government. He lunched with Secretary of State Dean Rusk and with Senator J. W. Fulbright, the chairman of the Foreign Relations Committee. He met with David Rockefeller, that paunchy symbol of American capitalism, at his Pocantico Hills home in Tarrytown, New York. He was given the key to the city of Washington. And he had an unpublicized, off-the-record luncheon with a spectrum of chief executive officers of the Fortune 500 companies.

The visit, from June 20 to 30, 1966, was Faisal's first to the U.S. as king of one of the world's most strategically important countries. The press covered his visit extensively, focusing on the customs and appearance of the bearded monarch.

On the first day of his visit, the *New York Times* ran a page-one story and three sidebars, one noting that at an all-male White House reception, guests drank only unspiked juice and Coke in deference to the nondrinking Moslem leader.

Two days later, even bigger headlines announced that Mayor John V. Lindsay of New York had withdrawn a dinner invitation to the king. The snub came after Faisal said at a press conference that friends of Israel are enemies of his people.

This prompted the *Times* to run two stories at the top of page one, plus two photographs on page one and three sidebars inside. One focused on James W. Symington, the U.S. chief of protocol.

"Used to important people," said the caption under a photo of Symington.

Unnoticed in the hoopla was a short, stocky Saudi who spoke fractured English and was balding at the age of thirty-one. Khashoggi was not a part of the official party, and he remained behind the scenes. In Washington, he booked into the Statler Hilton, while the king stayed at Blair House, the official U.S. government guest house. But in New York, he stayed at the Waldorf-Astoria, where the king stayed.

Khashoggi helped make the stay of the Saudi visitors more comfortable, arranging sight-seeing and business meetings, transportation, and sumptuous dinners for such dignitaries as Kamal Adham, the chief of Saudi intelligence. Always, there were gorgeous, available young women at Khashoggi's table.

On June 29, Khashoggi sat at a long table at New York's Metropolitan Club, where Faisal spoke to top business leaders.

On the forty-seven-item trip itinerary, the noon meeting at

One East 60th Street was listed only as a "private luncheon." Arranged by Charles B. (Tex) Thornton, chairman of Litton Industries Inc., the gathering had a guest list that read like a Who's Who of American industry: Chrysler's Lynn A. Townsend, Lockheed's Daniel J. Haughton, Deere's William A. Hewitt, McDonnell Douglas' Donald W. Douglas, Jr., Union Oil's Fred L. Hartley, Raytheon's Charles Francis Adams, TWA's Charles C. Tillinghast, Jr., and Litton's Roy L. Ash.

They heard a frank discussion about development prospects in Saudi Arabia.

Camille Nowfel, President Johnson's official Arabic interpreter, was impressed that Khashoggi seemed to be on close terms with all the members of the royal party, including Prince Sultan, the king's half brother, who was minister of defense and aviation. Khashoggi was beaming, almost as if he himself had arranged the king's visit to the U.S.

In fact, he had.

A few months earlier, Khashoggi had called his friend Gale Livingston, the president of Litton's Westrex subsidiary in Beverly Hills, California. Unlikely pals, they had met when Khashoggi arranged a contract for Westrex to operate the Dhahran International Airport in Saudi Arabia.

The dark, moustached Khashoggi had two ways of relaxing: gambling and beautiful women. Livingston, six feet tall, blue-eyed, and clean-shaven, liked to golf and thought the night was for sleeping.

Yet Livingston was impressed by Khashoggi. He was polished and urbane, and his big brown eyes radiated warmth and fun. Livingston found him to be honorable, forthright, and above all well connected.

Khashoggi didn't have to boast about his influence with the Saudi royal family. In Khashoggi's home at Riyadh or his flat in London, Livingston met Prince Sultan, the Saudi minister of defense and aviation, whose approval was needed on Litton contracts; Prince Talal, the finance minister; and Prince Fahd, the interior minister, who is now king.

Khashoggi looked to Livingston, who was twenty years older, to teach him about American ways of doing business. While attending college in California, Khashoggi had been taken with the free enterprise system and had embraced it as his own. When Khashoggi visited with Livingston, the older man introduced him to other U.S. business leaders and suggested he stay in a bungalow behind the Beverly Hills Hotel to create the right impression.

Usually, the two men met at the Los Angeles Country Club, where Livingston later was on the membership committee. And so it was when Khashoggi called Livingston in late 1965. Lunching with Livingston at the club, Khashoggi talked about his dreams for Saudi Arabia—dreams that Litton could share in.

When oil was still cheap and plentiful, Khashoggi foresaw the wealth that would soon descend on Saudi Arabia. But he also saw the need to sink the oil wealth back into the economy, to develop the land and its people, against the day when the wells ran dry.

"An example of the potential I saw with my own eyes," Khashoggi told him. "You people trained workers at the Dhahran airport to operate sophisticated electronic equipment. If this can be translated into other areas of the country, it would be magic."

Then he told Livingston how Litton could gain an edge in Saudi Arabia.

"King Faisal has always had a warm spot for America, ever since he came here as a guest of the government in 1943," he said. "If Litton could arrange to have the President invite His Majesty for an official state visit, it would enhance relations between the two countries."

Then, smiling, he said, "It would help Litton, too."

Already, Saudi Arabia was feeling the sting of playing second fiddle to Israel in its relations with the U.S. If Khashoggi could strengthen ties between the two countries, he would establish himself with Faisal as a man of influence and prestige.

To a middleman who made his money by selling arms and planes to the Saudi government, that kind of access meant the difference to his American clients between a signed contract and waiting for months for a call to be returned. Better relations between the two countries, in turn, would mean the U.S. would agree to sell more planes to the Saudis. And more planes would mean more commissions for Khashoggi.

But that was not the way he put it to Livingston. He presented the idea as a favor he was doing for Litton—a way of helping the company gain business in Saudi Arabia and ingratiate itself with the king.

Livingston agreed to present the proposal to his boss, Thornton. Thornton was an old friend of Lyndon Johnson's, ever since the two Texans had been government clerks in Washington in the 1930s. Later, as an originating sponsor of the National Independent Committee for President Johnson and Hubert Humphrey, Thornton helped raise money for Johnson's election in 1964.

A visionary, Thornton could be counted on to see the wider benefits of the plan. Yet when Livingston broached the idea, he hesitated. Thornton didn't want to get Litton involved in politics or in a controversy over the Middle East. But after several weeks, the prospect of winning the king as a friend became etched in Thornton's mind, and he met with Johnson and urged him to invite Faisal.

He found a receptive ear. Johnson was not a fan of Arabs. Privately, he made fun of their clothes and mannerisms. But the State Department already had Faisal's name on a list of dozens of other prospective state visits. For his friend, Johnson agreed to move Faisal to the top of the list.

When Faisal came to town, Livingston felt he had participated in an historic event. He never regretted the favor he had done for AK. In the ensuing years, Saudi Arabia renewed Litton's contracts. And in 1974, Khashoggi asked Livingston to retire from Litton and work for him.

For his part, Khashoggi could claim credit in Saudi Arabia for arranging the visit—and did.

The State Department knew nothing about Litton's intervention, much less Khashoggi's. In fact, no State Department officials were invited to the luncheon at the Metropolitan Club. It was always that way with Khashoggi. When asked about him, the State Department would warn that he was in disfavor with the king, that he was a corrupting influence on the royal family, that he was a man who used mirrors to magnify his own importance—a man to stay away from.

Then Prince Sultan or Prince Fahd would show up on one of Khashoggi's three commercial-size aircraft, in one of his twelve sumptuous homes, or on one of his two fabulous yachts. And Khashoggi would meet with King Faisal in his palace, with President Richard M. Nixon at his Key Biscayne compound in Florida, with President Jimmy Carter on Khashoggi's plane, or with President Ronald Reagan in the White House.

Always, the meetings were secret, as was the commission King Faisal gave him in 1962: to walk in the Western world on behalf of his king.

•  •  •

When Khashoggi was born on July 25, 1935, the desolate kingdom of Saudi Arabia was three years old, carved from the Arabian peninsula by Faisal's father, King Abdul-Aziz.

Standing six feet four inches tall, Abdul-Aziz had an aquiline profile, full-fleshed nostrils, and heavy-lidded eyes. He exuded charm and dignity. When he wanted to emphasize a point, he dropped his voice to a whisper.

He was a descendant of the House of Saud, a nomadic but proud family that once occupied Riyadh near the center of the Arabian peninsula. When Abdul-Aziz was eleven, the Rasheed family, a powerful tribe, drove his family from the city, leaving them to wander the Empty Quarter, a vast, uninhabited wasteland of sand in the southeastern portion of the country.

As he grew up, the affront to his family tore at Abdul-Aziz. When he was twenty-two, Abdul-Aziz told his father he was determined to retake their homeland.

"You will either see me victorious or never see me again," he told him.

With a band of forty men riding on camels, he stole toward Riyadh. Their swords flashing, they overtook the Rasheed governor while he slept, reclaiming the city for the Al Saud.

As in a tale from the *Arabian Nights*, Abdul-Aziz soon set about conquering the feuding tribes and sheikhdoms that populated the land between the Red Sea and the Persian Gulf.

In accomplishing his mission, Abdul-Aziz knew how to use the carrot as well as the stick. One of his favorite techniques was to marry the loveliest daughter of an intransigent leader, and so bring him into his inner circle as a member of his family.

During his lifetime, Abdul-Aziz managed to take three hundred wives and countless concubines. The wives—never more than four at a time—bore him forty-three sons and an estimated fifty daughters.

By 1932, Abdul-Aziz proclaimed Saudi Arabia an Islamic monarchy.

It hardly seemed worth taking. The size of the United States east of the Mississippi, it was nearly all desert—endless miles of searing, shifting sands. From the air, the land looked like corrugated cardboard. By day, the temperatures rose to 120 degrees. At night, they could plummet to zero.

Beyond mysterious underground springs and shifting oases, there were no permanent bodies of water.

The few inhabitants were bedouin—illiterate nomadic tribesmen who wandered from oasis to oasis looking for blades of grass for their camels and goats. The camel was their primary tangible asset. It provided transportation, meat, and frothy milk.

The bedouin had no fixed allegiances and tended to flock to those in power. They could always be counted upon to provide hospitality to strangers they met in the desert. Tradition demanded that they defend a stranger they chose to travel with, be he Christian, Jew, or slave. No word left a nastier taste in the mouth of the bedouin than *bakhil*—stingy one.

The bedouin understood raids on other tribes according to strict protocol: Camels could be taken, but lives were spared and women were inviolate.

With no agricultural products except dates, the newly formed kingdom was perpetually strapped for cash. Dues levied on pilgrims who came for the *hajj*—the trip to Mecca required at least once in the lifetime of every able-bodied Moslem—provided the only other source of cash.

It was in Mecca and nearby Medina that the Prophet Mohamed lived and preached, receiving the word of God in the form of the Koran beginning in A.D. 610.

Into these impoverished circumstances ventured an unlikely savior—Charles R. Crane, the son of the American manufacturer of toilet fixtures.

Crane had visited the Middle East when he was appointed in 1919 by President Woodrow Wilson to a commission that was to make recommendations on U.S. policy toward the area. When he returned to California, he began dabbling in raising new strains of Arabian horses, the horses with oversize heads and eyes set wide apart that he had seen on his travels to the Middle East.

This passion took him back to Cairo, where he met Fauzan al-Sabik, the Saudi diplomatic liaison to Egypt. The Saudi diplomat was known for his fine Arabian horses, and he showed them off to Crane. When Crane asked if he could buy several, the Saudi gave him a mare and a stallion as gifts.

Staggered, Crane countered with his own offer. For some time, he had been thinking that Saudi Arabia must have some wealth beneath the ground, if only water. He offered to have a geologist survey the land.

Abdul-Aziz happily gave his approval.

The geologist, Karl S. Twitchell, was a bustling man who soon reported that the land held great promise. Based on his reports and reputation, the Standard Oil Co. of California (Socal) bought the rights to search for oil for $50,000 in gold.

After three years of fruitless drilling at Dammam on the Persian Gulf, a well designated as Number 7 began gushing at the rate of 1,585 barrels a day in 1938.

By Allah, it came just in time. Now even pilgrims' receipts had been cut in half by the worldwide depression. Yet Abdul-Aziz saw no need to reinvest the burgeoning profits in schools, roads, or factories.

Much later, in 1950, he was having lunch at the royal palace with Raymond A. Hare, the U.S. ambassador. Noting that 85 percent of Saudi government revenues were coming from oil, Hare said, "You're now getting a large income from oil, and perhaps it would be a good idea to use it to broaden your economic base."

Smiling, the king leaned over and tapped the ambassador on the arm sympathetically.

"You Americans can think about that," he said.

A generous man, Abdul-Aziz celebrated good fortune by feasting and throwing sacks of gold coins out the windows of his car.

"Hoarded money never does anyone any good," he told his friends.

Besides, he liked to see children and grown-ups as well scampering to pick up the coins.

If Abdul-Aziz was a simple man, he gathered advisers around him with a more sophisticated view of the world. One was his court physician, Dr. Mohamed Khaled Khashoggi.

A thin man with a thin beard, he was jocular and outgoing, entertained lavishly, and won friends easily. Originally Turkish, his family had lived in Kayseri, a city in the center of Turkey. In Turkish, his last name meant "spoon maker."

Like many pilgrims, the family had made the *hajj* to Mecca some four hundred years earlier and decided to stay, becoming *jarareem*—pilgrims who stayed behind.

After attending college at the Sorbonne in Paris and medical school in Damascus, Dr. Khashoggi became a surgeon and set up a practice in Mecca and Medina, where his father had been mayor. There, he met and married Samiha Ahmed Setti, a warm, engaging, and attractive Saudi whose family originally came from Syria.

As one of the few doctors in Saudi Arabia, Dr. Khashoggi

quickly became physician to the king and the royal family as well. As such, he was considered part of the royal cabinet. In the Riyadh telephone book, he was listed as "H.M.'s private doctor."

Fluent in French, Arabic, and English, Dr. Khashoggi was more fun-loving and worldly than the serious, insular bedouin surrounding the king. He traveled with him and acted as a sounding board when he had a problem, particularly if it involved money.

Dr. Khashoggi had a head for numbers and used it to good advantage. When one of the king's favorite wives fractured her hand in 1939, Dr. Khashoggi ordered Saudi Arabia's first X-ray machine for his clinic in Mecca. To power it, he bought an electrical generator with enough capacity to service nearby homes, along with a second generator for the royal palace in Riyadh.

He charged ten riyals a month for each lamp hooked up to the system in Mecca. Soon, he had eight thousand lamps and more money than he needed.

The Khashoggis had six children: Adnan, Samira, Adil, Essam, Assia, and Soheir. As the eldest, Adnan Khashoggi was accorded special respect. He was the one who would lead the family upon his father's death.

Khashoggi worshiped his father, whom he called *baba*. If only because he loved to eat, he often went with him to the *majlis*, or receptions, given by the king and other members of the royal family.

With gleaming, expressive brown eyes and a soft voice, Khashoggi made a good impression. He was relaxed and jovial. Yet he could hold his own in any philosophical discussion.

From his father, he learned to be loyal to his king. He learned, too, that a good deed is often repaid many times.

Dr. Khashoggi told him how he had obtained his first car. On a hunt for gazelle in the desert with King Abdul-Aziz, he brought along a pair of 30-power, 50-millimeter binoculars purchased in France.

"What would you take in barter for these binoculars?" the king asked Dr. Khashoggi.

"They're yours, Your Majesty," his father said. "Please accept them as a present."

When they returned to the royal palace, the king gave him the keys to a gleaming white Packard.

If Khashoggi got his business sense from his father, he

learned to talk politics and world affairs from his uncle Yussuf Yassin.

Married to a sister of Khashoggi's mother, Yassin was a Syrian who was second only to Abdullah Suleiman, Abdul-Aziz' finance minister, as the king's most powerful aide. Yassin was secretary to the king and national security adviser. Wily, thin, and often brooding, he had another job as well.

As Abdul-Aziz aged, he worried about his potency, and it was one of Yassin's assignments to provide the king with ever-younger nubile maidens to help him prove his manhood.

From Khashoggi's birth, Yassin was his mentor. He taught him how to show deference to the king, yet always to speak his mind when his opinions were sought, how to banter and crack jokes while dreaming up political strategies—schemes that others thought too ambitious.

Always, there was a money angle, a way of achieving political ends through financial means.

From Yassin, too, Khashoggi learned to downplay his access to the king lest other courtiers became jealous.

Khashoggi loved his uncle and kissed his hand.

When he was eight, Khashoggi's father sent him to attend school in Egypt. Egypt was the heart of the Arab world, the place where the future leaders of Arab countries were educated and Saudis could relax in nightclubs and bars.

Khashoggi attended Victoria College in Alexandria, a boarding school that taught all its classes in English. Here, as a young boy, Khashoggi met Hussein, the future king of Jordan, and Hisham Nazir, who became Saudi Arabia's minister of planning. Here, too, he made his first deal as a middleman.

The father of a Libyan classmate told Khashoggi his father wanted to import some towels. So Khashoggi introduced him to an Egyptian classmate whose father made towels.

To Khashoggi's surprise, he received two hundred dollars for making the introduction.

In 1952, Khashoggi graduated with highest honors at age seventeen, then helped Anas Yassin, one of his uncle's sons, set up a company for importing goods to Saudi Arabia. Based in Jeddah, Saudi Arabia, it was called Alnasr Office, meaning "victory." Later, Khashoggi used the corporate name "Triad."

At first, the company sold mainly to the Ministry of Health, where Khashoggi's father had just been named deputy minister, and to the Saudi Ministry of Agriculture and Water. But

Khashoggi wanted to become a professional like his father. After a few months in Saudi Arabia, he enrolled at the Colorado School of Mines in Golden, Colorado, planning on becoming a petroleum engineer.

Khashoggi arrived in New York in a blizzard. It was his first taste of snow, and he complained to Omar A. Khadra, the Saudi official who helped students in the United States.

"Colorado will be even colder," Khadra warned.

"Where can I go where it's warmer?" Khashoggi asked.

Khadra suggested Chico State University, where other Saudis were studying, and Khashoggi changed his plans.

At the foot of the Sierra Nevada 170 miles northeast of San Francisco, the wooded campus of Chico State was a pleasant change from Saudi Arabia, and it had something else as well: girls.

Khashoggi could scarcely believe his eyes. Growing up in Saudi Arabia, he had seen the unveiled faces of perhaps twenty women—his mother, his sisters, and cousins. Dating and goodnight kisses didn't exist. Marriages were arranged.

Today, Western women visiting the kingdom are advised to wear clothing that conceals their arms and legs. On the theory that darkness might excite men and women who sit together, movie theaters are banned. Mixing of the sexes in swimming pools is prohibited.

The Koran is explicit on the subject: "Tell the believing women to lower their gaze and be modest," it says, "and to display of their adornment only that which is apparent, and to draw their veils over their bosoms... and let them not stamp their feet so as to reveal what they hide of their adornment."

Yet men are permitted to have as many as four wives, so long as they can care for them equally. A man can divorce a wife by pronouncing "I divorce thee" three times. (A woman must have grounds—such as impotence or inability to provide support—to obtain a divorce.)

Islam has never restricted sexual pleasure, providing it doesn't lead to adultery by women. The Prophet Mohamed had ten wives and at least three concubines.

Sexual intercourse is regarded as being no different from any other bodily function. It is discussed freely even when children are present. Nor is there any stigma attached to sexual relations with young girls. Even a six-year-old is considered marriageable, although consummation is delayed until puberty.

Against this backdrop, Khashoggi could barely contain himself. Instead of being hidden by the *abaya*, a long cloak that covers their dresses, California girls were nubile young things who bounced down the halls wearing thin blouses and dresses ingeniously cut above their tanned knees.

Looking from just the right angle, Khashoggi could even see their bras under their short-sleeved tops or peer up their dresses while they sat in class. But there was a catch. One could never be sure if the pretty girls would go to bed with him. More than anything, Khashoggi hated uncertainty.

At parties, he carried a martini in his hand. At the end of the evening, it was still in his hand, half finished. It wasn't the Moslem prohibition on alcohol that bothered him. Most Saudis of stature had a bar concealed in their homes, to be opened for trusted friends or foreigners. Rather, Khashoggi's sparing use of alcohol was attributable to his compulsion to retain full control of his senses.

Khashoggi had seen how his uncle paid women for their favors, and he found that this gave him the control he wanted. One of his first experiences with this was during a school vacation, when he stopped in London and met Bertram Meadows, the jovial owner of the 21 Club.

Unrelated to New York's 21 Club, it was in a four-story mansion at 8 Chesterfield Gardens, an unimposing, block-long cul-de-sac in London's Mayfair section. There, Bertie, as he was known to his friends, and his brother, Harry, served steak, lobster, and the best drinks in town. In the rear, they operated a gambling casino suffused with smoke and gypsy music.

For the customers he got to know, Meadows provided a special service. He would shuttle them in a Rolls-Royce to Churchills, another club he owned nearby.

There, the most beautiful women in London acted as hostesses. They came from all over the world—Sweden, the U.S., Denmark, Germany—as well as England. When they turned twenty-four, he retired them.

Before sending customers to Churchills, Meadows personally selected the right women to help them enjoy their evening. The women greeted the customers at the door and sat with them while they drank champagne. By the end of the evening, the customers were ready to negotiate more convivial activities.

When a new Chevrolet cost $2,081 and lamb chops cost 59 cents a pound, the charge was $300. If customers wished, they could even make use of bedrooms on the upper floors of the 21 Club.

For Khashoggi, "Sir Bertram," as he liked to call him, provided an oasis. When he flew in from the parched desert kingdom, he was guaranteed sex, and he could guarantee it for his friends as well, including key Saudi princes who approved his contracts. Unsophisticated desert foxes, they gaped at the revealing dresses of the women at Churchills.

Khashoggi learned he could take the women on trips to gambling casinos and hire them for parties, adding an element of glamour and excitement that was missing from the entertainment provided by his competitors.

So central was Meadows to his operations that his name appears on a Chance card in a Monopoly set designed around his assets as a gag by Khashoggi's brother Essam.

Announcing that the holder and Meadows have just tied for first on the best-dressed list, the card, picturing a champagne bottle nestled in a bucket, instructs the holder to collect his share of $25,000.

Khashoggi's life-style at Chico State amazed his fellow students from Saudi Arabia. Like him, they received a stipend from the Saudi government of $200 a month for living expenses. Yet Khashoggi soon moved from a dormitory to a hotel room, which he divided with a curtain, calling it a suite. There, he gave catered parties, creating an impression of wealth. He hired a student as his secretary, giving her his school papers to type. When he ate out with friends, he always picked up the tab. He enjoyed spending money so much that his friends *wanted* him to have more of it. To uninformed Americans, he seemed to be a prince himself.

One night, after treating a Saudi friend to dinner, he borrowed the friend's last five dollars to buy a pack of cigarettes from the hotel desk clerk, whom he told to keep the change.

To his shocked friend, Khashoggi explained, "You see, my hotel bill comes due tomorrow, and I don't have the money now. But if I tip five dollars, it means I have plenty of money, and they won't ask for immediate payment."

Soon, Khashoggi rented a house with a swimming pool and moved in his friends on condition they serve as his butler, chauffeur, and gardener. It was the last time Khashoggi would ever mow the lawn, take out the garbage, go grocery shopping, or do the other mundane things that occupy others' lives.

When he once attempted to use a camera, the photos didn't come out.

Enrolled at Chico in engineering and geology courses, he had little time for learning about rocks and got average grades. While he became interested in a marketing course, he needed little instruction in that arena.

From Roy Eidal, a Seattle maker of trailers and equipment used for desert travel in Saudi Arabia, Khashoggi learned that American companies often lease their trucks instead of buying them.

When his father sent him $10,000 to buy himself a car, Khashoggi used it instead to buy a truck from Eidal's friend Henry P. Oswin, the international sales representative for Kenworth Truck Co. in Bellevue, Washington. He leased it, complete with driver, to companies in Saudi Arabia. The payments raised his monthly income by $200.

Then Mohamed Binladen, a patient of his father's, needed some trucks in a hurry for his construction business in Saudi Arabia. A few weeks after he made the $500,000 purchase from Kenworth, Khashoggi got a $50,000 check in the mail.

Meanwhile, Eidal introduced Khashoggi to Las Vegas, where Khashoggi developed the habit of sharing chips worth thousands of dollars with friends, business associates, corporate executives, or Saudi princes at the roulette tables.

After three semesters at Chico, Khashoggi decided to become a businessman instead of an engineer. He transferred to Stanford University in Palo Alto, California.

Yet each time he returned to Saudi Arabia, he got more orders for merchandise from the U.S., including trailers from Eidal's company, which he eventually bought. Telling his customers they must put down a large deposit, he then used the float to finance other deals.

Already on his way to becoming a millionaire, he quit Stanford after a semester and returned to Saudi Arabia, opening offices in Jeddah and then Riyadh.

At the time, Saudi Arabia had a cement plant, five bakeries, three dairies, and two date processing plants. A national currency had just been adopted, and slavery was still legal. Khashoggi's company, Alnasr Trading & Industrial Corp., had business registration number 3 and Riyadh post-office box number 6.

King Abdul-Aziz died in 1953, but Khashoggi's royal connections remained intact. His uncle and his father continued as advisers to his successor, King Saud. With the new king, Khashoggi spent many hours talking about the opportunities he had seen in America and the need to develop Saudi Arabia's industries—industries that Khashoggi would own.

He convinced Saud to give him a franchise to build a factory to supply bricks to the government. A tire recapping factory would follow, then a furniture factory operated by Khashoggi's artistic brother, Essam.

Shortly, the king granted Khashoggi a fifty-year monopoly on the production of gypsum board for interior and exterior walls. Khashoggi's partners in the venture, called National Gypsum Co., included two friends from Chico State, Prince Nawwaf and Prince Abdul Rahman, both half brothers of the king.

At the age of twenty-one, Khashoggi got his first taste of selling military supplies. This was in 1956, just after Israel invaded the Gaza Strip. Saudi Arabia needed trucks to help send supplies to Egypt. Khashoggi had noticed that the trucks used by the military sank in the sand. He noticed, too, that the Kenworth trucks used by Arabian American Oil Co. (ARAMCO), which had the rights to drill for Saudi oil, had wide tires that negotiated the desert like camels.

King Saud and his defense minister ordered $3 million in Kenworth trucks from Khashoggi. Khashoggi's commission was $150,000.

Before Khashoggi had even received the money, he threw a lavish party at the Hôtel George V in Paris. Complete with champagne, caviar, and the lovely girls who became Khashoggi's trademark, it was so spectacular that the princes and businessmen who attended still talk about it.

The party nearly wiped out his net worth. But he was only following his father's advice. While his son watched, Dr. Khashoggi once dropped a coin on a carpet, then dropped the same coin on a marble floor.

"You can spend your money quietly or with a bang," his father had said.

Khashoggi chose the loud way, with style. It was the gambler's instinct in him to blow at least half his income on lavish living. Like bees around honey, people figured there was more money where that came from, that he had connections, that he was successful. They wanted to become a part of that success.

The strategy came naturally to Khashoggi, and it worked.

The parties gave him access. No longer did Khashoggi have to go looking for business. Business came to him.

By the end of 1961, he had negotiated a contract for an American firm, Commonwealth Services International Inc., to help maintain Dhahran International Airport. Soon, he had the agencies for Rolls-Royce Ltd. of Britain, Marconi Wireless Co., Fiat, Westland Helicopter Ltd. in England, and Chrysler as well.

In September 1962, a civil war erupted in the Yemen Arab Republic. Faisal, then crown prince under King Saud, summoned Khashoggi to his office and handed him a check made out to him for a million British pounds.

The money was to buy arms for the royalist forces who supported the Imam Badr, from a dynasty that had ruled since 1918. With Soviet-made weapons, Egypt was supplying the opposing revolutionaries, consisting of units of the Yemeni Army.

The war on Saudi Arabia's southern border was a threat to the royal family, yet Saudi Arabia didn't want to openly support the guerrillas against Egypt.

Faisal said he didn't care where Khashoggi got the weapons, how he got them to the royalists, or how much they cost. But the name of the Al Saud must not be associated with the purchase.

It was Khashoggi's first assignment as a trusted intermediary. He bought the arms—mainly rifles—from Great Britain. The mission successfully completed, he told Faisal he wanted no commission, and so gained stature in his eyes, just when Faisal was gathering the reins of power and preparing to be king.

Fearing that Arabia would become encircled by pro-Egyptian, pro-Soviet governments, Faisal embarked upon a reorganization of his government, a buildup of its defenses, and a new direction in foreign policy.

He decided that his country's future lay in closer ties with the U.S. To win American support, he banned slavery in the kingdom and started a modernization program to improve education, health, housing, and roads.

As his allies, Faisal chose Prince Sultan and Prince Fahd, two of seven sons of King Abdul-Aziz and Hassa Sudairi, one of the king's favorite wives. In October 1962, Sultan, thirty-eight, became minister of defense and aviation, while Fahd, forty-one, became minister of the interior.

These two princes and a third, Prince Abdullah, the thirteenth son of Abdul-Aziz, rule the kingdom today—Fahd as king, Abdullah as crown prince, and Sultan as defense minister.

As part of his plan, Faisal secretly commissioned the twenty-seven-year-old Khashoggi to act in an unofficial capacity to strengthen ties with the U.S. and Western countries. Later, Faisal's successors reaffirmed the commission and extended it to Third World countries as well.

Khashoggi was to obtain arms, invest to win friends and influence, and serve as the royal family's eyes and ears in the U.S. In short, he was to "build bridges" between the backward kingdom of Saudi Arabia and potential allies.

He would, of course, charge his usual fee for the passage.

Almost immediately, Khashoggi began dickering with Lockheed Corp. and Raytheon Co. to supply Saudi Arabia with an integrated defense system—contracts that would reap Khashoggi commissions in the hundreds of millions of dollars. On a sale of French tanks, he got a commission of $45 million.

Oil was then selling for less than two dollars a barrel, and Saudi Arabia was shipping 2 million barrels a day. Within fifteen years, the price climbed to as much as thirty-two dollars a barrel, and production soared to 11 million barrels a day.

During that time span, total oil revenues increased from less than $1 billion a year to more than $100 billion—a hundredfold increase.

As revenues increased, so did the size of defense contracts. Instead of 5 percent of a $500,000 contract, Khashoggi got 5 percent of a $1.5-billion contract. No longer satisfied with 5 percent, he began charging up to 15 percent.

It was all done at the expense of the Saudis, who knew that the American companies simply increased their prices to cover the commissions they paid Khashoggi.

Never before, and probably never again, will one man make so much money so quickly.

# "My Integrity
# Is on the Line"

It is no sin for you that ye seek the bounty of your Lord
by trading.

—*The Koran*

**K**HASHOGGI was livid. In the infernal heat of the Saudi
Arabian city of Jeddah, he drove a white Chrysler to villa 101
in the Raytheon Co. missile compound. Glen A. Grubbs, the
Raytheon manager for Saudi Arabia, answered his knock.

"I have to talk with you. Not here," Khashoggi said.

As he always did when in Saudi Arabia, Khashoggi was
wearing a flowing poplin *thobe*, a sheetlike affair that came
to his ankles. On his head he wore a white *ghutra*, a headdress
that looked like a parted curtain framing his round face.

Khashoggi and Grubbs walked toward the Chrysler, parked
behind the well-tended grounds of the villa. Like the rest of
the homes in the compound, it looked like a concrete pillbox,
built to last forever.

The Saudis wanted the Raytheon compound as far away
from the capital of Riyadh as possible. They did not want the

American infidels with their loose-looking women with uncovered knees to taint the dignified atmosphere of the home of the king. So they placed Raytheon five miles northwest of Jeddah, a port city on the Red Sea five hundred miles across the desert from Riyadh. The compound was on a peninsula that jutted into the ocean.

Grubbs had never seen Khashoggi drive a car, and he did not trust him to do it.

"I'll drive, you talk," he said, sliding behind the wheel.

So Grubbs drove through the Raytheon compound gates, past swaying palm trees, and flipped on the air-conditioner. It was more than 100 degrees in the shade, and the air-conditioner made little headway against the heat.

Grubbs knew why Khashoggi was so agitated. Raytheon had dropped him as its agent for the HAWK, a supersonic, surface-to-air missile developed for the U.S. Army in the 1950s. Displeased by Khashoggi's ever-increasing demands for commissions, the Boston-based firm signed on a member of the royal family, a prince who was the eldest son of King Faisal. But Raytheon had annoyed the prince by criticizing him because he was doing little for Raytheon.

By Allah! It was blasphemy to criticize a prince, besmirching his honor and the honor of his family.

Because of that, Raytheon's decision to drop Khashoggi was unraveling before the company's eyes. In November 1971, when Khashoggi visited Grubbs at his home, the company was about to be tossed out of the country. Before the controversy subsided, the $2-billion-a-year company had to send its chairman, a descendant of both the second and the sixth president of the United States, to offer a personal apology. Raytheon had to reassign the president of a key subsidiary, banishing him forever from the austere Middle Eastern kingdom. And a variety of shadowy yet powerful Central Intelligence Agency agents and their Saudi counterparts had to be brought into play to restore Raytheon's reputation—and Khashoggi's commissions.

In the car, Khashoggi told Grubbs that by embarrassing the royal family, Raytheon had brought embarrassment to him as well.

"You have just done in three months what I told the Saudis I would never allow to happen," Khashoggi said as Grubbs dodged donkeys and potholes. "I told them I was bringing in an impeccable, conservative company that would respect the laws and would do a professional job, and would be worth what they were paid. You've just blown all of that," he said.

As he always did when he talked, Khashoggi was gesturing with his hands. Usually, they were expansive gestures to encompass a dream or plan, or confident gestures, made by spreading his hands out to either side or folding them comfortably in front of his paunch.

As the two men passed slender, unadorned minarets and sun-bleached buildings with woodwork faded in the burning sun, Khashoggi was making angry, sideways slashes.

"Now I'm obligated to straighten it out, whether you want me to or not," Khashoggi told Grubbs.

As Grubbs emerged from the Chrysler, he smiled to himself.

Khashoggi never took a breath without making more money, he thought.

When the dust finally settled, Khashoggi had regained his position as Raytheon's agent, entrenched even more strongly than before. His new contract provided for commissions two to three times higher than previously. Eventually, he made staggering sums from Raytheon—over a ten-year period, commissions of more than $100 million on sales to Saudi Arabia of $1.5 billion.

Almost simultaneously, Khashoggi negotiated a contract with Lockheed Corp. that brought him even more in commissions. The two contracts were his first megabucks deals.

Raytheon executives had no doubt they needed an agent to do business in Saudi Arabia.

The government and the royal family are virtually inseparable. Their relationship to the populace is much like the directors of a company to its stockholders. Like directors, each of the four thousand male members of the family receives a fee—a generous stipend that kicks in at the age of eighteen.

Who you know in the royal family—and how much you are willing to pay to know someone—remains crucial to doing business in the kingdom.

In Arab cultural terms, this is not looked upon as crude influence-peddling. The *wasta*, the Arab equivalent of the go-between, is a person with connections who can vouch for both sides and broker a business transaction or even a marriage. The concept was embodied in Islam: In making His will known to Mohamed, God used an intermediary in the form of Gabriel.

If the size of the fee determined the amount of service

rendered, it was only in good bedouin tradition. When a battle went against them, they were the first to pillage the tents of their chiefs, for they had served them longer and should be entitled to the spoils.

It is not that the Saudis have no standards. The Islamic *shariah* law that governs Saudi Arabia provides that a rapist may be killed without a trial, an adulteress stoned to death, and a thief may have his right hand cut off after more than one offense. It is just that Saudi standards are different from Western ones.

An agent was needed to explain these cultural differences, but more than that, he was needed so foreign businessmen could enter the country. Then and now, Saudi Arabia is a closed society. There are no Fodor's guidebooks, for there are no tourists. To enter, a visitor must obtain a letter of invitation from a Saudi company or citizen. Without it, there is no visa and no entry. For thousands of years, the bedouin had no visitors. There was no reason to start now.

Once inside the country, businessmen needed an agent just to stay alive. In the 1960s, it was almost impossible to get a reservation at the two hotels in Riyadh. Strangers shared rooms, and a visitor was lucky to pay one hundred dollars to sleep in the lobby—or in the backseat of a taxi.

Only a few agents—Suliman S. Olayan, the Alirezas, the Juffalis—represented foreign auto manufacturing or appliance companies.

Today, Baskin-Robbins ice-cream parlors and bold white skyscrapers have replaced the open sewers that once fouled the streets. Yet for all the signs of development, the old ways continue. In fact, whereas previously an agent was optional, the Saudi government now *requires* the use of a Saudi agent on all but military products.

It was against this backdrop that Raytheon first ventured into Saudi Arabia. Founded in 1922 by MIT professor Vannevar Bush and other Boston scientists, Raytheon was originally formed to make refrigerators. But the iceman was still delivering ice, and there seemed little need to replace him.

The company turned instead to production of the S-tube, a gaseous rectifier developed by inventor C. G. Smith. It permitted radios to operate on household current instead of batteries. Helped by its proximity to MIT, Harvard, and Tufts, Raytheon branched into other high technology areas, including television receivers, radar and missile systems.

But if Raytheon knew its diodes, it knew nothing about the world outside Boston. Raytheon's executives were engineers; Thomas L. Phillips, Raytheon's executive vice-president in the early 1960s and later its president, had developed the HAWK missile from the bench up.

Khashoggi had sold several Lockheed planes to the kingdom, but he had no ongoing relationship with the aerospace company. Raytheon wanted to sell its HAWK to Saudi Arabia, and the company tried to team up with Lockheed to offer a complete defense package.

When that fell through, the company dispatched Joseph F. Alibrandi, Raytheon's senior vice-president, to meet with Khashoggi. From Lockheed officials, Raytheon had learned that Khashoggi was on extremely good terms with Prince Sultan, the minister of defense, who was the eighteenth son of King Abdul-Aziz.

Over six feet tall and portly, Sultan was a robust man with a goatee, even white teeth, and penetrating brown eyes. Seven years older than Khashoggi, he had a taste for beautiful women and night life. His support and the support of other key princes who were Khashoggi's friends were needed to obtain a contract with the Saudi government.

A high-strung man who remained slim no matter how much he ate, Alibrandi saw Khashoggi a number of times before a contract was signed in late 1965. Beside the pool at Khashoggi's Riyadh house, the two men talked about Saudi Arabia's future and how Raytheon could share in it.

"My country is going through a tremendous change," Khashoggi told Alibrandi. "We're trying to bootstrap ourselves into the twentieth century. Even in your country, it took two hundred years from the time of the tremendous immigration from Europe, and we are now where you were then. We're going to have to accomplish this same thing in twenty or thirty years," he said.

Khashoggi had a dual personality, demonstrated by a double photo displayed in his homes. One half shows him in a *thobe*, the other half in a white shirt, dark business suit, and tie. He was comfortable in both cultures and could bridge the gap between Saudi and American ways of doing things.

When he met later with top Raytheon officials, including Raytheon's chairman, Charles Francis Adams, he impressed them as a man who operated on their level. Instead of taking him to lunch, they were invited by Khashoggi to opulent dinners at the Waldorf-Astoria in New York or the Tour d'Argent in Paris.

Other agents wanted to know when they would get their money. Khashoggi didn't seem to care. He talked politics for an hour and a half. He asked questions and remembered the answers. He established lots of eye contact. He threw his head back and laughed. His guests relaxed. He was almost as royal as the king himself.

It was not an act. The Saudis punctuated their sentences by saying *inshallah*—"God willing." If Allah wanted Khashoggi to get his contract, he would get it.

Khashoggi's father had taught him how to negotiate. Khashoggi wanted to buy a shiny flashlight at the *souq*, or market. His father taught him to point out imagined deficiencies—the metal is cheap or the switch is rusty. Then he taught him to pretend to walk away. Khashoggi loved the act of negotiating, and the Moslem fatalist approach enhanced his skill at it.

When Khashoggi met with Raytheon executives, he was the little boy buying a flashlight. There was no edge to his voice. The contract at hand seemed to be the farthest thing from his mind—an afterthought, like a handkerchief stuffed in a suit pocket.

*Inshallah.*

Glen Grubbs did not want to go to Saudi Arabia. A ruddy-faced man with a salt-and-pepper pompadour, the thirty-seven-year-old Grubbs was the quality control manager for the HAWK. He had lived all his life in Pennsylvania or New England. He had eight children. He did not know where Saudi Arabia was, nor did he care.

But Grubbs was skillful at dealing with people. There seemed to be a roundness to everything he said—never any rough edges to bruise egos.

Raytheon wanted him to head its operations in the kingdom. His superiors at Raytheon headquarters—a low-slung, plain-looking brick building on rolling hills eleven miles west of Boston along Route 128—hinted that there were bigger things in store for him at Raytheon. Eventually, he agreed to go.

Grubbs oversaw the installation and operation of the HAWK, an acronym for "homing-all-the-way killer." Weighing 1,279 pounds, the missiles measured nearly six yards long and rose like Magic Markers embedded in the sky.

Unlike refrigerators, they couldn't be shipped and plugged in. Before they arrived, Raytheon had to build bases for them and train three thousand Saudis to use them. Before doing that, the Lexington, Massachusetts, company had to teach them English, since Arabic is almost devoid of the needed technical terms.

For the purpose, Saudi Arabia granted Raytheon its own compound adjacent to a military base on the Red Sea in Jeddah. All the foreign embassies and companies were located in or around the ancient city.

Here, Grubbs found himself in charge of 750 employees and their families. During the day, he supervised the construction of barracks for Saudi military men, and of schools, homes, and recreation centers for Raytheon people. At night, he was like the mayor of a small town, dispensing justice, laying down rules, settling disputes, and dispensing favors.

He quickly learned that living in Saudi Arabia would be more difficult than he ever imagined. Besides the language barrier and the oppressive heat, there were cultural chasms. To an American, frankness and even bluntness are prized. To a Saudi, the avoidance of negative statements is a virtue. For someone to suggest that he could "help with a problem" implies that there is one. It is therefore offensive. An American might cross his legs, showing the bottom of his shoes in the presence of a Saudi, never realizing he is committing an act of disrespect.

Time has a different meaning in Saudi Arabia. It is shaped by events, rather than events being shaped to conform with existing schedules. Saudi businessmen or bureaucrats took weeks to return a call, and the Americans learned to mentally add two hours to any appointment with a Saudi.

The wives of Raytheon employees were taught to conform. To avoid attracting undue attention when outside the compound, they were told to wear long dresses with long sleeves. Lest they be mistaken for prostitutes, they could not go out alone. When greeting their husbands in public, they were not to display any affection. Nor could they make friends with Saudi women.

The Saudis kept their wives veiled and at home. As they could not be seen with their husbands in public, they could not go with them to parties or other nonfamily events. Mixed dancing was scandalous and out of the question.

Since liquor was forbidden in Saudi Arabia, some employees distilled their own. They fermented sugar for a month, then diluted the pure alcohol and colored the mixture. One evening, a Raytheon engineer flipped on an electric light switch in the shed where he kept his still. A ball of flame engulfed him, and he died two days later. After that, Grubbs banned all stills and confiscated the existing ones, burying them in the sand with a bulldozer.

Grubbs' immediate concern was that the Americans could not practice their own religions. As the location of Mecca and Medina, Saudi Arabia was the unofficial homeland of Islam, the second largest religion in the world, and no other religion was allowed.

Meaning "submission," Islam requires allegiance to one all-powerful God, who revealed his will and commandments to the Prophet Mohamed at Mecca and Medina in the seventh century A.D. Those who practice it are called Moslems ("one who submits").

There are more than 600 million Moslems, primarily in seventy-seven countries where Islam is the predominant religion. Even though the Koran is written in Arabic, some of the largest Moslem populations are in non-Arab countries like Indonesia and Pakistan.

Within Islam, there are several sects, including the Shiites, who periodically burst into the headlines when planes are hijacked or barracks bombed. Most Moslems belong to a more conservative sect called the Sunnis.

In Saudi Arabia, Sunnis follow the teachings of Mohamed ibn Abdul Wahhab, a religious teacher who interpreted the Koran literally. King Abdul-Aziz owed his support in large measure to a liaison with the Wahhabis, who continue to dominate Saudi life and fight to preserve the status quo.

While Islam has no priesthood, it has the *ulema*—fundamentalist religious scholars who meet weekly with the king and exercise authority in religious matters. Usually, they object to any change, as they did to the satanic innovation of the radio. To overcome their objections, Saudi authorities demonstrated that it could convey the word of God through the reading of the Koran.

In 1967, they objected to the introduction of television as well. In their faith, human images of any kind are prohibited. The Islamic God has no physical form. To allow portrayal of the human likeness could lead to worship of idols, as the Israelites had done before Moses brought forth the Ten Commandments. What's more, portraying the faces of women without their veils, and without their husbands, violated other koranic interpretations. To placate the religious leaders, Saudi television emphasized religious programming.

Today, during the five daily calls to prayer, bearded members of the Committees for the Propagation of Virtue and the Prevention of Vice still patrol the streets of Riyadh. Calling out *salaat*—"prayer"—they rattle their staves on the windows of any shop that has not closed up.

Grubbs decided that the issue of religious freedom for the Americans residing at the Raytheon compound was important enough for an audience with the king. At his request, Hermann F. Eilts, the U.S. ambassador, arranged for him to meet with Faisal at the king's office in Jeddah.

Before discussing the business at hand, the king ordered his servants to begin the coffee ceremony, a symbol of Arab hospitality. The coffee beans, already roasted over a fire, were poured into a mortar and pounded with a pestle.

Meanwhile, a servant began boiling water in a *dallah*, an hourglass-shaped brass pot with a large open spout. The boiling water was then poured into a second *dallah* containing the ground beans. It was then put back on the fire to boil. Finally, the brew was mixed with freshly ground cardamom. A servant gave Grubbs the steaming coffee in a small cup.

After two cups, Grubbs shook the cup one or two times when giving it back to a servant, the traditional way of signaling that a guest has had enough.

Through an interpreter, Faisal bantered with Grubbs. Grubbs could tell that Faisal understood his words. Still, Faisal waited for the translation. It gave him more time to frame a response.

Grubbs said to the king, "Your Majesty, we intend to respect your customs and religion, but we have needs, too, and one is the free practice of our religion."

After the translation was finished, Faisal spoke. "You may hold services so long as they take place on the grounds of the American embassy," he said.

The exercise had been painless. Grubbs drove back to the Raytheon compound and arranged to fly a Protestant minister and a Catholic priest in from Beirut once a week.

There was no need to arrange for a rabbi. By design, Raytheon had not sent any Jews to Saudi Arabia.

•  •  •

Even before the missiles began arriving on ships, Raytheon's original $126-million contract with Khashoggi had been modified dozens of times. The Saudis wanted additional items—more missiles, better educational facilities, or improved electronic components.

When proposing these changes, Khashoggi told Grubbs which government officials to approach, and he delivered Raytheon's "white papers" outlining the proposals.

Khashoggi always used the add-ons to drive up his commissions. Even before the missiles were delivered, he had gotten a $500,000 advance on his fees.

One morning, Khashoggi met with Alibrandi and Grubbs in the lobby of the King Abdul-Aziz Hotel in Taif. On the edge of the Hejaz Mountains high above the Red Sea, Taif is where the Saudi government conducts business in the summer to get away from the oppressive heat of Riyadh.

Khashoggi and the two Raytheon men were about to meet with Prince Sultan to discuss a $51-million add-on for spare parts. They sat down at a coffee table and went over the proposal. After a few minutes, Khashoggi excused himself and met with some other people in a corner of the lobby. After he came back, he excused himself again, this time to confer with some people in another corner of the lobby.

"It's obvious we don't have your attention," Alibrandi finally said. "What could be so important that you can lose interest in this $51 million?"

"I'm sorry," said Khashoggi, "but in my meeting this afternoon, not only am I going to talk about your deal, but I'm also going to try to sell three commercial jet planes." He pointed to the other people in the lobby. "Over there is Lockheed, and over there is Lear, and over there are the French," he said.

Grubbs and Alibrandi exchanged glances. Khashoggi never made any secret about the fact that he represented Raytheon's competitors. He always mentioned it when haggling for higher commissions. He said Raytheon could easily be replaced as a supplier to Saudi Arabia. He made the same point when Grubbs told him a shipment of missiles would be delayed.

"I don't ask for concessions," Khashoggi would tell Grubbs at these times. "I only ask for two things: the contract and my commission. This is my country and I value my integrity more than yours. I am never going to be accused of bringing in a poor performer or a money-grubber."

The new company might not be American—it could be

British or French or German. And Khashoggi would still get his commission.

It was during these negotiations that Khashoggi told the Raytheon executives he needed higher commissions to cover "other things." The "other things" were never spelled out, but to Harry A. Loebel, the president of the Raytheon subsidiary with responsibility for the HAWK contract, the meaning was clear: In his view, it was Khashoggi's code for bribes to Saudi officials.

Loebel and Grubbs consciously avoided referring to the subject in memos or letters. They didn't want to know too much about it. But the question of bribes was something they discussed in hotel rooms and planes, just as they speculated about Khashoggi's life-style. They figured it cost him $10,000 a day just for personal expenses.

Still, they did not want to be left entirely in the dark. Both men were under increasing pressure from Raytheon headquarters to explain where the money was going. Khashoggi's fees could be justified when they were in the hundreds of thousands of dollars. But as the HAWK program expanded, they were running into the tens of millions of dollars. It was beyond the comprehension of the Boston blue bloods and Irish Catholics who ran Raytheon. Khashoggi could not be keeping it all.

On several occasions, Khashoggi explained to Grubbs that he considered it honorable to help a government official who had helped him with a contract.

"Perhaps," Khashoggi said, "I sold a Saudi general a house for $10,000, then immediately leased it back for $50,000 over ten years—the $50,000 to be paid in a lump sum at the beginning of the contract." Khashoggi would never occupy the house. He called it his "connection with that guy."

"He has helped me as an agent, and I think I owe him that," Khashoggi told Grubbs. "I'm not going to give him money in brown bags, nor will he get in trouble if it comes out. I would not object to going to Prince Sultan and telling him."

Grubbs could empathize with that. On a smaller scale, he had found it expedient to help out Saudi officials by lending them a Raytheon car for a few years or helping to remodel their homes.

At other times, Khashoggi told Grubbs that he furnished Sultan's home overlooking Lake Geneva in Switzerland, or provided villas and palaces to other princes. These were tokens of esteem, like bottles of wine exchanged by Raytheon executives at dinner parties. In Saudi Arabia, the equivalent of a turkey at Christmas was a yacht.

Much later, when Prince Fahd became crown prince and was running the country while King Khalid was ailing, the prince decided to buy his own commercial-size airplane. Khashoggi provided his own chief pilot, Harold G. Renegar, to give him advice. At one point, Fahd was considering buying Khashoggi's Boeing 727.

Khashoggi told Renegar, "If he wants it, it's his as a gift."

This was the Arab way: "If you like it, it's yours."

If it happens to be a 727, so be it.

What most impressed the Raytheon executives were the late-night appearances of Prince Sultan at Khashoggi's home. He swept in at midnight with his robes flying and asked a few questions about a pending proposal. Then he and Khashoggi had dinner at 1 A.M., after Grubbs and Loebel had gone home.

Sultan put on the show a number of times, and it never failed to have an effect. Khashoggi was Sultan's boy, there was no doubt about it.

Khashoggi always insisted that offering a bribe to Sultan or other government officials would be an insult—like a beggar offering money to a king. These princes had all the money they wanted, he told Grubbs, and offering cash would be both gratuitous and demeaning.

In fact, the princes did not have all the money they wanted. While each member of the royal family had a stipend, no one except the king had unrestricted access to the royal treasury. Besides courting financial chaos, allowing any member of the family to dip his hands into the kingdom's coffers would unleash jealousies and rivalries within the clan.

On the other hand, it was not considered improper for members of the royal family to enhance their fortunes through partnerships with commoners like Khashoggi—even if the royals held government posts. The royal family and the government were inseparable in any case, so what difference did it make?

Over the years, Khashoggi invested, among others, with such princes as Talal, who was minister of finance until he was briefly exiled in Egypt for protesting the lethargic rule of King Saud; Prince Nawwaf, a special adviser to King Faisal; Prince Misha'al, who was minister of defense in the early 1950s; and Prince Abdul Rahman ibn Abdul-Aziz, a businessman who plays a key role in allocating power and money within the royal family.

Still, Khashoggi kept his place. He was the commoner, and the princes were royalty. The Raytheon executives saw an example of that when they invited Prince Talal to Boston to discuss a possible contract to supply the Saudi National Guard with arms.

Talal, King Abdul-Aziz' twenty-third son, who later became special envoy to the United Nations International Children's Emergency Fund (UNICEF), is a close friend of Khashoggi's. Yet Khashoggi refused to stay at the Ritz-Carlton, where Talal was staying in Boston. Khashoggi did not want to infringe on his princely territory.

When Raytheon invited Talal and his attractive multilingual wife to dinner at Boston's venerable Locke-Ober Restaurant, Khashoggi at first said he would not attend. He did not want to divert attention from the prince. He wound up going, but in the car on the way over, he snapped at his wife, the spectacular-looking Soraya Khashoggi.

"Take off the makeup and jewels," Khashoggi said.

He didn't want her to upstage Talal's wife.

Khashoggi and his wife argued, but when she appeared at the restaurant, Soraya Khashoggi had removed her jewelry and makeup. As she entered the private dining room on the second floor, a hush fell over the guests.

She was beautiful without makeup.

Officials at Raytheon headquarters knew that Khashoggi's commissions were paid directly to several Swiss bank accounts, usually at the Swiss Bank Corp. in Geneva. Khashoggi used the bank so routinely that its name appears on a Chance card in the Monopoly game tailored around his assets.

"Advance to Swiss Bank Corp., pay $200,000," the card says.

Through assignments of Khashoggi's commissions, portions of the proceeds were designated to Liechtenstein companies whose principals had been helpful to Khashoggi. The funds went directly from the American companies to their Swiss accounts.

Sometimes the assignments amounted to as much as 5 percent of a contract and even equaled Khashoggi's commission. At other times, they were expressed as lump-sum payments per plane or per phase of a contract. One from a segment of a Lockheed contract alone was for $5.5 million.

What Raytheon officials did not know was the identity of the individuals behind the companies that were the ultimate recipients of the money.

That was Khashoggi's secret.

Tight-lipped and loyal Swiss accountants handled the accounts. Only three or four others knew that money placed in several of the accounts went directly to key Saudi princes who approved Khashoggi's contracts.

It was not that the princes were being bribed. They were Khashoggi's partners—and senior partners at that. Khashoggi did not say, "I'll give you 5 percent if you give me the contract." Instead, the idea was, "Let's get together and market this together, and we'll split the commission."

Whether his partners were government officials or members of the ruling family made no difference. The royal family owned the country. They decided what was their proper fealty. It was simple bedouin logic: The House of Saud had conquered Saudi Arabia. Shouldn't the family members be entitled to some of the spoils?

The secret of the Swiss accounts remained so inviolate that neither investigations by the Securities and Exchange Commission nor the Watergate Special Prosecution Force ever focused on the accounts and uncovered the facts.

To this day, Khashoggi insists that the assignments of his commissions went to members of the royal family who were businessmen and not government officials—even when the payments equaled half of his own commission.

When the SEC questioned Raytheon officials under oath in 1977, they could say they knew nothing about any questionable activities. There was virtually nothing in writing, and there was never any *quid pro quo* so far as they knew.

It was much like Khashoggi's penchant for call girls. The Raytheon executives could not help but notice the stunning, sophisticated young hostesses who showed up at parties given by Khashoggi in London, Cannes, and on his yacht. And they believed them to be call girls.

But Khashoggi never fixed up any executives with a call girl. When a guest chose to take one home, that was his business. If the guest felt obligated or compromised, it was purely in the mind of the executive who had enjoyed a lovely evening.

Loebel had never seen such a smooth operator.

• • •

As time went on, Khashoggi became more insistent in his never-ending negotiations with Raytheon. He had started with a commission of 5 percent, and now he was demanding 10 to 15 percent on services and spares to replace worn-out parts.

At the same time, Grubbs needed Khashoggi less. The Raytheon manager had established his own relationships with Saudi officials, particularly with Prince Turki, the vice-minister of defense.

When Grubbs did need Khashoggi, he was difficult to find. Successful beyond the plot of the most fanciful novel, Khashoggi now rarely returned to Saudi Arabia. When Grubbs needed him in Saudi Arabia, Khashoggi was in New York with Lockheed. Like a parent looking for his child, Grubbs would leave messages for Khashoggi at his homes and offices, which were already beginning to spread across the globe like spilled molasses. Several days later, Khashoggi would get back to him.

As Raytheon's disenchantment with Khashoggi festered, a new agent appeared on the scene. Originally an Egyptian journalist, Mohamed Habib wore brown-rimmed glasses, smoked Honduran cigars, and had a voice like Charles Boyer. For twelve years, he served as the information counselor at the Egyptian embassy in Washington. When the U.S. broke relations with Egypt in 1967, Habib stayed behind, becoming an American agent for Arab companies.

While in Saudi Arabia in 1968, Habib met Prince Abdullah al-Faisal ibn Abdul-Aziz, the eldest son of King Faisal. The prince was a businessman with considerable clout by virtue of his order of birth. With four thousand members, the royal family had to establish strict lines of authority to maintain tranquillity within the clan. Age was the unquestioned determinant of power. Even when lining up for family pictures, the youngest always shuffled to the back.

Six feet three inches tall, lean, with erect posture, Abdullah had a kindly, almost scholarly expression. Indeed, he was a poet of considerable talent, a facility that is highly esteemed by the bedouin. They consider poetry to be of supernatural origin.

"What is poetry but pure honey, magic and ecstasy, spurring on hope, expanding and intoxicating the mind," Abdullah waxed eloquently in a Saudi newsletter.

Besides helping to organize Saudi soccer teams, Abdullah acted as the Saudi equivalent of a public relations man for his father, who needed to unify the disparate tribes conquered by King Abdul-Aziz.

Even though Saudi Arabia is a monarchy, the royal family is sensitive to pressures from the populace and can be surprisingly democratic. Each day, the king holds a *majlis*, where any citizen can present his grievances or requests directly. Prince Abdullah held his own *majlis* in the form of a feast that was open to all.

Each day, the prince had 100 to 120 bedouin in for lunch served from massive tables laden with *kharuf mahshi*—roast lamb stuffed with pieces of chicken, fruits, nuts, onions, and cracked wheat, sautéed in coriander-and-ginger-spiced butter. In a week, the bedouin consumed two tons of rice, two hundred chickens, and forty sheep.

One day, Abdullah invited Habib to the lunch, and he was placed at the prince's table. Habib sat entranced as Abdullah related how Arabian American Oil Co. (ARAMCO), the American oil consortium that eventually obtained the rights to drill for Saudi oil, had paid royalties in gold. As a child, he and other princes played in a room of the royal palace where the gold was heaped, Abdullah recalled.

"We threw it at each other," he laughed.

Four days after the lunch, Abdullah's son, Khalid, called at Habib's hotel.

"My father would like to see you," he said to Habib.

It was close to midnight, but Habib accompanied the son to the prince's Moorish-style palace just a quarter of a mile from the Raytheon compound. The palace sat amid twenty acres of gardens with water fountains illuminated by hidden lighting. Inside the palace were spacious reception rooms with high arches.

One side of the house was for the prince's wives. The other side was for the prince. Other buildings housed servants, kitchens, and guards. Everywhere, there were Persian rugs, mother-of-pearl furnishings, and burnished carvings.

Abdullah ushered Habib into his den, a small but finely appointed room with a tiny desk and books on walnut shelves. Under the shelves was a bar with an ice maker and glasses.

On either side of the prince stood two huge black bodyguards, like bulls with shining swords.

Motioning with his hands as if shaking a martini tumbler, the prince asked, "Would you like a martini?"

"Perhaps some of the scotch," Habib said, pointing to the bottle of Johnnie Walker.

As the prince began speaking in Arabic, Habib thought his accent was clearly that of the Nejdi, the bedouin tribesmen who populated most of the country. The other major group was the Hejazi, who live near the Hejaz Mountains along the Red Sea. The Nejdi viewed the Hejazi as virtual foreigners—spoiled flotsam from other countries who, like Khashoggi's family, came for the trek to Mecca and stayed. The Hejazi, on the other hand, considered themselves more sophisticated and worldly than the nomadic Nejdi.

"My father, the king, believes Adnan is no good," Abdullah told Habib. "He is demanding fees that are too high."

Citing Khashoggi's well-known friendship with Abdullah's uncles Prince Sultan and Prince Fahd, then the interior minister and second deputy premier, Abdullah said his father was troubled by the stories he had heard.

"The king feels he corrupts my uncles," he said. "My father wants to protect them and stop the stories about gambling and women."

Turning to the bodyguards, Abdullah said, "I could send these black guards to drag Adnan from his house and give him two hundred lashes on the back. We don't want to. We just want to stop his business activities.

"Do you think these companies would refrain from doing business with us if he were out of business?" he asked.

Abdullah looked intently at Habib. Abdullah knew nothing about Western ways, and Habib could interpret them for the prince.

"They will work as long as you are paying," Habib said.

"Okay," said the prince, his voice rising. "Go to Raytheon and tell them in my name I want the agency immediately. You will receive 20 percent of the commissions I receive."

"What will be the rationale?" Habib said.

"The logic is we want the defense business to remain in our hands. It's the defense of the country and of the family. Defense is essential," he replied.

Habib knew how the Saudis felt about defense. The oil under their feet was both a blessing and a curse. The country had the highest petroleum reserves in the world—twice as much as the Soviet Union and four times as much as the United States.

That meant the country was vulnerable to any nation that

decided it did not have enough oil to meet its needs. That, plus the perceived threat posed by Israel, meant the Saudi per capita defense budget was second in the world only to the tiny country of Qatar. Saudi Arabia spent $1,837 per capita a year on defense, compared with $543 spent by the U.S. and $433 by the Soviet Union.

That night, Habib couldn't sleep. The son of an Egyptian judge, he had lived most of his life on a salary. Now a prince had proclaimed that he would get 20 percent of hundreds of millions of dollars. Like the Prophet Mohamed, Habib felt he was being sent on a mission.

Allah be praised!

Habib called Harry Loebel and arranged to meet with him at Raytheon's Burlington, Massachusetts, offices. Green buds were beginning to emerge on the branches of the elm and maple trees outside his window.

Already, Loebel was under pressure from his superiors to reduce Khashoggi's commissions. A technocrat, he did not like the nagging questions, always accompanied by a wink, about where the money *really* was going. When Habib told him of Abdullah's proposal, Loebel grabbed for it as if it were a life raft in the ocean.

He called Grubbs to tell him of his decision, but Grubbs was on vacation with his wife in Italy. When Loebel finally reached him, Grubbs said, "I think it's a mistake."

He couldn't visualize dealing with a prince as an agent. But Loebel said the Raytheon hierarchy had already approved it.

Loebel and Grubbs broke the news to Khashoggi at the Phoenicia Hotel in Beirut. It was past midnight, when Khashoggi usually did business. Normally jovial, Khashoggi turned somber. This was the first American company to reject him.

"If that is the wish of the prince, so be it," he said. "But you are making a serious mistake."

Without missing a beat, he immediately launched into a discussion of a new $100-million Saudi National Guard contract that he could arrange for Raytheon to get. It was under the control of Prince Abdullah ibn Abdul-Aziz, the commander of the National Guard and now crown prince.

Ironically, he had the same name as the prince who had just taken the Raytheon contract from Khashoggi. The Al Saud named their sons for distinguished forebears, and there were only about twenty names to go around for four thousand family members. At last count, there were forty Prince Faisals and twenty-eight Prince Mohameds. Abdullah, one of the more prized names, meant "servant of God."

As the head of the National Guard, this Abdullah was in competition with Prince Sultan for Saudi defense dollars. Giving each some firepower was a way of hedging bets and making sure no one minister became too powerful.

When Khashoggi mentioned the National Guard contract, it was clear he had known about it all along but had not told Raytheon. Now he was trying to win back Raytheon by offering to arrange a new contract. But it was too late. Khashoggi was no longer Raytheon's agent.

On May 14, 1971, Loebel signed on Prince Abdullah as Raytheon's new agent. Almost immediately, there were problems. When Grubbs went to see the prince, he was told to deal with his subordinates. When he tried to see him again, the same thing happened. Grubbs was miffed, and he called Loebel in Burlington.

"Khashoggi at least pretends to take orders," Grubbs said. "Abdullah is a prince and has to act like a prince at all times. He's not hungry like Khashoggi. He expects to be treated with royal deference," he said.

Loebel picked up the phone and called Habib in Washington. He relayed what Grubbs had said, and Habib diligently took notes. Then Habib called Prince Abdullah in Jeddah and told him of the complaints.

"God willing," Abdullah said, "you will come here in six weeks' time and we will go over this whole thing and resolve everything to everyone's satisfaction. There is nothing to be concerned about. This time, you must stay in my palace," he said.

But the complaints circling the globe were beginning to circulate in Saudi Arabia. A copy of Habib's notes surfaced in the country. When Abdullah heard about this from others, he became enraged. Raytheon dared to criticize a prince!

In Saudi Arabia, there is nothing as important as the family, which replaced the earlier tribes as the fulcrum of Saudi society. By involving Abdullah in public controversy, Raytheon was besmirching his reputation and, by extension, the honor of his family.

*"Wallahi!"*—"By God!"—he barked at Habib. "This commotion is not worth the dust on my shoes."

Then Abdullah met with his father, King Faisal. He told him the Raytheon representatives were abrasive and incorrigible. Soon, Prince Fahd, the interior minister who later became king, mentioned to Nicholas G. Thacher, the U.S. ambassador, that Raytheon seemed to be having a lot of problems in Saudi Arabia.

"Perhaps this is not the best time for Raytheon to be seeking more contracts in Saudi Arabia," Fahd told Thacher.

It was typical Saudi understatement. The Saudis never intruded more than needed. But the message was unmistakable.

From other sources, Grubbs learned that the king wanted Loebel removed from the HAWK contract and was unhappy with him. When talking with Faisal, Abdullah had accused Grubbs of "telling lies."

Now Raytheon's entire business in Saudi Arabia was at stake. The HAWK was one of Raytheon's most profitable items, and Saudi Arabia accounted for the greatest share of HAWK sales outside the U.S.

In a state of shock, Grubbs caught the next plane to Beirut. He wanted to call Raytheon without being monitored in Saudi Arabia. Checking into the Phoenicia Hotel, he called D. Brainerd Holmes, then executive vice-president and now president of Raytheon.

At forty-nine, Holmes was a boyish electrical engineer whose suit jackets always seemed too big for him. Before being tapped by Raytheon in 1963 to become a senior vice-president, Holmes had been deputy associate administrator of manned space flight at the National Aeronautics and Space Administration. There, he had worked with Wernher von Braun. In 1962, he made the cover of a *Time* magazine issue devoted to the conquest of space.

Grubbs called Holmes on a Saturday. The peripatetic executive was at the aircraft hangar where he kept his own plane. Immediately, he understood the gravity of the situation. Holmes had been pressuring Loebel to clamp down on Khashoggi's commissions. But now Raytheon's business was being threatened. The king, the second deputy premier, even the American ambassador were involved.

"Stay where you are," Holmes told Grubbs. "I'll get back to you within twenty-four hours."

Grubbs spent the time in his room or in the lobby. That

wasn't unusual. Sometimes, Raytheon executives waited in their hotels for weeks for important calls.

Grubbs heard from Holmes the next day. "Loebel will be removed and will never enter Saudi Arabia again," Holmes stated. "We will not comment on you at all. I'll rely on you to see how much sensitivity surrounds you."

Somewhat relieved, Grubbs returned to Jeddah, only to be summoned two days later by Prince Turki, the vice-minister of defense.

"If you wanted to fire Adnan, fine," he said, "but you don't need another agent, especially not a prince."

Then Turki looked directly at Grubbs. "You should disregard the comment about you," he said. "We are not unhappy with you, and I would like you to convey that to Raytheon."

Grubbs, based in Saudi Arabia, had managed to make friends in the right places. Loebel, based in Massachusetts, became the scapegoat.

"I'm here to say I told you so," Khashoggi said as he and Grubbs got into the Chrysler behind Grubbs' villa. "It happened quicker than I thought it would." Referring to the complaints made to Habib, he asked, "How could you do that with a rebel Egyptian in Washington, D.C.?

"I want you to know this all reflects on me," Khashoggi said. "I know Sultan and Fahd will come and say to me that I caused this. My integrity is on the line."

Having regained his composure, Khashoggi met with Grubbs the next day at Khashoggi's house in Jeddah. He already knew how Raytheon was going to extricate itself from its own foolhardiness, while he would regain his commissions. Khashoggi said the plan required a face-to-face apology to Prince Abdullah by Charles Francis Adams, Raytheon's chairman.

That was not as easy as it sounded. A Saudi who feels he has been insulted would not wish to face the offender. So Khashoggi told Grubbs of a grand strategy that would enlist the aid of his friend Kamal Adham.

Seven years older than Khashoggi, Kamal Adham was the chief of Saudi intelligence and the liaison with the American CIA. A portly, personable man, he had blond hair—unusual in a Saudi but not unheard of. Educated at Cambridge University, he got along well with Westerners and Saudis alike. As the half brother of Queen Iffat, King Faisal's favorite wife, he was favored by Faisal as his own son.

Kamal Adham played an important role in Egypt, where he was close to Egyptian President Anwar Sadat. As an intermediary between the two countries, he negotiated hundreds of millions of dollars in Saudi subsidies in return for Sadat's decision to expel fifteen thousand Soviet military advisers in 1972.

Besides directing Saudi intelligence activities, Kamal Adham was a businessman who had acquired considerable wealth acting as an agent on sales to the Saudi government.

In 1981, he and several other Middle Eastern investors bought control of First American Bankshares Inc. in Washington, D.C. The investors installed Robert A. Altman, the husband of Lynda Carter, television's "Wonder Woman," as president of the holding company that owns the banks.

Khashoggi told Grubbs that he would ask Kamal Adham to use his influence with King Faisal to smooth the rough waters.

As part of the plan, Raytheon also obtained the help of James H. Critchfield, the CIA's chief of Near East affairs. Critchfield was in charge of the Middle East for the CIA from 1959 to 1969. Later, he was national intelligence officer for international energy affairs in the Nixon White House.

Critchfield was a friend of Khashoggi's and spent many hours with him in Washington, Beirut, and other parts of the world. At the time, he considered Khashoggi to be the best-informed person on Saudi Arabia and its foreign affairs.

Critchfield knew the Raytheon chairman as well. Within Raytheon, Adams had a reputation for liking to communicate with spooks. Critchfield thought the reputation unfair. Although Critchfield knew people who got their thrills by having clandestine meetings with CIA agents, Adams was not of that ilk. He was a patriot, a descendant of John Adams and of his eldest son, John Quincy Adams—a distinguished man of breeding.

When Adams told Critchfield about the bleeding wound in Saudi Arabia, the CIA man agreed to help. He already knew about the problem, and he felt that an embarrassment between the U.S. and the royal family was reason enough to become involved. Critchfield had dealt with Kamal Adham for years. Meeting with him at his home in London, he suggested that he go along with Khashoggi's plan.

"Neither we nor you need a problem," Critchfield told him.

Kamal Adham agreed to help.

As Raymond H. Close, the CIA station chief in Saudi Arabia, kept Grubbs informed, Adams enlisted the aid of still another spook, Kermit (Kim) Roosevelt, Sr. The grandson of President Theodore Roosevelt, he was an impish, ruddy-faced man with a mischievous grin and an intellectual demeanor. As head of the CIA's Middle East operations in 1953, he engineered the return to the throne of Mohamed Reza Pahlavi, the shah of Iran.

After leaving the CIA in 1958 as assistant deputy director of clandestine services, Roosevelt consulted for companies on the Middle East, and Raytheon was one of his clients. While Roosevelt was no longer with the CIA, he still kept in touch with his former colleagues, and that was one of the assets he brought to any consulting arrangement.

In reporting back to his clients, he would say he "talked with a friend at my old place of employment." No one knew for sure where his CIA connections began or ended, magnifying his importance.

Roosevelt also knew Khashoggi, who claimed that he had considerable influence with the king. In fact, Khashoggi boasted he could get Raytheon almost anything it wanted in Saudi Arabia. Roosevelt had his doubts. Later, when he brought up Khashoggi's name with the king, Faisal almost choked.

But that was more public relations than reality. Repeatedly, key members of the royal family claimed they would have nothing to do with Khashoggi, or that he was out of favor with the king or the crown prince, or that he had just gone too far. On one occasion, Prince Sultan even told U.S. Ambassador Eilts that he didn't want Khashoggi to have any American contracts.

Then Khashoggi would show up in Geneva with Prince Sultan on vacation, or Prince Fahd would appear on Khashoggi's yacht, in his plane, or at his Olympic Tower home in New York.

Repeatedly, Khashoggi arranged meetings between Saudi rulers and U.S. presidents, beginning with King Faisal's visit to see President Johnson in 1966. On October 14, 1969, Khashoggi organized a visit to President Nixon by Prince Fahd, then interior minister and second deputy prime minister. It was Nixon's first year in the White House, and the thirty-minute meeting started a new phase in U.S.–Saudi relations.

As king, Fahd met with Khashoggi before leaving for talks with President Reagan at the White House in February 1985.

Now Raytheon assigned Roosevelt to meet with Habib at his office on Connecticut Avenue in Washington. Roosevelt knew him from the days when Habib was in the Egyptian embassy. To Raytheon, Habib was like a jumping bean that had to be contained.

On November 4, 1971, Habib opened a telegram from Prince Abdullah summoning him to meet with him in Jeddah. A visa was waiting at the Saudi embassy in Washington.

But Roosevelt told him to stay out of the developing fracas in Saudi Arabia. Habib agreed to ignore the telegram and stay where he was.

He later regretted his decision.

During the first week of February 1972, Adams traveled to Saudi Arabia. According to plan, Kamal Adham had smoothed things out with Prince Abdullah. With Kamal Adham present, Adams met with the prince, who showed him around his palace and grounds.

Still frazzled from his experience, the prince said he would like to resign the Raytheon account but be kept informed on the company's progress. Adams thanked him for his kindness.

The entire matter was kept secret. At Kamal Adham's suggestion, Raytheon wrote the prince a letter after the meeting. Alluding to Kamal Adham without using his name, the February 23, 1972, letter said, "We shall continue to call on Your Highness through our common friend and in the manner in which you have directed us, and are looking forward to the opportunity to do so."

Raytheon then signed a new contract with Khashoggi and restored his commissions covering sales of the HAWK and improved HAWK missile. The new agreement called for commissions as high as 15 percent on some items, well above the 5 percent rate in the old contract.

Recognizing he was an impediment to Raytheon's dealings in Saudi Arabia, Loebel voluntarily withdrew from having anything to do with the contract or Saudi Arabia. With Abdullah out of the picture, Habib was out in the cold.

Looking back, Loebel thought that Khashoggi probably set up the whole house of cards so it would fall apart and restore him as agent with even higher commissions.

He was just that shrewd.

# Code Cupid

ANCHOR: U.S. Ambassador Nicholas G. Thacher
BLOSSOM: Prince Fahd, Saudi minister of interior,
      later king
CUPID: Adnan Khashoggi (later WISHBONE)
DAISY: Samyr P. Souki, Northrop Corp. consultant
GERANIUM: Saudi Brigadier General Zuhair
NIGHTRIDER: Prince Khalid ibn Abdullah ibn Abdul
      Rahman, businessman
PILGRIM: Prince Turki, vice-minister of defense
PRUNE: Manuel G. Gonzalez, Northrop Corp. vice-president
TIDE: Prince Sultan, Saudi minister of defense and aviation
TRUMPET: Saudi Brigadier General Hashim S. Hashim
UNCLE: U.S. government personnel based in
      Washington, D.C.
WAVE: Saudi King Faisal

*—Northrop telex codes*

**K**ERMIT Roosevelt, Sr., flipped on his tape recorder. Ever the spook, the former CIA agent wanted to make sure he got every word of the incoming call from Khashoggi.

A year earlier, Khashoggi had regained his commissions from Raytheon Co. Besides Raytheon, he now represented a dozen other American, German, British, and French firms, including Northrop Corp. Roosevelt was a consultant to Northrop.

Calling from the Majestic Hotel in Cannes, Khashoggi wanted Roosevelt to pass along a message to the Los Angeles aircraft maker.

It concerned a $250,000 bribe.

Khashoggi insisted the money was needed to pay off the commander of the Saudi Royal Air Force, Brigadier General Hashim S. Hashim, "Hashim Squared" as Khashoggi's American executives called him among themselves.

Hashim was about to retire, and Northrop executives saw little point in bribing a retired general.

Now Roosevelt heard Khashoggi's dulcet voice come on the line. Khashoggi waived the pleasantries. His tone was deadly serious.

"I am just putting it to you," he said, "that we don't play these games in our part of the world. We don't, maybe this guy tomorrow will become a minister or anything, so we just cannot..." His voice trailed off. "Anything we promised, even if he is in his job or out of the job, he gets it. Do you follow me?" he asked.

"Yes, I do," Roosevelt answered.

Roosevelt was purposely noncommittal. As he put down the receiver, he shut off the tape recorder. He never knew for sure when Khashoggi was acting and when he was serious. Sometimes he thought Khashoggi didn't know himself. But Roosevelt passed along the message to Northrop anyway.

By this time, Khashoggi had removed his mask. Unfinished sentences and suggestive smiles had given way to explicit demands preceded by dollar signs. Khashoggi had become too successful to waste time with subtlety. His Swiss bank accounts were awash with money from companies all over the world. He had already decided to project an image as an international businessman—much preferable to the persona of a middleman.

Besides, Northrop executives from California seemed far more amenable to going along with his schemes than were the stuffy Raytheon officials from Boston. Maybe it was the climate.

After Raytheon and Lockheed, Northrop was his biggest contract. Eventually, Khashoggi profited from Northrop beyond his fondest dreams. In the space of nine years, he accrued commissions of $184 million on an astounding $4.2 billion in sales to Saudi Arabia.

While a later court challenge reduced the sum to $42 million (and the exact amount is still being disputed in the courts), his commissions still averaged nearly $9 million a year from Northrop alone—or $25,000 a day.

From these commissions alone, he could have bought a Mercedes-Benz 500 SEC every other day and never have had to finance it.

The colossal profits had their roots in a meeting in Khashoggi's Beirut home on December 1, 1969. He had already established the habit of multiple homes—a London apartment, a home in Riyadh, and another in Jeddah. The Beirut home was a sprawling, five-bedroom affair that overlooked the city from a hillside in the Yarze section. Two years earlier, he moved there from a two-bedroom apartment on Hamra Street, where he still had his main office.

Khashoggi's guest was Samyr P. Souki, a former Middle East correspondent for *Newsweek* who had drifted into consulting work and now represented Northrop.

Souki had rapport with King Faisal and other Arab leaders, and his crisply written reports and letters informing Northrop of developments in the Middle East never failed to catch the attention of Northrop executives, including Thomas V. Jones, Northrop's chairman.

Born in Cairo of Egyptian parents, the soft-spoken Souki had an office across the street from Khashoggi's. In the past, Souki had expressed reservations about Khashoggi as a prospective Northrop agent. He represented too many of Northrop's competitors.

But Souki liked Khashoggi. He always had something interesting to say about a wide range of topics. He was a gracious host and a good listener. And the fact that there were often beautiful young women at Khashoggi's table made dinners with him far more interesting than with some of his competitors.

As Khashoggi poured Souki a drink, they looked out at the city spread beneath Khashoggi's home. Quickly, Khashoggi filled Souki in on a visit he had just had with Prince Sultan.

While he was with the Saudi defense minister, a small war had broken out with South Yemen. On the spot, Sultan decided he wanted seventeen of Northrop's F-5 tactical fighters as soon as possible. From the Iranian military officials, he had heard that they were good planes.

Northrop developed the F-5 as a simple and inexpensive plane primarily for use by Third World countries. An entire engine could be replaced in twenty-five minutes. It was the Volkswagen of the defense industry. Each cost $1.2 million including spare parts—just right for a country on a tight budget.

It was clear to Souki that Khashoggi had the inside track on a purchase that could easily mean $20 million in sales by Northrop. Khashoggi even gave Souki some helpful advice: He said Northrop should add 10 percent to the price it quoted the Saudis. This would allow for Khashoggi's 5 percent commission and free up another 5 percent as a "cushion."

"There may be a certain amount of bargaining," Khashoggi explained, "at which time you can then show your goodwill by reducing the price by 5 percent."

Khashoggi was playing nice guy to get his foot in the door. There would be plenty of time later to talk about terms and a commission of 10 to 15 percent. Like a practiced fisherman, he cast his line into the stream, then slowly brought it back, patiently waiting for a solid bite so he could yank the line and hook his fish.

The next morning at 9:30, a forty-nine-word telex describing Khashoggi's proposal of the previous night came clattering into Northrop's sandstone headquarters at 1800 Century Park East in Century City.

Like everything else about Northrop, the building on the corner of Santa Monica Boulevard was starkly efficient. The company had been founded by John K. Northrop, an architectural draftsman. Originally, he was a partner of Allan and Malcolm Loughead, two brothers who later changed their name to Lockheed. Thirteen years after the Wright brothers' first, twelve-second flight in 1903, the partners used an abandoned garage on the Santa Barbara waterfront to build airplanes. In 1939, Northrop left Lockheed Aircraft Co. to found the company that bears his name. The company never really became a major competitor until Thomas V. Jones became its president in 1959.

Jones grew up in the Los Angeles suburb of Pomona, majored in architectural engineering at Stanford University, and graduated magna cum laude in 1942. A scholarship student, he earned his way by waiting on tables.

He became a wartime engineer for Douglas Aircraft Co. and gained a reputation as a cost cutter. After working for the Brazilian Air Ministry, he took a job at the Rand Corp., the West Coast think tank. In 1953, he joined Northrop Corp. as assistant chief engineer.

By 1958, he had risen to vice-president for development planning. In 1963, he was named chairman.

A man with a high forehead, big ears, and black-rimmed glasses, he was an aggressive businessman who collected modern French paintings, was a wine connoisseur, and socialized with politicians and Hollywood stars.

Jones insisted on an "honest pricing" policy that did little to enhance Northrop's U.S. government sales. In Washington, government contractors often bid low to win contracts, then increased the price later through cost overruns.

The government's labyrinthine budgetary process encouraged the deception. Congress appropriated Defense Department funds for one year. At the end of the year, new funding had to be approved. If the Pentagon came in with a low price in the first year, the project had more chance of being funded. There was always room later to milk Congress for more money. The Pentagon knew that once a plane was being built, Congress would not cut off funds.

Jones bid the true price from the start, establishing Northrop's reputation for delivering planes on time and within cost. As Northrop's work for the U.S. government slid, Jones began looking for new markets overseas.

He decided the way to do it was to hire consultants who knew each country.

"Agents open doors and keep you apprised," he told his executives. "They are a stethoscope on the workings of the government."

He appointed agents to sell planes in Greece, Iran, Taiwan, and Germany, among other places. By the early 1970s, Northrop's sales had swelled to more than half a billion dollars a year. Northrop had opened offices in London, Paris, Taipei, Tehran, Beirut, Oslo, Bangkok, Rome, Zurich, Madrid, and Athens.

The method was working.

Jones ran Northrop as his personal fiefdom, which he directed from an entire floor of offices decorated with the help of his wife, Ruth, the daughter of the late movie actor Conrad Nagel. He entrusted the most important tasks to a few "stars."

One of them was C. Robert Gates, Northrop's international vice-president. Gates had rugged, movie-star good looks. Tall, with gray hair and steely blue eyes, he had a sense of humor that attracted people to him. Gates had been with Northrop since 1955, in charge of all foreign contracts.

When he received Souki's telex, Gates had Northrop's Washington office gauge State and Defense Department reaction to the idea of a sale to Saudi Arabia. Military sales to foreign governments were an arm of U.S. foreign policy and could not be done without approval from Washington.

Then Gates called Northrop's scheduling section and learned the first deliveries could begin within seven months. Finally, he ran the idea by Roosevelt, the former CIA agent.

Roosevelt was particularly effective in Iran, where he handed back the throne to the shah. But he dealt in other Middle Eastern countries as well. He reported directly to Jones, with whom he frequently socialized. For devoting half his time to Northrop, he got $60,000 a year from the company.

Roosevelt's blessing counted for a lot at Northrop, and he gave it to Khashoggi, saying Northrop should try him and see if he brought results.

To the casual observer, Khashoggi seemed disorganized— an Arab riding his magic carpet without benefit of the communications or support staff of a company like Northrop. The appearance was deceptive. Intelligence on developments around the world, on new contracts, and on his competitors was crucial to his success. Before it hit the wire services, Khashoggi knew from sources on the staff of his friend Prince Rainier of Monaco that Princess Grace had been killed in a car accident.

Intrigue, gossip, mystery—they were all grist for Khashoggi's mill.

As soon as it became technically feasible, he hired two computer whizzes to design an electronic mail system that would link him to all his toys throughout the world. Each of his homes, countless offices, helicopters, planes, and yachts, plus the homes and offices of all his executives and consultants, had a portable terminal. A computer in Geneva kept track of Khashoggi's location and the location of every executive.

Using a modem, a Khashoggi operative in Washington who obtained information about a new contract with Egypt could hook his portable computer to his home telephone, type out the information, and send it to the central computer. In real time, the computer instantly routed the message to Khashoggi.

Picking up some more information on the same contract at the air force procurement office in Dayton, Ohio, another Khashoggi operative used the same procedure. Padding around his plane or yacht, Khashoggi often wound up with several messages on the same subject from different aides stationed all over the world.

Usually, an assistant read the messages to him. Khashoggi did not like to read.

Northrop later developed its own electronic mail system, but Northrop executives had to play chain-of-command. A Northrop executive in the Washington office gave a memo to his boss, who gave it to his boss. Two days later, Jones got it.

In the meantime, Khashoggi would shuffle down the deck of his yacht in his white *thobe* and mention to a Northrop executive traveling with him, "I feel the air force will be awarding a contract in Egypt."

Four days later, when the Northrop executive found out that such a contract was in the works, he thought it was black magic.

Now Khashoggi was laying the groundwork to snare the Northrop contract. It was by no means guaranteed. Northrop could try to go around him to Sultan, or Sultan could enlist the aid of another agent.

At the time, Khashoggi was agent on at least 80 percent of the defense contracts with Saudi Arabia. But others got their share: Suliman S. Olayan, a former employee of ARAMCO; Ghaith R. Pharaon, the son of another physician to the Saudi royal family; or Akram Ojjeh, a Syrian-born agent who sometimes worked with Khashoggi.

Each had his own style and focus, and each amassed fabulous wealth. Swarthy, born in 1918, Ojjeh was Khashoggi's opposite when it came to polish. His father died when he was eight, and his mother supported her four children by working as a seamstress. The family drifted from Damascus to Lebanon, where French monks taught Ojjeh to read and arranged a scholarship for him to study law in Paris.

But he got a job with the French government and was put in charge of Arab broadcasts to North America and the Middle East. In that role, he met Prince Mansour, Saudi Arabia's first minister of defense, and they became friends. Ojjeh began selling arms to Saudi Arabia. When he became bankrupt, Khashoggi helped him out by getting him a new contract for pistols.

Based in France, Ojjeh founded Technique Avant-Garde, known as the TAG Group, which bought interests in the Air Alpes regional airline, Dumex public works group, and the Crédit Commercial de France.

To burnish his image, Ojjeh dabbled in the art world. In 1977, he purchased the ocean liner *France* for $16.5 million to serve as a hotel and museum for French antiquities. To furnish it, he bought a collection of eighteenth-century French furniture, only to learn the pieces would become damaged by the moist, salty atmosphere. In 1979, he sold the furniture at auction in Monte Carlo, realizing $1.7 million on one Louis XV ormolu-encrusted corner cabinet.

With two Boeing 707s at his command, four Paris residences, a country château, and beautiful women always hovering, Ojjeh comes the closest to emulating Khashoggi's lifestyle. Still, he lacks both the flare and the wealth of Khashoggi, who, with his twelve homes and international operations, makes Ojjeh look like a member of the Kiwanis Club.

By contrast with them, Pharaon and Olayan are colorless conservatives. Born in 1940, Pharaon received a Harvard MBA before embarking on a career as a Saudi agent. Through his Saudi Arabia Research & Development Corp., he got a lock on much of the country's construction business.

Looking to the U.S. to invest, he bought a $30-million interest in Detroit's Bank of the Commonwealth in 1975, then teamed up with former Treasury Secretary John Connolly to buy a controlling interest in Houston's Main Bank. After Bert Lance got in trouble with the controller of the currency, Pharaon bought his stock in the National Bank of Georgia.

With only two Lear jets and a French château, Pharaon leads a spartan life-style compared with Khashoggi, but it's more than Olayan allows himself. Born in 1918 in a small town 250 miles northeast of Riyadh, Olayan worked for ARAMCO as a truck dispatcher and warehouse manager. In 1947, he took a ninety-day leave of absence to start his own importing firm and never returned.

Investing jointly with Saudi princes, his Olayan Group took positions in a number of U.S. banks, including Mellon, Bankers Trust, and Chase Manhattan, acquiring more stock in Chase than any other holder except David Rockefeller. Olayan's reputation as a solid businessman got him on the board of Mobil Oil Corp. and the international council of Morgan Guaranty Trust Co.

Yet he spends most of his time in Saudi Arabia and takes the Concorde when he wants to oversee investments in the U.S., where he indulges in one of his few temporal pleasures: hamburgers.

Still, when it came to defense contracts in Saudi Arabia, Khashoggi was the man to see. If only for the sake of appearances, Sultan occasionally let some other agents share in them. It would not look right if Khashoggi were the agent on 100 percent of the defense contracts. Yet he openly called Khashoggi the "research arm" of his ministry.

Like a magician pulling a rabbit from a hat, Khashoggi arranged for the Northrop executives to meet in Paris with

Sultan himself. Khashoggi passed the word that Sultan was considering buying thirty-six planes—more than double the original order.

Meanwhile, Gates sent telexes to Northrop outposts in Paris, Rome, Washington, and Beirut, with copies to thirteen executives in the "Blood Distribution"—California marketing executives on a list compiled by Arlie J. Blood of the aircraft division. Gates wanted them to know that a sale was imminent.

Artfully, Khashoggi built the suspense as he arranged for Northrop executives to meet with Prince Sultan. He did not want them to think it was too easy to get their contract.

The meeting was to take place while King Faisal was in Paris to meet with French President Georges Pompidou. Sultan was with King Faisal, staying at the Hôtel Crillon. Khashoggi set the appointment for Friday, January 9, 1970.

On Thursday, Khashoggi sat down with Geoffrey Parsons, the leader of the Northrop group. Northrop's Paris chief, Parsons was a sophisticated man of letters who had a wide range of social contacts in Europe, including Prince Bernhard of the Netherlands and an assortment of dukes and earls.

Khashoggi told him the Saudis were unhappy with their past dealings with the U.S. on defense matters. They would never forgive a switch the Americans pulled in the early 1960s: The Saudis wanted Lockheed's F-104 fighters, but the U.S. government arranged instead to have Great Britain sell them Lightnings.

It was the kind of complicated deal that often pervades the arms business, which is governed as much by political considerations as by cost and quality. Returning the favor, the British bought F-111s from the United States.

In Saudi Arabia, where the harsh climate wreaked havoc with the sophisticated British planes, the Lightning bombed, so to speak.

Parsons listened impassively. Did this mean Northrop was not going to get the contract?

Then there was the 1969 visit of Robert J. Pranger, deputy assistant secretary of defense, Khashoggi went on. On a tour of the Middle East, Pranger stopped off at Sultan's ministry. New to his job, he asked Sultan why he wanted ships to defend his waters.

*Wallahi!* This was an insult to the defense minister and the royal family. The Americans had so little concern about

Saudi defense that they sent a neophyte who knew nothing about the Middle East and its tensions.

More recently, Khashoggi told Parsons, the Saudis had had to wait six months to get clearance from the U.S. government to buy some American-made machine guns.

"As you know," he added, "we could have obtained similar machine guns immediately from almost anywhere in the world—the U.K., Czechoslovakia, or Rumania."

Parsons assured Khashoggi that Northrop would not stand for any delays. But then Khashoggi raised a new obstacle. He said the Saudis would like the closest possible relationship with the U.S. but often found it difficult because American companies competed against each other.

In Saudi Arabia, companies and even agents formed alliances so they would all benefit from a contract award, no matter who won it. Thus Khashoggi and Ojjeh, working different parts of the world, were often inseparable. When a company wanted to switch agents from Ghaith Pharaon to Khashoggi, Khashoggi would call Pharaon and ask what he thought. Often, they would agree to let the company switch, then split the commission. Or they might throw the company out of the country entirely. All the while they gave the impression they were competitors.

Khashoggi said Northrop should team up with its archrival, Lockheed, to offer a better package to the Saudis. Lockheed already had maintenance facilities in Saudi Arabia, he said, and had been doing a good job of servicing planes. He suggested that Lockheed, acting as subcontractor to Northrop, maintain Northrop's planes.

Parsons knew Northrop was perfectly capable of servicing its own airplanes. But he did not want to lose the contract. He told Khashoggi that Northrop would consider it.

The idea was a standard Khashoggi technique for swelling his commissions exponentially. He got a commission on the full price from the contractor, and he got a commission from the subcontractor, whose price was included in the full contract. So Khashoggi layered commissions on his own commissions.

The math was simple. Let's assume Khashoggi's commission was 10 percent and the subcontract represented half the contract. On every $100 in sales, he then got a total commission of $15 instead of $10—$5 from the subcontractor and $10 from the contractor. In some cases, he got more because he piled on other clients as subcontractors.

In a private dining room of the Hôtel Crillon, Khashoggi portrayed the package idea at lunch on Friday as a patriotic gesture. The British had not serviced the Lightnings properly, he told the executives he invited from both Northrop and Lockheed. The marriage of Northrop and Lockheed would guarantee good products and good service.

"Although commissions are important to me," he said at the lunch, "I am a loyal Saudi, and the good of my country comes first."

Khashoggi watched his guests. He had a way of tilting his head back and to the side so that his face looked like a very steep ski slope. Instead of giving him a haughty appearance, it made him look relaxed and jovial.

Later, Khashoggi analyzed the reactions. To Khashoggi, every human being was a new book to be read and savored. It was one reason he listed "philosophical games" and "people" as his hobbies in his biographical data.

"Why did he smile at that moment? Why did he respond that way? Did you see the way, just after I mentioned commissions and offered him the fruit, he couldn't finish the banana? He only ate half of it! Do you know what that means?"

Khashoggi's analysis often confounded his aides. He took seriously things that passed them by. He always seemed to interpret favorably what he perceived: If someone dropped a glass, Khashoggi would find an excuse for it.

"He was not normal then. He had a fight with his wife," he would say. A certain comment by the man was not outrageous: "You didn't understand what he was saying," Khashoggi told his aides.

Khashoggi could tell the meetings in Paris were having their effect. The Northrop executives were impressed by the private dining rooms, the tab he always deftly picked up, and the entourage that went wherever he went.

The entourage was a uniquely Khashoggi phenomenon. It was a ready-made claque of aides, associates, and glitterati who moved on a wave generated by Shaheen, Khashoggi's assistant.

If only to transact a given piece of business, the Northrop executives became part of the entourage. They learned to leave all type-A behavior behind, to close their eyes and float. It was like being in the army. When the sergeant wanted them to move, they moved.

The sergeant was Shaheen, who happened to have been a

civilian in the U.S. Army Signal Corps when he met Khashoggi in 1960. Thin, with wire-rimmed glasses and a receding hairline, Robert Andrew Shaheen was born in Canton, Ohio, to Syrian parents on October 6, 1933.

Shaheen was the youngest of nine children; his father died when he was three. At age six, he began selling newspapers to help put food on the table. He dreamed of one day owning Cadillacs, diamonds, and gold. His mother, Selma Shaheen, still lives in the house where he was raised in Canton.

Shaheen attended Mount Union College in Ohio, a Methodist-affiliated school not far from Canton. He majored in political science and graduated in 1955. After two years in the army, he enrolled in Georgetown University's doctoral program in international relations. He interrupted his studies to advise the U.S. military in Saudi Arabia on how to teach English to Saudi Arabians.

He was considered *dumo khafif*—light-blooded or light-hearted. Early on, he showed a propensity for attending to people's needs. In his free time, he lent first-run American films to Saudi princes and made himself a number of friends, including Khashoggi. He first met him when dispatched by the U.S. military to deliver a letter to him at the Yamama Hotel in Riyadh. They had dinner, and soon Shaheen was supplying him with 16-millimeter copies of *La Dolce Vita*, *Never on Sunday*, and *Psycho*.

In 1960, Shaheen began working for him as a consultant. In 1971, he became his full-time personal assistant.

Shaheen called Khashoggi "the chief" and considered him a demigod. He spent twenty-four hours of every day working for him, or on call, and he named three of his four daughters after Khashoggi or his wives—Sueraya for Khashoggi's first wife, Nanda for Adnan spelled backward, and Laradona for Khashoggi's second wife, Lamia, whose original name was Laura. (He claimed to have forgotten the origin of Daveeda, the name he gave his fourth daughter.) Shaheen never lost his sense of wonder at what Khashoggi's riches could buy, or the access that Khashoggi enjoyed.

Driving in Paris, Shaheen told a guest, Khashoggi got a call on the limousine telephone from King Carlos of Spain. A letter to Khashoggi just came in from Richard M. Nixon. It's just a polite reply to a letter Khashoggi had written after Nixon gave a speech, but Shaheen reads it anyway.

"The man is unique, the way he deals with people. I'm struck with awe," he confides.

If Khashoggi is constantly enveloped by controversy, it is to be expected. "It happened to Caesar, to Jesus, and it happens today when a man has great visions and dares to be different," he says.

In his most inspired moments, Shaheen calls Khashoggi a "merchant statesman."

Usually, Shaheen is on the phone, juggling three calls on three different phones at the same time. One day, he was talking on one line with an aide to the prime minister of Jamaica, a man worried about where he was going to park his Rolls-Royce when he visits Khashoggi in New York. On a second line, he was hiring a plane to fly some businessmen from Paris to Bologna. On a third, he was consoling a love-struck girl.

"You're too young to be in love," he told her.

Each party could hear what he was saying to the others.

In carrying out Khashoggi's wishes, money was no object.

"Get the job done" was one of his mottoes, and he used crisp, new bills to help in that regard. He prided himself on the way he discreetly took care of restaurant checks, always excusing himself and settling accounts out of sight of his boss.

"Security," he would whisper when explaining why frogmen checked out the *Nabila*'s berth before it docked, just as he explained why he had obtained from New York publishing sources a copy of the proposal for this book.

As a token of appreciation, Khashoggi gave Shaheen a birthday present every October of one thousand times his age in the currency of the country where they happened to be at the time. Shaheen always fretted that they would be in the Philippines or Spain instead of the U.S. or Great Britain. Khashoggi played on his fears by leaving him messages instructing him to meet him in Mexico.

Over time, Shaheen got to share in Khashoggi's wealth. Khashoggi cut him in on deals, and he became a millionaire.

But the money he made from Khashoggi meant little to him. His biggest fear was that Khashoggi would die. For all the money Shaheen accumulated, it didn't give him the power he derived from being the personal assistant to the richest man in the world. In unguarded moments, he likened his position to being chief of staff at the White House.

Shaheen knew that people around Khashoggi were envious of his position. As the gatekeeper to a modern King Croesus, he had to apportion Khashoggi's time among family, friends, and business associates. That led to palace intrigues—family members trying to gang up on him, trying to unseat him from the foot of the throne. He knew how petty people could be and he was always on guard—sifting rumors, looking for hints, never quite sure that his enemies were failing in their mission.

Shaheen was Khashoggi's alter ego. "Never in the way, and never out of the way" was another of his many mottoes. Deftly, he used his authority, sometimes hinting that he spoke for Khashoggi, other times giving the impression he was acting on his own. Usually, he spoke without quoting Khashoggi. He never signed letters, never socialized with the people around Khashoggi, never told anyone but family members where Khashoggi was. No one knew where Shaheen ended and Khashoggi began, but it mattered little. After twenty-five years with Khashoggi, he knew what his reactions would be on a given subject.

On important matters involving current business, Shaheen did nothing without Khashoggi's approval, even giving him the benefit of tape recordings of his telephone conversations so Khashoggi could get his own feel for them. On other matters, like publicity or new business proposals, Shaheen often acted on his own, going to his boss only when it became absolutely necessary to get approval. He knew how to sell Khashoggi on an idea by feeding it to him slowly, in small chunks, over time.

Shaheen was a shrewd judge of people and knew immediately who were the hangers-on and who were the people with class, who were the ones who wanted his job and who were the ones who could be trusted. If he didn't like someone, he didn't return his calls. Usually, there was no way to get to Khashoggi without going through Shaheen. All phone messages and mail went through him, and he would tell secretaries to rip up messages if he didn't think his boss should see them.

Shaheen insisted that every hotel supply him with an extra-long extension cord for the telephone, so he could conduct conversations while walking around. In leaving tips at the end of Khashoggi's visits, he included hotel operators, usually giving them two hundred dollars.

On the phone, he was an actor, first sounding threatening and abrupt, then ending on a mellow note. When inviting guests to a party at Khashoggi's Olympic Tower apartment in New York, he would spit out the consonants and make his voice sound breathless to get across the enormity of the favor being bestowed.

While Shaheen could terrorize employees with a strident delivery, his strongest imprecation was "goofs." Only rarely did he discard his manners, as he did with former Florida Governor Claude Kirk. Kirk had joined the entourage for several months and seemed to think he had a permanent meal ticket.

The end came after Kirk, flying on Khashoggi's stretched Boeing 727 from Riyadh to London one day, told a former Northrop Corp. executive in Khashoggi's presence that he would like to talk with Khashoggi alone.

Flabbergasted, Khashoggi told Kirk the man was a guest of his.

When they landed in London, Kirk asked Shaheen when he should be back at the plane. Shaheen told him Khashoggi's plans didn't include Kirk.

"The party's over," he told the former governor.

If the power went to his head, Shaheen never showed it. He was always nattily dressed, always the dark suit or navy blazer, always the very starched collar or the dazzling white shirt. When addressing people, he used their last names preceded by "Mr." long after most people would have begun using a first name. The way to get Shaheen to drop his formal exterior was to call him "Mr." back.

On the rare occasions when Shaheen took off his clothes to don a bathing suit, Khashoggi's entourage would whistle and applaud. But at Christmas, he loved to dress up as Santa Claus, puff up his belly, and put on a show for Khashoggi's children.

He was a born performer who became a jaunty host when Khashoggi threw parties and then did not attend. When Khashoggi gave a speech, Shaheen was effusively attentive and the first to break into applause, setting off a wave of accolades from the audience.

As the leader of the entourage, Shaheen managed to be a brilliant organizer and people-mover while being charming, remembering names, introducing everyone, overseeing caterers, arranging appointments, procuring theater tickets, and hinting that good news was in the offing.

The latter was the most important. Everyone in the entourage was after something, and Shaheen knew it. He had an ironic wit: If he knew he had you where he wanted you, he let you know he was enjoying it.

When Spiro T. Agnew briefly joined the entourage, Shaheen chortled when Agnew called one day at the Waldorf-Astoria Towers looking for Khashoggi.

"What's that, Mr. Vice President?" Shaheen asked, winking at Edward K. Moss, Khashoggi's public affairs consultant. "I can't hear you, would you speak up, please? Ah, I don't think that would be possible. Try another approach, Mr. Vice President."

Khashoggi never invited just anyone to join the entourage. If it was an actress, she was the stuff of men's dreams—Gina Lollobrigida, Farrah Fawcett, Brooke Shields, Jane Seymour, Raquel Welch, or Cheryl Tiegs. The males were always dashing or famous and preferably both—Sean Connery, Christopher Reeve, Frank Sinatra, William Holden, Robert De Niro, Roger Moore, or Pierre Trudeau.

Khashoggi always found time to go to every table, to introduce all the guests, and when the evening was over, to see even the lesser ones to the door or to their cars.

One night, after the Northrop contract was signed, the cast of thousands descended on Khashoggi's Paris home at 11 Avenue Montaigne. Complete with a pool, it was a magnificent piece of real estate once owned by Ferdinand de Lesseps, the French promoter who won the concession to build the Suez Canal.

When Khashoggi bought the house, the walls were covered with bookshelves from floor to ceiling, but the shelves were empty. Khashoggi told an aide to buy books to fill the shelves.

The aide asked what kind he should buy.

Noting that the decor was done in reddish browns, Khashoggi replied, "Mahogany ones."

As Khashoggi was making the rounds of the tables at the dinner party, William I. Lightfoot, an energetic Northrop executive with steel-gray eyes and a Boston accent, introduced Khashoggi to his wife, Mary.

"Your wife is very attractive," Khashoggi said.

"She should be. It's her birthday," Lightfoot said.

"Why didn't you tell me?" Khashoggi said. He turned to an aide and whispered that he wanted a birthday cake.

A few minutes later, the aide returned, saying the chef could not make a cake on such short notice.

Khashoggi thought about his twelve homes, each fully staffed at all times, and the fact that he only spends about a week a year in each one.

"I want a cake in ten minutes, or I'm going to restaff the kitchen," Khashoggi commanded.

Mrs. Lightfoot was blushing.

Ten minutes later, the chef brought out different-colored melons cut in geometric shapes and arranged like a cake on a silver platter. On top was whipped cream dotted with birthday candles.

"See? They can make a cake in ten minutes," Khashoggi said.

When the Northrop executives met with Sultan that Friday afternoon in Paris, it was anticlimactic. Almost word for word, Sultan reiterated what Khashoggi had already told them.

That was hardly surprising. Khashoggi was more than a commissioned agent. He played a major role in Saudi defense. Saudi Arabia was still a country of desert nomads. Slavery had only recently been abolished. Airplanes were still fearsome winged behemoths. In the 1960s, Sultan needed someone to suggest what he should buy, and from whom.

Khashoggi helped develop the need for the product, and then he supplied it. If he made more money doing it than anyone in history, wasn't that just the free enterprise system at work?

On Friday evening, Souki met with King Faisal and Sultan. Sultan mentioned the previous conversations with Northrop officials and Khashoggi.

At the mention of Khashoggi, Faisal turned to face Sultan.

"That's your responsibility; the main thing is that Saudi Arabia should maintain its close association with the U.S.," he said.

The comment was holy water sprinkled on Khashoggi. King Faisal—who ultimately would have to approve the contract—had raised no objection to Khashoggi as the agent. He had left it to Sultan, who was Khashoggi's buddy.

After the meetings, Parsons was convinced Northrop should sign Khashoggi as its agent. He later urged Gates to do anything "within reason" to obtain Khashoggi's services and win the contract.

That summer, Souki learned that King Faisal had told Sultan to drop Khashoggi. The news came from a princess who saw Sultan in Geneva.

She told Souki, "If he does not, Sultan may be out of a job."

Quickly, the telexes went out to Century City: "Sultan must

drop his fat friend." Gates instructed his executives, "Stall all negotiations."

The report was typical of the smoke constantly swirling around Khashoggi. Although not a blood relative, he was like a member of the royal family. As in any family, squabbles arise, and this was one of them. The argument was not over whether Khashoggi should get commissions; it was over the size of his fees and how they were split among the princes.

Khashoggi delicately balanced the aspirations of one member of the royal family against another, striving to make them all happy. He always took care to instruct Northrop not to send him anything in Saudi Arabia referring to his commissions. If the size of his fees got out, it would disrupt his role as ballast within the family.

When Khashoggi later signed a contract with Northrop, it consisted of two parts: a public one that provided for a modest monthly retainer, and a private one that listed his percentage commissions.

The latter documents were "secret and under no circumstances are to be discussed outside of the key responsible people within Northrop," Robert B. Watts, Jr., Northrop's assistant general counsel, wrote in a memo after he prepared the papers.

Whenever Khashoggi heard rumors that he was in disfavor with the king, he always took care to bring it directly to Faisal's attention, often in a letter. Then Faisal would write back a glowing letter full of praise for the work Khashoggi was doing. His contracts in Saudi Arabia were never disturbed.

Within a few weeks of the princess's visit, Souki was told that Khashoggi was no longer in disfavor. He told Gates, who told his people: "Fatman's cloud has passed over."

As if to underline the point, Souki reported to Gates that Khashoggi was on vacation with Sultan. By then, Souki had checked further into Khashoggi's relationship with Prince Sultan and his method of operating.

"As he is on such good terms with Sultan," he wrote to Gates, "we should try to work with him," adding, "On such delicate matters as 'extraordinary expenses,' Mr. K knows how to maneuver. It is not . . . just a matter of Sultan. There are many persons, at various echelons, who have to be persuaded."

On August 20, Khashoggi arranged another meeting for Northrop executives with Sultan. His access seemed to be limitless. This time, Gates himself attended. The meeting took place in Khashoggi's suite at the Hôtel Président in Geneva.

Sultan was three hours late, but the reason pleased the Northrop crowd: He had been lunching with the crown prince, Khalid, who would later become king.

Again Sultan discussed his misgivings about the way the Defense Department had treated him. But he ended by telling Northrop he intended to buy the F-5s. On October 4, 1970, Northrop signed Khashoggi as its agent for what would later become known as the Peace Hawk Program.

The contract—which would eventually supply the Saudis with 150 planes—seemed to be in the bag. Yet the squeeze was just beginning.

Soon, Khashoggi began telling Northrop about "other people" who had to be taken care of. This was a surprise to Northrop. Khashoggi was supposed to handle any such demands. But this request came from Prince Khalid ibn Abdullah ibn Abdul Rahman.

A brother-in-law of Prince Fahd, then interior minister, Khalid was a businessman whose position within the royal family required that he be placated. As the husband of Fahd's full sister, he qualified for membership in Saudi Arabia's most exclusive and powerful club: the Sudairi clan. Understanding the Sudairis was crucial to understanding power relationships in Saudi Arabia.

The Sudairis were the seven sons of King Abdul-Aziz born of Hassa bint Ahmad al-Sudairi. Having divorced and married her again, the king considered her one of his favorite wives. Her offspring tended to be more aggressive and ambitious than the rest of Abdul-Aziz' forty-three sons.

These seven became the elite of the royal family and wound up ruling the country. They were Prince Fahd, her first son who is now king; Prince Sultan, the defense minister; Prince Abdul Rahman, a businessman; Prince Turki, the vice-minister of defense at the time; Prince Naif, the former governor of Riyadh; Prince Salman, the governor of Riyadh; and Prince Ahmad, the vice-minister of the interior.

Until their mother died in 1969, the seven brothers had lunch with her almost every day. By Western standards, that is hard for even a mother to fathom. But to the Saudis, it was expected.

To this day, the Sudairis gather once a week for dinner, usually at one of their sisters' homes. Included in this inner circle are their wives and brothers-in-law, Prince Khalid among them. Besides the social chitchat, important business deals are struck over coffee. It would be inadvisable to have a detractor within that auspicious group.

Khashoggi told Northrop that Khalid was asking for a cut of 10 percent, claiming he had helped Khashoggi work out the Northrop deal. Khalid wanted to meet with Northrop executives about it. But Khashoggi told Northrop to cool Khalid.

"Tell the prince that Northrop is annoyed with my demands," Khashoggi advised R. Grant Rogan, Northrop's Beirut chief, on January 11 at the Mayfair Hotel in London. Besides, he told Rogan, there are other players to worry about—General Hashim, for instance, who was asking for 5 percent. And his replacement could add another player, Khashoggi said.

It was the first time Northrop had heard about the need to pay off air force commanders. Rogan felt he had just stepped off a very fast merry-go-round. The number of Saudi officials with their hands out made his head spin.

When Gates got Rogan's report, he ordered his executives to code all their international messages. Discussions of bribes were too sensitive to leave in plain English. Because Khashoggi was attempting to mate Northrop with Lockheed, he was called Cupid in Northrop's code book.

On May 14, 1971, Gates got a message from his executives in Saudi Arabia: "Cupid expects . . . green light for roses [Saturday]." It meant Khashoggi expects approval of the F-5 sale by Saturday.

A week later, Sultan told the U.S. embassy that he wanted a total of fifty F-5s—thirty-three more planes than the original number. By now, the price had escalated to $140 million, including extras the Saudis wanted. Sultan saw the F-5 as the backbone of the air force he wanted to build.

Northrop executives were jubilant, if puzzled. Originally, the deal was to be made directly between Saudi Arabia and Northrop. Khashoggi was to get a 12 percent commission. But Sultan told the U.S. embassy he wanted the sale to be made through the U.S. Foreign Military Sales Program.

This is the way foreign governments usually buy arms from U.S. manufacturers. They go through the Defense Department, which awards the contract to the manufacturer and ensures that prices are reasonable.

For the thirty years beginning in 1950, Saudi Arabia accounted for more FMS sales than any other country—$23 billion, including construction of military facilities.

Now that the sale would be made through the FMS program, Khashoggi's commission was cut to 5 percent. That was fine with Northrop, but Northrop executives wondered how Khashoggi would react.

It turned out Khashoggi had urged Sultan to use the FMS program. He told him it would mean less paperwork than contracting directly with Northrop. But he had another reason. It eliminated the clamor from his competitors. He already had a guaranteed commission. The Defense Department would not allow the additional commissions being requested; the FMS program would cut them out and allow him to get his foot in the door with Northrop.

Later, there would be time to increase his commissions on subsequent phases of the contract. Khashoggi knew how to wait. Patience was one of his greatest assets.

The signing was to take place on July 27 in Sultan's office in Riyadh. Fifteen minutes before the 11:45 A.M. appointment, Hashim appeared in Sultan's reception room, where the Northrop officials and U.S. Ambassador Nicholas G. Thacher were already waiting. Hashim said the signing was being delayed until the next day.

The executives were dumbfounded. No explanation was given.

That night, Manuel G. Gonzalez, a Northrop vice-president, got a call at his hotel from Khalid. Saying he was at the home of Prince Turki, the vice-minister of defense, Khalid said he wanted to see him.

Half an hour later, Khalid showed up, visibly upset. He said he had worked behind the scenes with Khashoggi to help win the contract for Northrop. He was supposed to get a share of the commission. Now that it was to go through the FMS program, he would get nothing. He threatened to get Sultan to delay the signing unless he got a cut.

"If I get nothing, then I will make sure that Adnan gets nothing," he said. "If he gets one dollar, I want fifty cents. Otherwise, I will take steps to see that he never gets any more business in this area."

Gonzalez told Khalid he should talk to Khashoggi.

After the nighttime visit, Khalid became Nightrider in Northrop's code book.

• • •

The next day at 1 P.M., Prince Sultan strode into his office at the defense ministry in Riyadh. After thumbing through the contract, he turned to Gonzalez, the senior Northrop official at the meeting.

"Do you have any agent in Saudi Arabia?" he asked.

Khashoggi had prepared Gonzalez for this question. He said Sultan would ask it, and he told Gonzalez to answer in the negative.

As instructed, Gonzalez answered, "No, not in Saudi Arabia."

Then he asked if any middlemen were involved. Sitting next to Gonzalez, Thacher, the U.S. ambassador, answered that no middlemen were involved in the FMS program.

Thacher knew Khashoggi was involved but later said he had misunderstood the question.

Sultan signed on the dotted line, but before the Northrop executives could uncross their fingers, General Hashim took Gonzalez aside.

"His Royal Highness wants to see you," he said.

His Royal Highness was Prince Turki, whose office was one flight down.

Even though Turki was vice-minister of finance and presumably an important player in Khashoggi's business dealings, Khashoggi avoided him as much as possible. Ever alert for changes in the status of members of the royal family, Khashoggi had decided that Turki had no future.

Turki had made the mistake of hitching himself to a non-Saudi wife after divorcing one of the royal family's favorite daughters. What's more, the father of his new bride, Hind al-Fassi, had been jailed by King Faisal himself for practicing witchcraft.

Known as "Dr. Sheikh," her father was from Morocco, where the entire family made potions that were supposed to cure everything from heart disease to wandering husbands. In 1969, Dr. Sheikh decided that Saudi Arabia held more promise, and he emigrated with his flock to Jeddah. There, the family opened a tobacco shop and continued to dabble in the black arts. Meanwhile, they began attracting a following of dissidents who embraced the family as spiritual leaders, disturbing Islamic authorities and the Saudi royal family.

While Dr. Sheikh was in jail, Turki fell for Hind, with her porcelain features and almond-shaped eyes. He held off marrying her until King Faisal died, but meanwhile he traveled with her and her four brothers and shared his wealth with them. First in London, then in Geneva, and finally in Los Angeles, the brothers vied with each other to spend as ostentatiously as possible.

In 1978, the oldest brother, Mohamed al-Fassi, won the contest by buying a $2.4-million home on Sunset Boulevard in Beverly Hills. He painted it mint green and placed lifelike nude statues on the lawn, painting the genitals pink and pubic hairs black.

Later, he was arrested in Hollywood, Florida, for allegedly failing to pay a $1.4-million hotel bill. Al-Fassi became so unpopular that Walter Reed Martindale III, a former State Department official, was convicted in 1984 of conspiring to kill him on behalf of unnamed Saudis.

Eventually, the royal family had had enough. Turki was asked to resign as vice-minister of defense.

But now he was chatting with the Northrop executives about seeing their chairman at the annual air show in Paris. Edging into the events of the previous evening, he said, "Speaking as a friend, and not in any official capacity, I understand that there was a disagreement with Prince Khalid." Calling it "most unfortunate," Turki said he hoped "things will be worked out to his satisfaction."

As he spoke, Gonzalez decided he knew why Sultan had delayed the signing: It was to put pressure on Northrop to accept Khalid's demands. It was the same reason Sultan asked if Northrop had an agent *inside* Saudi Arabia, Gonzalez thought. Khalid was inside Saudi Arabia, and Sultan wanted him signed on.

Gonzalez was not sure whom Khalid represented: Khalid had said he represented Prince Turki, who was his brother-in-law. Later, he said he represented himself. It mattered little. They all wanted him to get a cut.

Immediately, Northrop told Khashoggi about Prince Turki's comment, and Khashoggi agreed to assign half of 1 percent of the contract price to Khalid's company, Cantona Establishment. It was all done through Swiss bank accounts and came from Khashoggi's funds.

The payment was only the beginning of the "extraordinary expenses" and set the stage for demands that Khashoggi did not cover.

• • •

On October 9, 1971, Jones was in Saudi Arabia to meet with King Faisal. The first phase of the contract had been signed, but now there were other phases to discuss. The Saudis wanted Northrop to provide more maintenance services and build military bases and barracks. In the meantime, the U.S. government had turned thumbs down on the idea of Lockheed servicing Northrop planes.

Khashoggi invited Jones to his home in Riyadh for dinner, along with Souki, Gates, and Roosevelt. After dinner, they adjourned to the business end of the home.

Turning to Gates, Khashoggi said, "Bob, are you ready to meet with Hashim and take care of that? Hashim is not happy and has to be taken care of." He mentioned $250,000.

Jones was surprised and muttered that he knew nothing about that.

"Northrop honors its commitments, but not everybody in the company can make them," Jones said to Khashoggi.

The exchange broke up the meeting, and Jones and the others went back to their hotels. Gates, meanwhile, told Khashoggi that Hashim was his problem.

The disturbing incident focused more attention on Khashoggi's demands, as the Northrop executives debated what to do. Was it a ploy by Khashoggi to raise his commissions? Or was he serious when he said Hashim must be taken care of?

Ironically, Lockheed executives were facing a similar dilemma. For some time, Khashoggi had told them that various Saudis had to be paid off.

In an internal memo, a Lockheed official referred to the fact that the company added $100,000 to $200,000 to the price of each Hercules C-130 jet sold to Saudi Arabia. This money was for a "contingency" fund, according to the memo.

"This contingency fund...mostly has been used by the consultant [Khashoggi] for so-called 'under-the-table' compensation to Saudi officials in order to get the contract signed," the memo said. Lockheed has "no way of knowing if the so-called 'under-the-table' compensation is ever disbursed to Saudi officials or stops at our consultant's bank account."

Back in Century City, Northrop officials hit upon a ploy to try to resolve the question. A Northrop check would be drawn for $250,000, payable to Hashim. Gonzalez would present it to Khashoggi and watch his reaction. Presumably, if the money were really intended for Hashim, Khashoggi would accept the check.

Gonzalez and Gates went ahead with the plan on February 6, 1972. When they showed Khashoggi the check in his dark-paneled Beirut office, he hit the ceiling and did not come down for several minutes.

"You personally might get arrested," he said. "You just can't do it this way."

Then, sensing their purpose, he said, "Look, you don't trust me. You're doing this because you don't trust me."

Khashoggi suggested they give him the money. Khashoggi would take care of it properly.

In retrospect, Gonzalez, a lawyer and a native Californian, decided showing the check to Khashoggi was the stupidest idea he had ever had.

But the exercise had focused attention on Khashoggi's demand. The next month, Northrop did as Khashoggi had asked. It sent him $250,000 in his account at Swiss Bank Corp. in Geneva, the bank that appears at the "Go" position on the Monopoly set designed around Khashoggi's assets.

Six months later, General Zuhair replaced Hashim as commander and the same scene was replayed. Khashoggi told Northrop another $150,000 was needed to pay off the new commander. Gates decided all the payments should be taken out of Khashoggi's commission. As far as Gates was concerned, Northrop was not going to reimburse anyone for paying off a retired general.

It was then that Khashoggi called Roosevelt from Cannes to complain.

The fact that Hashim had retired was irrelevant, Khashoggi told him in the March 1, 1973, taped call.

"...even if he died, we give his family the thing," he insisted.

A week later, Northrop executives in Saudi Arabia began reporting that government officials were acting coolly. Plans for going ahead with the next phase of the contract were being delayed.

Lockheed had had much the same experience.

"Strongly suspect machinery stalled for lack of grease," Lockheed executives told headquarters. Another payoff was not being made according to Khashoggi's instructions.

At the Defense Department, Air Force Major General Robert F. Trimble was reviewing the agent fees paid under the Northrop contract. The director of procurement policy, Trimble had been with the air force since 1951. He wore white shirts and walked erect like a soldier. He spoke few words and got his point across like a knife slicing through butter.

Now he was in his office in the C-ring on the fourth floor of the Pentagon. Flipping through countless documents, he noticed the 5 percent fee to Khashoggi. To Trimble, it seemed high. Ultimately, all costs are passed along to the government making the purchase. But a major purpose of the FMS program is to assure the purchaser that the costs are reasonable.

Trimble saw no reason for any agent fees in any case; usually on FMS sales, there weren't any.

Instead of writing a memo to the Peace Hawk program manager, he called him. He knew him personally and didn't want to embarrass him. The officer had already signed off on the fees.

"I'm sorry," Trimble said. "I cannot agree to it. Five percent doesn't sound high," he said, "but when you multiply it out, it's $6 million in commissions on one phase alone."

Then he quoted a regulation—ASPR 1-505.4 (a)—that says commissions should bear a relationship to the cost of the services received. Were there airline tickets and hotel room bills to justify $6 million in fees?

Privately, the procurement officers smiled at the question. Everyone at the Pentagon knew the answer, or thought they did: The money was for bribes.

Trimble decided there was nothing that could be done about the fees already paid to Khashoggi. But he said he would hold up approval of the third phase of the contract, a segment that could mean another $200 million in sales to Northrop.

The Pentagon held meetings and more meetings. Each time, fifteen people attended. Then they sent memos on the meetings to another fifteen people. Trimble's decision stuck. The contract was stalled.

When Gonzalez heard about this, he suggested to Khashoggi that he meet with the generals. It seemed like a harebrained scheme at first—a Saudi with a reputation as a fixer subjecting himself to grilling by American officials. But Khashoggi had unlimited confidence in his ability to persuade, and he agreed to do it. The generals consented, in part because they respected Gonzalez.

On August 9, 1973, Khashoggi showed up at the Pentagon with his lawyer, Daniel G. Zerfas. In the secretary of defense's suite, across the table from Khashoggi, sat seven Pentagon officials, including Trimble.

Khashoggi immediately defused them with an account of how he had become an agent—attending Chico State, knowing the Saudi princes, and selling Kenworth trucks to the Saudi military.

"In every case," he said, the companies he contracted with provided "excellent products and good services. I never had to develop excuses for poor performance."

Scribbling notes in a corner, Gonzalez thought the brass understood the point and accepted it: that he had not achieved a favored position with Prince Sultan solely through personal friendship.

Khashoggi described the king as a firm believer in the free enterprise system and the Saudi royal family as a "stabilizing force" in the Middle East. He said the king was concerned that Saudi Arabia could be the target of a communist takeover.

The king could distribute the oil wealth directly to the people, but instead chose to foster business development. Since few hard goods were manufactured in Saudi Arabia, the only way to build business was by encouraging Saudis to represent foreign companies.

Khashoggi seemed to be saying he was a foreign aid program. Several of the people at the table were holding back smiles.

Then Khashoggi pointed out that the role of a sales representative is accepted in all areas of the economy except defense.

"Defense equipment manufacturers get an unusual amount of publicity throughout the world," he said. "When I sell Chrysler products to the government, I openly mark them up 15 percent," he said. On the other hand, commissions on military sales must be kept secret.

Khashoggi had hit another nerve.

"Yes," said David Alne, a high-ranking defense official. FMS officials have to use "carefully selected and artful" words when dealing with the subject of commissions.

Khashoggi ran through the types of fees he received and listed some: 5 percent from Raytheon on hardware and 15 percent on spares and services; 8 percent from Lockheed; 15 percent from Chrysler on $50 million in sales.

The brass was fascinated.

Khashoggi said he would never offer Prince Sultan any

money—only "truth, sound advice, and good products." On the other hand, he said, the Saudi culture is different from American culture. It is based on a bedouin philosophy.

"They only recognize loyalty based on material values," he said.

Khashoggi said he has often been called upon to demonstrate his loyalty to the royal family by offering goods or services free. For example, he said a bedouin school needed textbooks. He donated them. A family needed trucks to transport their goats. He gave them twelve.

He had other costs, he said, offering to let the generals look at audits of his books.

Khashoggi conceded that when arms purchases were not made through the FMS program, improper payoffs did occur. That was why commissions were higher on these sales.

"Americans are ethical, and if I had my way, all the world would be. But all the world is not like that. You should adjust to it. Unless you do, you're not going to be particularly successful," he said.

The point was that his charges on the Northrop contract would only cover his costs and tokens of allegiance to the royal family.

"Does that mean," Trimble asked, "that the king understands that you are receiving these fees?"

"Absolutely," Khashoggi said.

"If he does, does he realize that it increases costs?"

"Absolutely," Khashoggi repeated.

Trimble had expected Khashoggi to be a snake oil salesman. Instead, he found him to be very personable, very much at ease, and very accomplished and persuasive, but not in an objectionable sense.

After the meeting, Alne took Gonzalez aside.

"Manny, it was a stroke of genius to invite Khashoggi here today," he said. "Many people learned many things."

Trimble decided Khashoggi had a point: Agents are commonly used in foreign countries. He decided the fees were acceptable if Prince Sultan specifically approved them. If Sultan knew about Khashoggi's fees, let him verify that. If the Saudis wanted to pay Khashoggi's commissions, that was their business.

Trimble had changed his position from adamant opposition to conditional approval. From Northrop's and Khashoggi's standpoint, the meeting had been a success.

The same day, back in Los Angeles, Northrop formally agreed to Khashoggi's demands on behalf of General Zuhair. But instead of $150,000, Khashoggi told Northrop the general now required $200,000.

Two weeks after the meeting at the Pentagon, Gonzalez wired $200,000 from Northrop's bank to Swiss Bank Corp. in Geneva.

Like the $250,000 already spent for General Hashim, Northrop charged it to the Defense Department, which passed it along to the Saudi government.

It was another token of loyalty to Saudi officials. The charmed American generals never knew about it.

On October 1, 1973, James E. Akins replaced Thacher as U.S. ambassador to Saudi Arabia. The job of formally telling Prince Sultan about Khashoggi's fees fell to him.

A native of Akron, Ohio, Akins was a veteran diplomat who spoke Arabic, French, and German. He had previously served at the American embassies in Damascus, Kuwait, and Baghdad. Most recently, he had been on loan to the White House to work on President Nixon's Energy Message.

Six feet three inches tall, Akins combed his hair straight back. His eyes always seemed to be squinting, as if peering through a perpetual sandstorm.

A day after Akins was sworn in, he met with Gates in Washington and learned about the impasse over Khashoggi's fees.

Akins found the subject of agent fees distasteful. He had no use for Khashoggi, and he believed the Saudis really didn't know about Khashoggi's commissions and didn't care for him. He made it a point never to meet Khashoggi, citing somewhat contorted reasoning: He did not want to be accused of making a decision unfavorable to him out of personal animosity.

Now that his superiors were pressing him to meet with Sultan, Akins dragged his feet. He wanted Sultan to broach the subject first. In turn, Sultan let it be known that he would meet with Akins, but only if he initiated the meeting.

Round and round they went, a Ping-Pong game. Meanwhile, Sultan was flying on Khashoggi's plane, and Khashoggi lent his plane and pilot to Prince Fahd, Sultan's brother, so Fahd could go house hunting in Marbella, Spain.

While the game was being played out, the Pentagon approved new contracts subject to disclosure of the fees. *News-*

*day*, the Long Island, New York, tabloid, broke it up on May 8, 1975. It published a story saying Khashoggi was about to get a $45-million commission from Northrop. The newspaper called it the biggest agent's fee in history.

This was the first public glimpse of the size of Khashoggi's commissions. It put Sultan on the spot. An accountant wasn't needed to know that Saudi Arabia would wind up paying the bill for Khashoggi's commissions, and the news was circulating quickly there.

By now, the Defense Department had bypassed Akins. Sultan had a letter on his desk from Assistant Secretary of Defense Robert F. Ellsworth asking for his approval of Khashoggi's fees.

Publicly, at least, Sultan could not approve such astronomical sums. On May 17, he told the Defense Department that intermediaries should not be allowed on arms sales between governments.

Yet Sultan wanted to leave the question perfectly unclear. So on June 11, he told Thomas C. Barger, a Northrop director who formerly headed ARAMCO, that he had nothing against agents, as long as the cost was not passed along to the Saudi government. When Barger explained that all costs are eventually paid for by the purchaser, Sultan shifted his ground, saying he only opposed bribes.

In an interview with *Al-Anwar*, a Saudi newspaper, Sultan clouded the issue still further. This time, he said he condemned bribery but insisted on the right of an agent to remuneration.

From reading a column by Joseph Kraft in July 1975, Akins learned that he had been fired.

Henry Kissinger, secretary of state, had never liked him. He did not take instructions from higher-ups, and Kissinger thought he was too close to the Saudis. Besides, Akins had publicly labeled a "madman" the person who suggested the U.S. should invade Saudi Arabia if necessary to preserve U.S. oil supplies.

Later, Akins learned the "madman" was Kissinger.

But if Akins was a thorn in the side of the State Department, his relations with the Saudis were excellent. Even though he had been fired, the State Department asked him to return to Riyadh on a special mission concocted by Northrop and Lockheed.

Fearful that they would wind up paying Khashoggi's bills themselves, the two companies told the State Department that they would go bankrupt if the Defense Department refused to approve his fees and pass them along to the Saudis. Already, the amounts owed to him exceeded their current worldwide profits.

The two companies urged the State Department to seek from the Saudis a ban on payment of any commissions—past, present, or future. They wanted the Saudis either to condone commissions, so the cost could be passed along through the FMS program, or to prohibit them, so the companies would not have to pay them from their profits.

In March 1975, Faisal had been assassinated by Faisal ibn Musa'id, his twenty-six-year-old nephew, who had hopped from college to college in America smoking pot and taking LSD. As Faisal was about to meet with a Kuwaiti delegation, the nephew pulled a pistol from beneath his *thobe* and shot the king three times. No one knew why he did it.

Akins arranged to meet with the new king, Khalid, to convey the request for a retroactive ban on commissions. A simple man who was sick much of the time, Khalid preferred camel racing and hunting falcons in the desert to matters of state.

Altogether he had 104 falcons, each with its own handler. In caravans of sixty or seventy four-wheel drive vehicles, Khalid and other Saudi princes scoured the countryside so the falcons could hunt the houbara bustard, a game bird. As many as 2,700 camels took part in the races, twice around a 7.5-mile course, while Khalid and his brothers and nephews cheered them on.

By default, the administration of the country fell to Fahd, the highly competent crown prince.

Akins met with Khalid at his palace in Riyadh, a marble and granite affair with Chinese rugs on the floor. Khalid wanted to know why the Americans could not take care of their own problems. Akins explained an American law could not ban payments retroactively.

Khashoggi had hoped to head off any action by his government, but it was too late. Now that the commissions were becoming public, there was no way to justify such immense figures. And the disclosures were just beginning.

On September 12, 1975, Lockheed disclosed that Khashoggi had received $106 million in commissions from the company and that much of it was to be paid to Saudi officials. The numbers were numbing, and they represented only a part of the cash Khashoggi got from Lockheed.

Four days after the first disclosure of the fees from Lockheed, the Saudi Council of Ministers, acting at Akins' request, banned "any middleman, sales agent, representative or broker" from receiving payments on arms sales, even under a preexisting agreement.

If the princes had to bow to public opinion, they were not about to throw Khashoggi overboard. In an interview with *Al-Anwar*, Fahd, the crown prince and chairman of the council, emphasized that Saudi Arabia encourages the use of agents and pointed out the decree applies only to weapons purchases.

The operative word was *weapons*. By then, most of the commissions owed Khashoggi covered construction of barracks and military bases in Taif and Dhahran—not purchases of weapons.

When Northrop and Lockheed subsequently withheld his fees, Khashoggi tried to use what seemed like a loophole in the decree to win back much of it in secret proceedings before the American Arbitration Association. He lost on that point but won on others, obtaining another $100 million in fees from Lockheed, on top of the $106 million he had already received.

By comparison, the 149 other worldwide consultants paid by Lockheed from 1970 to 1974 got a total of $64 million, or an average of just $430,000.

Ultimately, the Saudis backpedaled by passing a law *requiring* the use of local agents on every contract except those covering weapons actually used for killing or purchases by the Saudi government from other governments.

As his fees became public, Khashoggi gave interviews in which he portrayed himself as a reluctant bagman. To this day, he insists the Americans thought the Saudis had to be bribed and urged him to do it. He recalls saying at the meeting with Northrop officials in his home in Riyadh, "Did you inform Jones that you made a commitment to Hashim?"

While his version is contradicted by Northrop memos written at the time, his story was made more believable by the fact that Northrop officials *did* resent the fact that Khashoggi made more in a year than they made in their lifetimes. They wanted to feel they were paying for something tangible—like bribes to Saudi officials.

As for the $450,000 in bribes intended for the still-unnamed Saudi generals, Khashoggi said he put the money "in my pocket." Asked why he did that, he told *The Wall Street Journal*: "I just penalized" Northrop for wanting to bribe Saudi generals.

It was an appealing tale that made Khashoggi sound like

Robin Hood. If a giant corporation insisted on giving him $450,000, he was glad to take it.

The story preserved the honor of Saudi officials and served Khashoggi's purpose. It extracted more money from Northrop and diverted attention from the real payments. They were made to his princely partners through assignments among Swiss bank accounts.

Khashoggi had gambled and won.

# Triad

But as for how a prince can assess his minister, here is an infallible guide: when you see a minister thinking more of himself than of you, and seeking his own profit in everything he does, such a one will never be a good minister; you will never be able to trust him.

—*Niccolò Machiavelli, The Prince*

AS his wealth grew, Khashoggi dreamed of an international conglomerate, with offices in every major country and investments the world over.

To staff the company, he began hiring Harvard MBAs and Princeton Phi Beta Kappas. Intense white males, they looked more like Boy Scouts than aides to an arms merchant.

Khashoggi needed very little help in arranging defense deals. A lawyer, an accountant, perhaps an engineer were enough to make sure the contracts he negotiated as a middleman would stand up. What Khashoggi hired most of the aides for was to invest the money he made on these contracts. Eventually, he had 140 employees and owned businesses in thirty-eight countries.

But like waves rolling over a sandy beach, the bright young men came and went. Some became disenchanted with the flying-circus atmosphere that Khashoggi relished. Some were offended by the waste and drift or by the nagging questions about how Khashoggi made his money. Still others became disappointed when they didn't get to share in Khashoggi's wealth.

Khashoggi was like a playful cat with its claws extended, or so felt Jan Stenbeck, a Morgan Stanley & Co. investment banker who often traveled with Khashoggi. He found him genuinely gracious and charming. But the people around him imagined limitless riches out there, and they became corrupted by their own greed.

When Khashoggi rubbed up against them, they got scratched: They lost their integrity.

A Harvard Business School graduate and vice-president of Morgan Stanley, Stenbeck faulted Khashoggi for failing to stick with his investments outside the U.S. long enough to see them pay off. He traveled with him to see heads of state about projects to turn deserts into Gardens of Eden. But when the trips were over and the glitter gone, there was little to show for it. The grandiose plans came to nothing or withered for lack of nurturing.

There were the exceptions: Khashoggi's investment in a $1-billion development in Salt Lake City, for example, and a similar project on twenty-two acres of prime land in the Galeria area of Houston. But by and large, the investments made at an accelerating rate produced minimal returns or lost millions of dollars in operating income.

Yet Khashoggi didn't become the richest man in the world by losing money. He knew that the quickest way to get from A to B was sometimes through C. Business to Khashoggi was not just a matter of profit margins and balance sheets, which he rarely looked at and had trouble understanding.

There was a human element that most people overlooked— of one hand washing the other, of politics, and of making friends in high places.

Behind what sometimes seemed like madness, there was a plan and a purpose that enabled him to make even more money as a middleman.

The vehicle for that plan was Triad.

Khashoggi adopted the corporate name Triad for the three brothers who owned it. Younger than their famous brother, the two others resemble him with high forehead and moustache.

The youngest, Essam Khashoggi, is a paler version of Adnan. Born in 1939, he graduated from California State University at San Jose with a BA in industrial design. An art collector, he runs Triad's custom furniture and architectural design subsidiaries, among other ventures.

After living in London, Beirut, and the San Francisco area, he settled in Santa Barbara. With his blond, willowy second wife, Layla, he moved into a $10-million Spanish-style mansion on fifty-one verdant acres overlooking the Pacific. The mansion is guarded by electronically controlled gates and Korean bodyguards, placed there after three men tried to ambush him and singer Paul Anka in 1982 in London as they drove with their families in two Rolls-Royces to Heathrow Airport.

Soon, the mansion will become a guest house, as Essam Khashoggi builds an even bigger home next to it. His instructions to Triad's architect, Alain Cavro, were terse: Create the finest villa in California, and, if possible, in the U.S. This in addition to Essam's white-pillared home outside London— called Elk Meadows, in Chandlers Hills, Berkshire County— and his Honolulu home, called Katimona.

Khashoggi's second brother, Adil, is Khashoggi's opposite in almost every respect. While Khashoggi travels around the world and has twelve homes, Adil, born in 1936, lives primarily in Riyadh, where he invests in real estate.

While Khashoggi is constantly surrounded by beautiful women, Adil has remained with his first wife, Aida. While Khashoggi dropped out of college, Adil earned a B.A. in political science and economics from the University of California at Berkeley, then did graduate work at the University of Geneva.

Khashoggi gave each of his brothers a 20 percent interest in his Triad Financial Establishment, a Luxembourg company. When Adil went off on his own, Khashoggi bought out both brothers' interest in Triad, now called Triad Holding Corp., a Cayman Islands company.

The real force behind Triad was always Khashoggi, but no one was more important to him in building it than Morton P. MacLeod.

One afternoon in 1954, Edward Hardy poked his head into the law library at his firm, Hardy, Carley and Thompson, in Palo Alto, California.

"There's a guy out there in a white robe," he told MacLeod. "I'm going to the ball game. Would you take care of him?"

MacLeod had gotten hired by the skin of his teeth. He had a

B.A. from San Jose State College, and his law degree was from the University of California at Hastings College of Law. Hardy was a former judge who taught at Stanford University School of Law. Usually, the firm took only Stanford graduates, certainly not Hastings graduates. But MacLeod had written a brief that Hardy liked, and he brought him in. Yet MacLeod still didn't have an office of his own. Instead, he used the law library.

Hardy told MacLeod he could use his office to see the eighteen-year-old visitor. As they sat down, the visitor introduced himself as Khashoggi, a student at Stanford University. He said he came to see Hardy because the older man taught at the school.

Khashoggi immediately liked MacLeod. Six feet one inch tall, MacLeod had a friendly, direct manner and a deep, booming voice that engendered trust.

"What can I do for you?" the thirty-year-old MacLeod asked.

Khashoggi explained that he had given some printing plates to a local firm to produce brochures for his business. When the brochures came back, he couldn't make out the decimal points—crucial to understanding the prices and weights listed for pharmaceutical products he was selling in Saudi Arabia.

When he complained, the firm insisted he pay for the brochures anyway, refusing to return his plates.

"Let me see that," MacLeod said, noticing that Khashoggi had some samples with him.

He couldn't make out the decimal points either.

"Wait a minute," MacLeod said, as he began dialing a number on the phone.

It just so happened he knew the president of the printing firm.

"John," he said, when he had him on the line, "I can't make out the decimals in this brochure."

The man apologized and said he would return the plates.

"John," MacLeod persisted, "do you think you could bring them over here in fifteen minutes?"

Khashoggi had his plates, and when he asked how much he owed in legal fees, he was surprised that the charge was only twenty-five dollars.

Khashoggi remembered the favor, and when he obtained a contract to ship Kenworth trucks to Saudi Arabia, he called MacLeod.

There were other contracts—one in Germany, then one with Litton Industries Inc. Based in part on Khashoggi's business, MacLeod opened his own practice in Los Altos. In 1965, just as he was closing deals with Lockheed Corp. and Raytheon Co., Khashoggi offered MacLeod more money than he was then making to work for him full-time.

Besides putting ribbons around defense contracts, MacLeod was a visionary who could help Khashoggi achieve his dream of building a worldwide business empire. Khashoggi wanted people in his organization from each of the countries he did business with, seeing that as a way to develop the kinds of relationships he needed to make deals.

As in a Martian landing, Khashoggi had alighted in Los Altos and recruited this tall American with a law degree to populate his plush offices with MacLeod replicas.

MacLeod was the first to admit he had no business experience and no knowledge of the world beyond Los Altos. He pronounced the word *garçon* as if it had a *k* in it, drank J&B scotch, insisted on using Maxwell House coffee in Beirut, and managed to find Khashoggi's home in Riyadh one night by repeating the word *gyps*—hoping the taxi driver would understand he wanted the manufacturer of gypsum board.

MacLeod was the prototypical ugly American. He could always be found quickly in a hotel because he had already succeeded in alienating half the staff. Because of his habit of yelling at the drivers for going too fast, taxicabs outside the Phoenicia Hotel in Beirut refused to take him.

But MacLeod understood Khashoggi's dreams and made them his. In his year and a half in America, Khashoggi had absorbed the free enterprise spirit like a dry sponge soaks up water. He understood that it gives people incentives to do their best, create, and grow. He wanted to import some of the spirit to Saudi Arabia, where businesses hardly existed.

Most of all, he knew the future and safety of Saudi Arabia lay in closer ties to the U.S. In a letter to his father, he said, "We are suddenly the richest people in the world, surrounded by a great sea of human misery."

MacLeod followed Khashoggi around with a yellow legal pad, sketching out his plans, represented by boxes with lines connecting them. The boxes were companies they could form all over the world. With hundreds of millions of dollars pouring in from Khashoggi's commissions, there was no limit to the number of boxes.

Some thought the boxes and the legal pads were to conceal MacLeod's lack of experience, but that didn't worry Khashoggi. A college dropout from a primitive land, Khashoggi was an outsider, just like MacLeod. Often, he felt, it is the outsiders who can make a greater contribution because they are unburdened by the conventional outlook.

Besides, MacLeod sounded like he knew what he was talking about. He spoke of game plans, venture capital, positioning, and CEOs. In a memo, he envisioned Triad as a "multinational diversified company capable of dealing effectively with the opportunities developing in the emerging nations of the Middle East, Africa, South America, Indonesia, and the Far East."

He told Khashoggi they needed chains of command, organization charts, titles, and business cards. To gain credibility with bankers and clients, Triad should be audited by an outside accounting firm, he said, and should hire the best talent money can buy.

This was to be MacLeod's first order of business.

His lack of imposing academic credentials didn't hinder MacLeod from hiring graduates of Harvard, Stanford, Princeton, Yale, and Amherst. Usually, they had multiple advanced degrees—in law and accounting or in business administration and law or engineering.

These were to be Khashoggi's advisers. They had to be gracious yet straightforward; good companions on trips, yet capable of speaking their minds.

Although pay was average, the opportunities for travel, adventure, and broad experience were unique.

Recruiting candidates through headhunters, MacLeod scheduled interviews at his Los Altos law office at 6 A.M., when he usually started work. He looked for the "Triad cut"—a tall, athletic-looking, Nordic appearance that he thought would give the right impression to Americans and Arabs alike. He peppered applicants with questions designed to reveal their character.

"How did you get the money to attend law school when your wife was going to law school?" he asked James C. Muir, a Stanford Law graduate, in 1969.

"My wife and I would make sandwiches at 5 A.M. We sold them to the students," Muir said.

Perfect guy for the case, MacLeod thought. To MacLeod, everything was a "case."

If an applicant met with his approval, he sent his résumé off to his short brown-eyed boss, inscribing at the top "has Triad cut."

Khashoggi scheduled interviews with the applicants wherever he happened to be. For Daniel M. Searby, it was Paris, where Khashoggi flew him for lunch.

Searby had the Triad cut—dazzling blue eyes and a square jaw. Then deputy assistant secretary of state for commercial affairs, he would make an impressive addition to Khashoggi's staff.

Khashoggi took him to Tour d'Argent, the four-hundred-year-old restaurant that pins a numbered certificate to each duck it serves. Looking out at Notre Dame Cathedral, the two men and another guest dined on quenelles and pressed duck, washed down with several noble burgundies from the 130,000-bottle wine cellar.

As the conversation turned to Israel, the other guest, a Triad consultant, commented that it wasn't really in the interests of the U.S. to support the Jewish state.

Searby disagreed.

"We have very definite interests in helping Israel," he said, "and there is a consensus in the country for doing it."

He wasn't sure he wanted the job anyway.

Later, after he was hired, Searby learned that Khashoggi liked what he had said because he hadn't taken the Arab line.

For Roger B. Godwin, the employment interview took place in the living room of the Waldorf-Astoria Towers' presidential suite.

Six feet tall, slim, with blue eyes, Godwin had the Triad cut, along with a deep, resonant voice reminiscent of Mac-Leod's. He also had enough credentials to fill the four-bedroom suite—a law degree from Stanford, an accounting degree from the University of Tulsa, a stint as a teaching fellow at Stanford, a clerkship with a U.S. court of appeals judge in San Francisco, a position with Lybrand Ross Bros. & Montgomery. Most recently, he had been a manager of U.S. Agency for International Development programs in Turkey.

As they discussed the needs of developing countries in the summer of 1970, it seemed to Godwin that Khashoggi was behind him for a few minutes, then with him, and finally beyond him—seeing relationships he had never seen.

In the middle of the interview, Khashoggi called room service and ordered steak tartare. When it came, he inspected it and told the waiter, "That's fine. Now take it back, fry it, and put it on a hamburger bun."

Khashoggi had a gentle manner—relaxed and relaxing, tactile and confiding. Godwin came away feeling he had never met anyone with so much intelligence and charm.

In 1970, Godwin became treasurer-controller of Triad International Marketing, the subsidiary that helped Khashoggi with his defense contracts. Based in Khashoggi's old apartment on Hamra Street in Beirut, the subsidiary consisted of MacLeod, Muir, a coffee boy, a telex operator, bookkeepers, and secretaries.

Godwin's job was to get the books in order so they could be audited by an outside accounting firm. But in Khashoggi's organization, titles and duties were constantly shifting. One day, Godwin would be called upon to deliver a document to the president of Raytheon Co. Another time, he would entertain a visiting Lockheed official.

Godwin drew the line when Soraya Khashoggi asked him to pick up eggs for her. He told her he worked for someone else.

He found the books a shambles. Payroll checks were often two months late, and there was no such thing as expense accounts. Employees simply took what they felt they needed.

When Godwin told Khashoggi that Triad needed expense accounts, he agreed and said he wanted one, too.

"What do you feel would be an appropriate limit to your expense account?" Godwin asked him.

"I think $10,000 a day," Khashoggi said. "As the chief, my needs are higher."

If Godwin found Khashoggi's attitude about money curious, his successor, Ronald J. Sorenson, was even more perplexed when he found that a businessman invited to stay at a hotel at Khashoggi's expense had charged several suits to his bill.

When Sorenson told him, Khashoggi indicated the boyish-looking Sorenson was wasting his time and shouldn't worry about it.

Later, when an employee embezzled $100,000 from him, Khashoggi told him to return half of it and he would not bring charges. They remained friends.

In explaining his response, Khashoggi cited the koranic injunction: "A kind word with forgiveness is better than alms-giving followed by injury." Yet some in Khashoggi's organization felt he obligated people to him by letting them get away with what to Khashoggi were petty sums.

Both Godwin and Sorenson, a Stanford graduate with a degree from Columbia University Graduate School of Business, realized that they had no real handle on Khashoggi's overall finances.

The books of the holding company were kept in Geneva by Gerard Boissier, a tight-lipped Swiss accountant. And Triad Holding Corp. represented only a sliver of Khashoggi's assets. It was the "public" portion of Khashoggi's holdings, the one audited by Price Waterhouse. There were dozens of other entities registered in places like Panama, the Bahamas, and the principality of Liechtenstein, bordered by Austria and Switzerland.

Driving in fog, the two accountants would come upon new forms and shapes that loomed out of the darkness and were not audited by anyone. No American, and few Arabs, felt they understood the extent of Khashoggi's wealth. Without explaining why, even Price Waterhouse withdrew from the account.

That was the way Khashoggi planned it. He was perfectly willing to let *House & Garden* take photographs of his lovely Olympic Tower home in New York, to permit *Town & Country* to photograph his luxurious yacht, or to parade himself before Robin Leach's cameras for *Lifestyles of the Rich and Famous.* But his finances were private.

Later, when he first tried out a worldwide computer system for keeping track of all his contracts, a worried look crossed his face as he called up the status of a contract on a terminal.

"Where's the brain to this?" he asked tersely.

He was assured that the computer with all its data was safely ensconced at 4 Rue du Mont-Blanc, Triad's Geneva office. But the idea of a centralized data bank continued to trouble him.

"Snoop eye is devoting a complete issue to you," says a Chance card in Khashoggi's customized Monopoly set. With the word "Exposed!" written across the front page of a newspaper, the card says $150,000 stops the presses.

Khashoggi had each member of his staff sign a four-page confidentiality agreement, barring them from talking with the press or book authors about what they learned on the job. The way he did business was his secret, and Triad was part of his mask. Outsiders were impressed by the apparent openness and qualifications of Triad's technocrats, diverting attention from Khashoggi's more Byzantine dealings with Saudi princes and his racy personal life.

Sensing his purpose, MacLeod never asked Khashoggi

questions, never pried. If Khashoggi wanted to tell him something, he would.

He gave similar advice to his "Vikings," as MacLeod called
them. He said Khashoggi was a generous host and would invite
them to parties. But he told them: Be professional. Be cour-
teous. And be on the 9 P.M. plane home.

Some Vikings didn't take the advice and found themselves
caught up in a vortex of women and gambling casinos, their
stature diminished as they shifted from the role of professional
to hanger-on.

For the most part, Khashoggi kept the two worlds separate,
but occasionally the gorgeous, sophisticated women who often
traveled with him turned up at business meetings.

One night, Khashoggi invited Godwin to dinner with several
other Triad executives at Rasputin, the Paris restaurant where
Khashoggi later met Richard M. Nixon. Khashoggi was trying to
impress a Los Angeles businessman who was his guest.

Sitting around the table with the men were five beautiful
women. Godwin had seen women of this caliber before in
Khashoggi's orbit. They were considered "hostesses," there to
ease the social circumstances.

If they went to bed, it was purely secondary to their main
function of creating a more amiable, glamorous atmosphere
while Khashoggi transacted business.

On this occasion, the guest from Los Angeles was seated
across from a particularly attractive young Swedish girl with
her décolletage held together by a string on a dress open down
the front to somewhere between her navel and her pubic hair.

All evening, the man was spilling soup on his tie to see
down her cleavage. Khashoggi couldn't get his attention to
discuss the business at hand.

At the end of the evening, the man went home. Godwin
thought he was doubtless tired after his exertions.

Khashoggi offered the Swedish girl to one of his longtime
employees, who said, "I don't think it would be fair to my
brother, who is visiting."

"Fine, take two," Khashoggi said.

Again the man demurred.

Afterward, Godwin saw all five girls drive off with Khashoggi in his limousine.

• • •

By October 1972, Khashoggi and MacLeod were ready with their grand investment scheme. They called a meeting of Triad executives at the Vendome Hotel in Beirut.

"My Kind of Man" MacLeod called the keynote speech that was delivered over the incessant rat-a-tat-tat of jackhammers outside and the ringing of telephones inside.

Some of the executives thought Louis J. Lauler, a Triad executive, had a hand in the interruptions. Lauler's views counted, because he was in charge of the Triad subsidiary that handled Khashoggi's arms contracts. Lauler had been with Khashoggi almost as long as MacLeod, and he had no use for long-winded speeches, corporate planning, or "game plans."

An engineer and former Lockheed Corp. executive, Lauler graduated Phi Beta Kappa from the University of Vermont. He had a round face and a soft voice. If he didn't have the Triad cut, he had a deadpan sense of humor and was fiercely loyal to Khashoggi. Besides Khashoggi, no one was considered smarter in the Triad organization than Lauler.

Even though MacLeod had hired Lauler in 1967, the two men saw the world from different eyes. MacLeod was offering a crystal ball. His commanding voice and confident tone made people believe in what he was saying. Lauler was a pragmatist. He thought MacLeod was already spending gobs of money, with little to show for it.

Within the organization, Lauler's subsidiary was known as the moneymaking side. It was the side that negotiated Khashoggi's contracts as a middleman and accounted for his growing wealth. All of the rest of Triad—comprising most of its employees—became known as the spending side of the company.

As de facto chief of staff, MacLeod, in theory, was Lauler's boss. In practice, everyone in Triad went around MacLeod and talked to Khashoggi.

Lauler let Khashoggi know what he thought about the spending side of Triad, and he and MacLeod had heated arguments. In 1973, the matter came to a head. Lauler resigned, but a day later, Khashoggi rehired him, putting him in complete charge of the moneymaking side.

It was a classic power struggle, and it would not end until one of the two men had won.

MacLeod moved back to California, where he still had a law practice, MacLeod, Fuller, Muir & Godwin. The firm, which primarily worked for Khashoggi, was at 175 South San Antonio

Road in Los Altos, less than an hour's drive south of San Francisco. A two-story pale pink stucco building, it became Triad's office as well. From the back, the building looked like a motel at the edge of the Sierra Nevada.

Now that he was in charge of the spending side, MacLeod decided the first major investments would be in banks. Besides making money, they would enable Khashoggi to bring banking know-how to Saudi Arabia, where consumer loans were unknown.

That was always a motivation of Khashoggi's—to learn something about the Western way of doing things and import some of it to Saudi Arabia. It was the reason he gave for buying Jungle Jap, a Parisian fashion house, although some thought he liked the idea of employing pretty models.

But banks had a special appeal. They could help establish him as a responsible businessman, a man of stature. For all his wealth, he was always the little boy with his nose pressed up against the store window, looking enviously at the glittering toys inside.

"The Rockefellers of the world have their own club," MacLeod told Khashoggi. "This is the way we'll do it."

MacLeod arranged to buy Security National Bank in Walnut Creek, California, which had $116 million in deposits and a gleaming, white eight-story building. Then came the smaller Bank of Contra Costa, based in the same town, with $34 million in deposits.

Khashoggi bought the first bank from U.S. Representative Fortney H. (Pete) Stark, a California Democrat, paying him $29 a share when the stock was trading over-the-counter for $10 to $12 a share. It galled MacLeod that Stark—marveling at the price he got—later introduced a bill to limit foreign holdings in U.S. banks.

As MacLeod continued to hire more people, the Triad employees began spilling out of MacLeod's law office. Soon, Triad filled nearly the entire building, and more space had to be rented down the street.

Late in the afternoon, MacLeod and his Vikings would adjourn to Mac's Tea Room, a nearby bar with a fake brick exterior. It was so much a part of Triad's ambiance that a printed card listing Triad offices worldwide included Mac's telephone number.

There, MacLeod held court far into the night, mapping strategy and relating anecdotes that sprung from his photographic

memory. All the while, he munched on the "MacLeod Special"—
generous slices of prime sirloin eaten with toothpicks and served
with fried onion rings and a side of Roquefort dressing.

Like a football coach giving a chalk talk on his players'
weaknesses and strengths, MacLeod held them in thrall as he
peered into the future and discussed his team.

Of Godwin, he said one evening: "I hired him when I asked
him about a legal problem, and he wrote a brilliant brief. He
is a walking encyclopedia, yet a country boy. He was a small-
town CPA. A braggart wouldn't sell. We gave him the whole
Far East. He could handle Brenda."

Brenda happened to be a smart, sassy, well-sculpted Stanford Law graduate who first married Muir and then married
Godwin, her Stanford classmate.

"Dan Searby," MacLeod went on, "is everything we expect
in a Washington, D.C., diplomat—articulate, gracious, a good
host and conversationalist. He has never decided what he wants
out of life, nor what his focus is, nor how to get from A to B.
Yet he plays an important role. He is a guy I can send with
Adnan to Egypt or Saudi Arabia, and he always conducts himself gracefully."

MacLeod wanted his Vikings to feel that they counted, that
they weren't just assistants.

"You're the top of the line," he told them. "You can make
anything happen."

As the energy crisis deepened in 1973, MacLeod hit upon
a plan to guarantee oil supplies to the U.S. He developed the
idea in July, three months before Saudi Arabia imposed a boy-
cott on oil shipments to the U.S.

MacLeod called it Petrosat.

The idea was that U.S. refiners would buy oil-preference
certificates from the Saudi government. When the oil was
pumped from the ground, the Americans would have first rights
to the oil. The Saudi government, in turn, would use several
hundred million dollars from the sale of the certificates to
build seven refineries in the U.S. These refineries would sell
the finished product to American utility companies.

Khashoggi approved the plan and began lining up support
from U.S. financial institutions, which would sell the certificates.

The job of drawing up the documents fell to Thomas L.
Barton, a Triad lawyer. A Yale graduate with a law degree from

Northwestern University Law School and an MBA from Stanford, the blue-eyed Barton was originally hired to manage Triad companies. But he quickly realized no one was going to manage them except Khashoggi, and he remained to practice law in the organization.

Barton took pride in the fact that no contract or deed drawn up by Triad lawyers had ever unraveled. While his peers were still writing briefs for partners, he was traveling all over the world, executing major deals.

As he tried to put the Petrosat proposal on paper, Barton realized he couldn't understand it. Then he found no one else at Triad understood it, either.

Later, he accompanied MacLeod as he presented the idea to thirty executives and economists from Bank of America, Merrill Lynch Fenner & Smith, and Schroders, the British merchant bank.

Seated at Bank of America headquarters in San Francisco around the biggest conference table Barton had ever seen, the executives first gave MacLeod their rapt attention. Soon, they began doodling on the pads in front of them. Then they began looking out the corners of their eyes at each other.

There were few questions.

Still, when Khashoggi arranged it, they traveled to Saudi Arabia to meet with Prince Fahd, then interior minister, to discuss the proposal.

"Why should we give you the right to issue these preferences?" the prince asked.

There was silence. In fact, there was no answer. If Saudi Arabia wanted to build refineries, it could do so without pledging its future oil production.

That was the end of Petrosat.

MacLeod and Khashoggi had other dreams—a plan to build a sewer system in the Iraqi city of Basra, which later became the battlefield for the war between Iran and Iraq, and a $9-million investment in Arizona-Colorado Land & Cattle Co., headquartered in Phoenix.

The latter investment illustrated their approach: They reasoned that one of the greatest problems in the Middle East was scarcity of food. Saudi Arabia had almost no farmland. Egypt, closely allied with Saudi Arabia, was always on the brink of starvation. The Sudan, just across the Red Sea from Saudi Arabia, could be the breadbasket of the Middle East, with both water and fertile land.

There must be a deal there somewhere.

Both Khashoggi and MacLeod had almost limitless faith in American know-how. If American expertise could be exported, the deserts could be made into grazing land. The perfect vehicle for this would be Arizona-Colorado Land, an agribusiness company listed on the American Stock Exchange. The company already controlled 1.1 million acres of land in Arizona, Colorado, Florida, Nevada, New Mexico, and Texas. It also owned a beef packing plant, two farms, two cattle feedlots, and nine ranches.

Khashoggi liked brand names, companies with visibility and an established track record. The Phoenix company would know what to do.

In April 1974, MacLeod advised Khashoggi to buy 15 percent of the stock, then form a joint venture called AZL International to undertake projects in Egypt and the Sudan.

But the Americans were not prepared for doing business in Third World countries. Khashoggi had arranged for the backing of President Anwar Sadat of Egypt and President Gaafar Nimeri of the Sudan, whose countries became joint venturers with AZL. Yet the bureaucracy of each country made it almost impossible to get approvals for the smallest needs.

A review panel from Egypt would look over the company's contracts, then the people would disappear for Ramadan, a month-long holiday marking the revealing of the Koran to Mohamed. After it was over, a new panel would appear.

The Sudan had 125 miles of paved roads, which didn't extend to the area where Khashoggi planned to create a million acres of farmland. For thousands of years, nomads had traversed those lands, and they weren't about to change their course, even if fences were erected. Efforts to enlist them in the project failed miserably. Then the company had to erect towns and mosques to lure the Sudanese from the towns to work the land.

Even if the company could produce beef and milk in Egypt at prices comparable to U.S. costs, the price per pound or per liter was far beyond the pocketbook of Egyptian citizens, who could buy powdered milk for far less. What's more, the Sudanese obtained milk free from water buffalo.

F. Michael Geddes, the president and chairman of the Phoenix company, was a Harvard Business School graduate who had been with the cattle company since 1964. He found Khashoggi soft-spoken if elusive at times, while MacLeod came on like gangbusters. Soon, conflicts developed between them.

Geddes listened patiently to MacLeod's ideas—combination plates, MacLeod called them—for melding different U.S. companies into joint ventures. He decided MacLeod was worth listening to if he had three other people holding him down and bringing him back to reality.

As the frustrations mounted, an economic downturn in the cattle business hit the company on the domestic front. The parent company began reporting losses, and its stock took a nose dive, bringing an end to its involvement in the Middle East and Africa.

The problems there had existed for thousands of years. It took more than some trips, conferences, and money to solve them.

When Khashoggi finally pulled out, the venture had cost him $8 million.

Spiro T. Agnew sat hunched on the floor of a suite at the Waldorf-Astoria Towers in New York, poring over a set of plans for a 1,600-acre land development in Kentucky. Less than a year earlier, on October 10, 1973, he had resigned as vice-president after pleading no contest to a felony charge of failing to report on his tax returns payoffs he received while in the White House.

Earlier in the day, Khashoggi, staying at the Waldorf as well, had instructed John McMahan, Triad's real estate consultant, to visit Agnew in his suite. Without saying who Agnew really was, he described him as a close personal friend and gave him his room number.

"He won't come to your suite; you should go to his suite," Khashoggi had said.

The blond, curly-haired McMahan often received assignments like this. A Harvard Business School graduate who taught at Stanford Graduate School of Business Administration, McMahan had sold a real estate consulting firm to Booze, Allen & Hamilton Inc. in 1970.

As his reputation spread, Khashoggi was besieged by businessmen and hangers-on looking for crumbs that might drop from his table. In lobbies of hotels, at parties—even in men's rooms—people would try to thrust proposals into his hands.

Khashoggi was particularly susceptible to business deals

referred by Arab friends and celebrities and politicians. People like former Florida Governor Claude Kirk would join his entourage for a month or more and smoke Khashoggi's cigars while whispering about schemes that struck Khashoggi's fancy—a hotel built underwater in the Mediterranean, for example. Usually, they received a fee for referring an investment to him, or shared in any profits that might be made.

The people who were already part of Khashoggi's inner circle eyed these requests warily. They measured their distance from the Sun King, and they regarded intruders as threats to their own favored positions in his castle. Yet they had little say in the matter.

Khashoggi hated to say no. He would touch the arms of the petitioners and say, "That's a wonderful idea. I'll put you in touch with my technical man."

As the technical man, McMahan felt he was on a treadmill, constantly being asked to check on off-the-wall ideas, with little time to look into more solid investment opportunities. After people wormed their way in, it was up to him to burst their balloons.

Now McMahan was knocking on Agnew's door. As it opened, he immediately recognized the graying man in shirt sleeves. They chatted at Agnew's desk, where the phones rang constantly. Then they adjourned to another room, where Agnew spread plans the size of a king-size bed on the floor.

Agnew pointed out the features of the proposal—a development of condominiums, marinas, and an eighteen-hole golf course on Lake Barkley in northwestern Kentucky.

McMahan asked him about sewer lines, lights, streets, and zoning. Agnew obviously knew the construction business. He had all the answers.

He invited McMahan to lunch, but McMahan declined. He already knew he would have to tell Khashoggi the plan didn't make sense. If Khashoggi wanted to invest in a waterfront development, Kentucky wasn't the place to do it.

McMahan told Agnew he would study it and research the site. Over the next several weeks, Shaheen and Agnew himself called him at home and at his San Francisco office to find out his decision. After a few weeks had elapsed, McMahan advised Khashoggi against the investment.

Khashoggi didn't object. If he wanted to invest, he would do it against any advice. But in this case, he was happy to be able to tell Agnew that his technical man was against it.

To McMahan, it was but another example of wasted effort. He noted that no other private developer chose to implement the plan. Later, Agnew used Khashoggi as his agent in selling prefabricated schools in Saudi Arabia. But McMahan had had enough. After two years with Khashoggi, he quit in frustration.

Ironically, one of Khashoggi's most successful projects originated with Shaheen.

Through F. William Gay, Howard Hughes' top lieutenant, Shaheen was introduced to a consultant who later put him in touch with an owner of an electrical firm that wanted to sell a piece of property in Salt Lake City.

In any given month, Shaheen received fifteen to twenty such investment proposals. Winnowing them, he usually allowed only three to four of the petitioners to see Khashoggi.

The Salt Lake City idea attracted Shaheen. He knew from Gay, a devout Mormon with close-cropped red hair, that Salt Lake City—where Brigham Young led his flock from persecution on July 24, 1847—was a stable, conservative environment where families and businesses could thrive.

Flying one day on a chartered Learjet from Beirut, Shaheen and the property owner began sketching out on a brown paper bag how the land two miles east of the airport could be turned into an industrial park.

When they landed in London, Shaheen sent a telex to Khashoggi outlining the idea. He got his approval to ask McMahan, Triad's real estate consultant, to look at it.

When McMahan arrived at the tract, it was like stepping on the moon. The entire area was alkaline wasteland. But McMahan found there was already a plan to expand the airport. The taxes were low, and the economy of the area was robust.

In August 1974, Khashoggi purchased 460 acres, later expanding his holdings to 900 acres. McMahan hired an engineering firm that designed an industrial park. Called Triad International Center, it was surrounded by a lake and fountains. To run it, McMahan got Shaheen's approval to hire Emanuel A. Floor. The son of a Greek Orthodox immigrant, he had good relations with local politicians and, more important, the Mormon Church.

Soon, the industrial park attracted tenants like American Telephone & Telegraph Co., Rockwell International Corp., Southland Corp., and Sperry Corp.

Khashoggi placed his youngest brother, Essam, in charge,

naming him chairman of Triad America Corp., the Triad subsidiary that owns the development. Essam has an ownership
interest in the subsidiary as well.

When the development opened in June 1977, Khashoggi
sent his father to give the speech, two years before Dr. Khashoggi died.

The city welcomed Khashoggi and welcomed his family.
And there were no nasty questions about being an arms dealer.

In June 1982, Khashoggi announced plans for a second,
$600-million project on once-blighted land in downtown Salt
Lake City. Part of the land came from a sale by the Mormon
Church.

Called Triad Center, it was the largest development ever
undertaken in Utah. It included two gold-colored forty-three-
story office towers, several high-rise buildings, a residential
apartment and condominium complex, retail stores, an outdoor
amphitheater, ice skating rink, five theaters, restaurants, sky-
walks, plazas, and parking.

As part of the development, Khashoggi agreed to renovate
a local landmark—Devereaux House. Once one of the most elegant mansions in the city, it was built in 1857 by William C.
Staines, supervisor of Brigham Young's orchards and gardens.
Then it was owned by Joseph Young, a son of the founder of
the Church of Jesus Christ of Latter-day Saints.

To help celebrate, Khashoggi booked the Utah Symphony
to play Beethoven's Ninth—also known as the Brotherhood
of Man Symphony—at the Mormon Salt Lake Tabernacle, importing soprano Roberta Peters for the occasion. The Brotherhood of Man theme is used by Khashoggi as well on the
"season's greetings" cards with real gold lettering that he
sends out to 5,000 friends and business contacts each year.

In June 1984, he flew in friends and family from all over the
world when he announced future plans for his Salt Lake City
holdings and a $1.2-million donation to the LDS Hospital to build
an international education center in honor of his father.

For lunch, Khashoggi loaded the guests on a bus that took
them from their hotel to La Caille, a country restaurant a half
hour's drive from Salt Lake City. As the guests walked up a
winding brick walk, they found themselves in a garden surrounded by lakes with swans. Waitresses attired in peasant
garb with revealing bodices served Piper-Heidsieck champagne. A lute played.

After Khashoggi arrived by helicopter, a hundred guests

entered the restaurant, built in 1935 as a mock seventeenth-century French château. There, they feasted on Russian sevruga and Colombian golden caviar, Strasbourg pâté de foie gras with a truffle core, Dungeness crab flown in that morning from Alaska, salad, and a fresh black raspberry tart.

That evening at Devereaux House, Khashoggi threw a lavish dinner attended by Utah Governor Scott M. Matheson, Salt Lake City Mayor Ted L. Wilson, and Gordon B. Hinckley, acting president of the Mormon Church. The ailing president of the church, Spencer W. Kimball, the twelfth prophet, seer, and revelator of the church, made a brief appearance.

In April 1985, Khashoggi bought the hotel where he put up his guests, renaming it Sheraton Triad Hotel and Towers. With more than $300 million in equity in the Salt Lake City ventures, Khashoggi had a $1-billion development that he could pass on to his children.

It was his Camelot.

In November 1974, Khashoggi tried to expand his bank holdings by offering to acquire a one-third interest in the First National Bank of San Jose, with deposits of $280 million. But after the directors agreed to issue new shares in return for his $14-million investment, an uproar ensued over the issue of Arab holdings in U.S. banks.

The idea of any foreign investment in the U.S. was still new, and people feared that foreigners would somehow take control of the country by buying companies and real estate. Yet the bank's directors had invited Khashoggi to make his offer. He never intruded where he wasn't wanted.

When the president of the Jewish Federation of San Jose threatened to withdraw his business account from the bank if Khashoggi bought into it, the directors changed their minds and decided to put the issue up for a stockholders' vote.

Khashoggi withdrew his offer in January 1975, saying that "individual fanatics" had waged a "hate campaign" against Arabs.

The town tried to make up with a luncheon for Khashoggi attended by the mayor and civic leaders. But it was too late. It was the first time Khashoggi had been confronted by anti-Arab sentiment in the U.S., and he never got over it. The incident soured him on banks and on California in general. He said he would invest his money elsewhere and did, plunging into a visionary investment in Egypt.

Called the Pyramids Oasis project, it was to be a $1-billion development a mile from the Pyramids of Giza on the outskirts of Cairo.

The project was the brainchild of Peter Munk and David Gilmour. Two Canadian entrepreneurs, they were already partners with Khashoggi in Southern Pacific Properties Ltd., a London-based operator of sixty hotels in Australia, Turkey, New Zealand, and several U.S. locations that form part of the Travelodge chain.

A balding Budapest-born engineer, Munk in the 1960s founded Clairtone Sound Corp., which built stereo equipment in Canada. Investment ideas spewed from him like water cascading from a fountain.

Munk and Gilmour envisioned a 2,000-room hotel, highrise condominiums and residences for 40,000 people, tourist and convention facilities, a museum, an artificial lake, and an eighteen-hole golf course.

Khashoggi took the idea directly to Egyptian President Anwar Sadat, who embraced it as an opening wedge in his "open door" policy designed to encourage Western investment.

Sadat gave the developers the right to use over 40,000 acres of land—then used by squatters—for ninety-nine years. In return, the Khashoggi group gave the Egyptian government a 40 percent interest in the project.

Besides Khashoggi, Munk, and Gilmour, the other owners included Prince Nawaf, a half brother of the then Saudi king, Saud.

To do the construction, Khashoggi hired Osman Ahmed Osman, a friend of Sadat's. A subsidiary of Howard R. Hughes' Summa Corp. was to design the buildings. And Robert Trent Jones, Jr., the Frank Lloyd Wright of championship golf courses, designed the golf course.

As construction of the golf course began, the project encountered a hailstorm of opposition, ostensibly from environmentalists, who said the buildings would cover up artifacts buried in the sands and damage the Pyramids through leakage from the lake. A previously obscure Egyptian professor, Nehmet Fouad, even wrote a book attacking the project.

In fact, the opposition was an indirect way for Sadat's political enemies to attack him over his peace overtures with Israel. Barred by law from criticizing the government's foreign policy through the press, they focused instead on domestic targets.

Leading the charge, the English-language *Egyptian Ga-zette* called the project the "most colossal rip-off of the 20th century." The paper said it "dwarfs every vile enterprise imposed on Egypt by adventurers and racketeers over the last 20 years."

In contrast to the Saudis, the Egyptians eschewed subtlety.

Jones was beside himself. He had invested his prestige in the golf course. Shaped like a cross, the Egyptian symbol of life, it was to appear from the air as a green oasis in the middle of the Sahara. In golfing and architectural circles, the golf course had already elicited widespread praise.

Jones knew that the land for the project sloped downward, away from the Pyramids. How could water flow uphill from the lake and damage the Pyramids?

Looking for artifacts, he had made borings in the sand. All he could find, according to a fact sheet put out by the developers, was "one decayed monkey and some honey-pot shards."

But after Sadat traveled to Jerusalem for a two-day visit in November 1977, the opposition intensified, and Sadat killed the project.

It was a hard blow for Jones. He had been accused of desecrating the Pyramids. Now all he had to show for it was a pile of sand.

More than a year later, in May 1978, Khashoggi arranged for John D. deButts, chairman of American Telephone & Telegraph Co., Charles Wohlstetter, his counterpart at Continental Telephone & Telegraph Co., and John Douglas, vice-chairman of GTE Corp., to see Sadat about a new telephone system for Egypt.

It didn't require an expert to know that one was needed. There was a backlist of fourteen years to get a new telephone installed. Because of crossed wires and bad connections, most attempts to make a call ended with wrong numbers or simply silence. It was faster to send a messenger through Cairo's tangled traffic jams than to pick up the phone and call.

Already, Continental Telephone had submitted an eight-volume study to Areto, Egypt's national telephone company, recommending a crash program to install 650,000 new lines, with a total of 5 million planned over twenty years at an estimated cost of $20 billion.

Khashoggi asked Max Helzel, a former Lockheed Corp. executive who was a consultant to Khashoggi and to Continental, to explore forming a joint venture of American telephone companies to do the work. Khashoggi decided to include GTE as well.

Helzel arranged meetings in New York with deButts and Wohlstetter, who agreed to form a consortium with GTE called Ameritech. Then Khashoggi set up the meeting with Sadat and got a commitment from King Khalid to provide Saudi financing. But the deal fell apart when Egypt signed the peace accords with Israel at Camp David. Khalid said he wouldn't give a nickel to help Egypt.

Beyond some improvements made by European companies, the system was never built.

For all their imposing academic degrees and intelligence, most of MacLeod's recruits possessed no more experience in business or investing than did he. They were lawyers, accountants, or Important People from Washington. Like MacLeod, they were receiving on-the-job training.

Those with an investing background quickly exited. One was Jack L. Melchor, who had started venture capital businesses with Hewlett-Packard Co. and later formed his own investment company. Another was Richard D. Nagel.

The son of Lebanese parents, Nagel had been recommended to MacLeod by John E. Thompson, who managed Khashoggi's banks. The two men had met at Kaufman & Broad Inc., a Los Angeles construction and insurance conglomerate where Nagel was vice-president for corporate development. Later, Nagel became chief of investments for the company's Sun Life subsidiary.

On his first day on the job, Nagel, an intense man with luminous brown eyes, asked to see the investment portfolio. He was shocked. There were shopping centers and restaurants that seemed to have been acquired with no plan in mind—a steak house here, a tract of undeveloped land there. Many were losing money and should have been written down in value. When he asked for the rationale behind the investments, he got mumbo jumbo.

Nagel listened while MacLeod held forth at Mac's Tea Room on the meaning of Life and Truth. It seemed to him that MacLeod was a guru who promised to lead his younger, inexperienced disciples to Aladdin's cave.

To Nagel, the Los Altos office was a wind tunnel with money rushing through it. At the drop of a hat, there were trips to the Sudan with all the secretaries, stays at the Dorchester Hotel in London, and lengthy international telexes that could have been mailed. Still, the furnishings in MacLeod's law office remained nicked and scruffy.

If there was a purpose to it all, Nagel never learned what it was.

One day, Nagel heard that Shaheen was visiting his mother in Ohio. He called him there and spoke with Shaheen's mother in Arabic. Then Shaheen picked up the phone.

"What's going on here?" Nagel asked. Then he described what he had found.

"Put it in a memo," Shaheen said, "and I'll give it to the chief."

Nagel mailed the memo to Shaheen but never learned what happened to it.

By the end of 1975, Nagel had left.

MacLeod managed to acquire or start seventy-nine businesses owned in whole or in part by Triad. He had organization charts that filled pages and an alphabet-soup list of Triad subsidiaries—TAG, THC, TCMI, TPC. Their nameplates covered a wall at Triad's office in the Adil Khashoggi Building on Airport Road in Riyadh.

MacLeod acknowledged that he didn't know a good business deal from a hole in the ground, at least not when he first met Khashoggi.

"There are smarter people than I," he would say. "I am not a good manager."

But he disagreed that his investments were a disaster and could point to some successes: He purchased Security National Bank, for example, for $12 million in 1973 and sold it in 1980 for $30 million. Later, he would talk about the $100 million that could have been made if Khashoggi had only kept the investments he had acquired for him.

Yet the failures seemed to outnumber the successes. "Great deal that really wasn't," says a Chance card in Khashoggi's customized Monopoly game, called Triopoly. The card was illustrated with a Rube Goldberg device and carried a penalty for drawing the card of $50,000.

There were too many penalties, and now MacLeod's enemies were beginning to circle. Influential Triad executives persuaded Khashoggi to hire McKinsey & Co. to study his operations. The consulting firm produced a thick report with impressive charts and cosmic conclusions. In essence, it said, Triad needed to be reorganized. The consulting company recommended chains of command, which MacLeod knew would never work. And it criticized MacLeod's method for compensating employees.

When he hired them, he told them they would receive a percentage of the gross revenues of the operation. But McKinsey pointed out that the method only encouraged sloppy investing. If a shopping center lost money, the Triad employees still received a percentage of the money put into it.

MacLeod never saw the McKinsey report, but he sensed a change in the wind when he had dinner one evening in Paris with Raja Sidawi, a shrewd Syrian friend and sometime partner of Khashoggi's in oil ventures.

"Do you know what the problem is?" Sidawi asked MacLeod.

"No, I don't. Tell me," he replied.

"There's a time for you to be a professor, and a time not to be. You have to realize that Adnan is now the professor, and you're the student," he said.

"It's over for you," Sidawi said. "Adnan is now the head of the class. In Arabic, we always say there can only be one guy in the tent. There's Adnan and you. How can there be two guys in the tent?

"You've been wonderful for Adnan," Sidawi continued. "You've given him high ideals about the world. You get an 'A' for that. Now it's time for you to relax and make some money. Let Adnan call the shots."

"Sidawi," MacLeod said in his deep voice, "it's very good of you to tell me that, because I guess you get myopic in life." But then MacLeod argued that he didn't pull all the strings.

"I don't even go to the head without Adnan's okay," he said.

"I don't like to be a pusher," Sidawi said, "but you take my advice. I think that you are exerting power and don't realize it."

MacLeod respected Sidawi and thought about what he had said. He realized Sidawi must have heard some rumbles—must have known Khashoggi was dissatisfied. He was saying he should flow with the tide.

But MacLeod wasn't made that way. He lived by objectives and goals. He and Khashoggi had dreamed of the first Arab conglomerate—a company that might make the Fortune 500. He had given up weekends and vacations to pursue that dream. He had even visualized retiring with his Vikings to a

Triad community in California. He wasn't going to watch it all float away.

MacLeod didn't change, and a year later, he was having lunch with Khashoggi in Paris. They were discussing the compensation plan, and Khashoggi was saying he couldn't understand why MacLeod was so insistent that it should be retained.

A founder, like MacLeod, or a brother should get a percentage, but not an employee.

"Why are you taking their side?" Khashoggi asked.

MacLeod said there was a principle involved. It was something he had promised his people. A corporate promise should be kept. Khashoggi announced that his brother, Essam, would now run the company, and Khashoggi would retire. But people should work for a company, not a man, MacLeod thought. MacLeod wasn't anybody's confidant or secretary, and he wasn't going to take orders from Essam Khashoggi or give up what he had worked for.

"I'm not taking anybody's side," MacLeod said. "What's fair is fair."

Nothing more was said about it, but MacLeod had known Khashoggi since Khashoggi was eighteen. He could tell what he was thinking. Khashoggi had a high tolerance for waste and even for theft but not for what he felt was disloyalty.

In October 1976, MacLeod was gone. Ostensibly, the Triad board of directors fired him. In fact, no one ran Triad except Khashoggi.

As a termination payment, MacLeod got a $1.6-million ranch near Gilroy, California. Called Castro-Escondido, it was property he had purchased for Triad. It produced no income and was a drain because of the maintenance costs.

But he had bought it for Khashoggi. Now he would have to live with it.

Soon, he sold it to meet the mortgage payments. Trying to survive as an independent businessman, he formed a company to sell mesquite chips for barbecues. It never really took off. Nine years later, on Shaheen's recommendation, Khashoggi agreed to put him back on his payroll temporarily as a consultant.

MacLeod was gone but the drifting continued. Khashoggi wasn't an administrator—didn't claim to be one and didn't want to be one. Triad seemed to continue to stumble from one losing proposition to another.

Yet the discerning observer could detect a pattern: Each

of the investments seemed to have an altruistic purpose that attracted publicity and engendered goodwill.

If Khashoggi were interested solely in making money, he could invest in the stock market or place his money with a professional investor. Instead, there was a land development in Gabon as large as the state of Delaware. In Turkey, a $100-million trading company.

If the ventures worked and made money, that was all to the good. But even if they didn't, they still accomplished their primary purpose, which was public relations—for Khashoggi and for Saudi Arabia.

Khashoggi hated to be called an arms dealer and considered it unfair: "Why don't they say, 'The chairman of Lockheed, the arms dealer'?" he would ask friends rhetorically.

A corporate umbrella covered him with respectability. Instead of being known as an arms merchant or a middleman, he became known as an investor. Chiefs of state appreciated the fact that he was investing in their countries. Then they received him more favorably when he tried to sell them on defense systems or bartering deals on which he made a commission.

He invested as other businessmen take prospects to lunch. When they pick up the tab, they hope the small favor may lead to a sale or provide greater access so they can make their pitch in the future.

"Merchantry," Khashoggi called it: trade for the sake of trade.

Always, it was with the approval of the Saudi royal family. Like a knight in King Arthur's Court, Khashoggi was entitled to collect tolls in return for doing the bidding of the king. As part of his special role, Khashoggi established closer relations for ever-vigilant Saudi Arabia with other countries like Belgium, South Korea, the Sudan, Turkey, and France.

By diverting attention from his role as a middleman, Khashoggi made even more money as a middleman. By making people around him happy, Khashoggi made himself happy. By investing in foreign countries, he fulfilled his mandate from King Faisal to win allies for Saudi Arabia. By playing to human needs, Khashoggi became the richest man in the world.

It was that simple—and that complex.

# The Planes

And let not those who hoard up that which Allah hath
bestowed upon them of His bounty think that it is better for
them. Nay, it is worse for them. That which they hoard will
be their collar on the Day of Resurrection.

—*The Koran*

**A**T the height of the controversy over his commissions
from Northrop Corp., Khashoggi took delivery of a gleaming
new Boeing 727. It was a commercial-size jet, a stretch that
normally seats 163 passengers. The sticker price was $11 mil-
lion—enough to fly first-class on Air France round trip from
New York to Paris four thousand times.

Khashoggi already owned a McDonnell-Douglas DC-9, a
medium-range, commercial, twin-engine jet that normally seats
90. In January 1978, he took delivery of a third commercial-
size plane, another Boeing 727.

At various times, he also had a Lear jet, a G-1 Gulfstream, a
Challenger jet, and a helicopter—enough to outfit the national
airlines of some countries. Each had a green horizontal stripe
the length of the plane and a gold "III" in a circle on the tail.

Critical to Khashoggi's success, the aircraft enabled him

to juggle dozens of business negotiations at the same time all over the globe and travel instead of wasting time in hotels. They gave him an aura of mystery and invincibility. And they were assets in his never-ending quest to cultivate princes and world leaders.

Instead of taking them to lunch, he gave them his Boeing 727.

With American pilots prepared to fly to any country in the world on a moment's notice, the planes gave Khashoggi the powers of a Superman in a *thobe.* He hopscotched around the globe the way other people drive to do their errands on Saturday.

From his plane's log in April 1985, the following two weeks of trips are typical. On Monday, he flew from New York to London. On Tuesday, he flew from London to Honolulu. On Wednesday, it was off to Brunei in Southeast Asia—a trip of twelve and a half hours. The day after, he left for Singapore, where he had six hours of business meetings. That same day, he flew back to Honolulu, then on to Los Angeles.

After a night's sleep in California, he flew to New York on Friday and then on to London, where he spent the night. The next day took him to Paris, then Nice. The following day, he returned to Paris and from there to New York and Washington.

On Monday of the second week, he flew back to New York and then to Acapulco, where he stayed four nights. On one of those nights, he flew to Mexico City for a formal dinner given by the U.S. ambassador. He returned to Acapulco the same night.

The following day, his plane took him from Acapulco to New York. The last day, a Saturday, he flew to Cannes.

Usually, as he hopped the world, Khashoggi saw heads of state. Like a customer of a store asking to see the manager, Khashoggi reflexively went to the top. If the top was Ronald Reagan or Egyptian President Hosni Mubarak or King Juan Carlos of Spain, then that is the person he would see.

Except for the Soviet Union, Libya, Israel, and the People's Republic of China, he has flown to every country. China is on the schedule, however, as he plans development projects in Shantou valued at $1 billion.

On the average, Khashoggi flies more than three quarters of a million miles a year. A grueling pace, but Khashoggi doesn't take the Eastern shuttle. While the rest of humanity rides bolt upright in uncomfortable chairs, Khashoggi sits on futuristic soft leather-and-silk banquettes or dozes in his ten-foot-wide bed, tucked in by a gold-plated seat belt.

On the plane, he naps, dines on French, Chinese, or Arabic delicacies, is shaved by his barber, or gets a massage from his masseur; then he showers and changes into a fresh suit and shirt.

Often, he has lovely young girls on board to make the trip even more enjoyable. One of the most stunning girls was Laura Biancolini. Known as the contessa, she began traveling with him when she was seventeen. After converting to Islam and changing her name to Lamia, she later became his second wife.

In his best-selling novel *The Pirate*, Khashoggi's friend Harold Robbins portrayed a thinly disguised Khashoggi as using women on board for diversion during long flights, much as others ordered in-flight movies. The portrayal was real, but the movies could be risqué as well. As soon as it was released, Khashoggi screened *Deep Throat* aboard his DC-9.

In flight, the atmosphere is the nearest thing to the Islamic conception of Paradise—believers reclining peacefully on silken couches, with an abundance of fruit and wine, in a garden of pure water, milk, and honey. The believers' companions are *houris*—virginal but amorous maidens with swelling breasts, their eyes downcast in modesty.

Khashoggi never seems to suffer from jet lag, which is probably a credit to his vitamin shots and his custom of living by European time regardless of hemisphere.

His doctor, Peter Butcher, a soft-spoken Brit, marveled at the man. At Butcher's London home, where he kept his office, the doctor would examine him at eleven at night, and Khashoggi would tell him he'd be in New York the next morning.

Despite an obvious weight problem and a typical regimen of four hours of sleep a night, Khashoggi had more vitality than any other patient he had ever seen. Beyond an allergy to shrimps and a slight tendency to diabetes, he had no health problems.

Besides a daily massage, Khashoggi got daily adjustments to his spinal column by chiropractors who were disciples of George J. Goodheart, Jr., of Detroit. The developer of applied kinesiology, Goodheart teaches that physical and psychological problems can be relieved by stimulating acupuncture points with pressure, manipulating reflex areas, and taking nutritional supplements like vitamins and minerals.

When Khashoggi emerged from a long flight, he looked like a million dollars—or more.

On the plane, Khashoggi and Shaheen constantly placed calls

to Khashoggi's executives, to world leaders, princes hunting falcons in Land-Rovers, or gorgeous women 35,000 feet below.

As the earthlings picked up their ringing phones, they heard a characteristic crackling noise. The next thing would be Shaheen's voice from somewhere over Monte Carlo or Zaire.

"The chief is calling," he would say, as if God were about to descend.

Shaheen never tired of hearing the reaction on the other end. They tried to suppress it, but Shaheen knew what was running through their minds: "The richest man in the world is calling from the lower stratosphere. He can make me rich and famous and happy. I won't ever have to work or mow the lawn or go grocery shopping again. I'll meet beautiful women/handsome men and dine on caviar and champagne."

It was a spectacular vision, but after a dozen such calls from the clouds, the novelty wore off. When they heard the crackling noise, Khashoggi's executives no longer asked where he was. They already knew the answer: He was over one of the 170 countries of the world.

Nor were the calls always cordial. Max B. Knudson, a Triad employee in Salt Lake City, had been asked by Shaheen to send copies of a videotape to each of Khashoggi's offices. The tape, of a dedication ceremony, was not in Triad's Abu Dhabi office. From the stretched Boeing 727, Shaheen called Knudson at home.

There was the crackling sound, then Shaheen's voice.

"Max, they didn't get the videotape here," he said from the clouds. "It's not here, Max. I'm disappointed, Max. The chief is disappointed."

The call cost forty dollars a minute.

Khashoggi bought his first plane from Las Vegas financier Kirk Kerkorian in September 1972. Kerkorian owned 47 percent of Metro-Goldwyn-Mayer Film Co. and later acquired 24 percent of Columbia Pictures Industries Inc. When he needed some cash, he sold Khashoggi the DC-9, along with his yacht.

The plane was already outfitted with two bedrooms, a lounge area, a kitchen, and a bathroom with shower. Khashoggi registered the plane in the U.S. as N-112AK.

With the plane came its pilot, Harold G. Renegar, who became Khashoggi's chief pilot. It was Renegar who built Khashoggi's small air force.

Renegar was a distinguished-looking gray-haired man with blue eyes and a booming voice; when he spoke, it was like crisp commands from a control tower. He was used to being obeyed in the cockpit and on the ground, and his erect bearing and confident smile showed it.

Originally an air force pilot, Renegar had flown the likes of Lyndon B. Johnson, Harry S. Truman, Everett M. Dirksen, Robert S. McNamara, and Nikita Khrushchev. Before going to work for Kerkorian, he was chief pilot for Xerox Corp.

Almost as soon as he took delivery of the plane, Khashoggi asked Renegar about bigger ones. On the back of a piece of hotel stationery in Paris, the pilot scribbled the advantages and disadvantages of three planes that would outdo the DC-9.

They were a used Boeing 707, a used Boeing 727, and a new Boeing 727. Each had good range and was easy to fly into airports with spotty ground services.

Renegar listed the approximate prices with finished interiors: $11 million for a new 727, $6 million for a 707, and $7 million for a used 727.

Like a kid choosing toy cars, Khashoggi picked the new Boeing 727.

To design and install the interior, Khashoggi hired AiResearch Aviation Co., a California company that custom-designs aircraft fittings. For his instructions, Richard A. Graser, the AiResearch vice-president assigned to the job, had to meet with Khashoggi wherever Khashoggi happened to be. As it turned out, the instructions were brief.

On one of his first meetings with him, Khashoggi was gambling at the Sands Hotel & Casino in Las Vegas. As Khashoggi came forward to meet him around midnight in a bar just off the casino, Shaheen was trailing close behind, holding four trays loaded with pink chips, each worth a thousand dollars.

"Chief, should I return the trays?" Shaheen asked.

"Keep one," Khashoggi answered.

As Shaheen took back the three trays, Graser started counting the chips on the fourth. That one tray held, he estimated, three hundred chips. At one thousand dollars a chip, Khashoggi must have been playing with over a million dollars.

Tearing his eyes from the chips, Graser asked Khashoggi, "What kind of interior do you want in the plane?"

Khashoggi motioned with his hands as if holding a bowl. "Make it plush," he said.

Khashoggi returned to the roulette tables, where he was known as the biggest high roller to ever hit Las Vegas. He never uttered another word about the design.

With those marching orders, AiResearch spent $2 million on an interior the likes of which had never been seen in any flying machine.

By itself, the plane was a gem of modern engineering. It was a Boeing 727/200, a series which was stretched by adding twenty feet to the length of the fuselage. Because of advanced sound suppression techniques, it was one of the quietest planes aloft.

Fully loaded at 199,005 pounds, it cruised at 570 miles per hour and could fly 3,600 miles without refueling.

AiResearch outfitted the interior like an opulent home. Taking 60,000 man-hours to complete, it was far more sumptuous than the DC-9.

The 727 had a living room, kitchen, bedroom suite, and a conference room. The conference room doubled as a bedroom that slept four in bunk beds. The living room was appointed with table lamps, coffee tables, and throw pillows. The seats and sofas were finished in soft leather.

When only television stations purchased video players, the plane had four of them.

In the kitchen were an ice maker, trash compactor, freezers, and conventional and microwave ovens. Usually, food was brought on board after being prepared by Khashoggi's three chefs—one French, one Chinese, and one Arabian.

Khashoggi's suite had a sable-covered bed and a bathroom with a shower and gold-plated faucets. The closets held a complete wardrobe. One held Western business attire—twelve suits by Cifonelli of Rome, the most expensive suits in Europe, twenty-four pairs of socks, fifteen shirts, ten pairs of shoes, and assorted ties and underwear.

In each of Khashoggi's twelve homes, complete wardrobes were kept as well—one closet in his Paris home held two hundred suits. When he flew, Khashoggi didn't need to pack. He just rose from his chair and walked on the plane.

A second closet in his flying suite held Middle Eastern clothing, including silken *thobes*. Because the loose-fitting garments are so comfortable, Khashoggi insisted his guests change into them on long flights, regardless of the guests' nationality.

One evening just after midnight, Khashoggi enlisted Kenneth J. Bialkin, one of his lawyers, to fly with him to Las Vegas to meet that morning with Roy R. Anderson, the new chairman of Lockheed Corp. The two men wanted to work out a settlement of Khashoggi's claim for fees owed him.

Besides being a lawyer, Bialkin wears other hats. He is national chairman of B'nai B'rith's Anti-Defamation League and chairman of the Conference of Presidents of Major Jewish Organizations, probably the most influential position in American Judaism.

Khashoggi often told Bialkin and others that when peace comes to the Middle East, his plane would be the first to land at the Tel Aviv airport.

When Bialkin boarded the Boeing 727 at Teterboro Airport in New Jersey just after midnight, he found the entourage was already there, including an elderly bearded gentleman introduced as a "holy man."

Khashoggi showed Bialkin to his room, the one with bunk beds near the back of the plane, and he gave him a *thobe* to wear. The holy man, who spoke only Arabic, had removed his sandals and was already asleep in a top bunk.

Donning the robe, Bialkin crawled into the bunk below and fell asleep. When he awoke, he was in Las Vegas.

Ultimately, Lockheed rejected Bialkin's settlement offer and wound up paying far more after his New York firm took the matter to arbitration.

Besides the flying closets full of clothes, Khashoggi had an office in his suite with a telex machine, copying machine, and telephone. Of all his offices throughout the world, this is where Khashoggi was most likely to do work.

By high frequency radio, the phone patched into a company in Berne or Stockholm that relayed the calls to any phone in the world. The reception was so good that even on the ground Khashoggi's executives often retreated to Khashoggi's planes to make international calls.

Including calls from the pilots' base of operations in California, the telephone bill for all three planes is $300,000 annually—more than most chief executive officers make in a year.

When Khashoggi took delivery of the stretched Boeing 727 in June 1975, Renegar assumed it would replace the DC-9. At the last minute, Khashoggi said, "We'll keep the 9, too."

The same thing happened when Khashoggi bought the third plane, a Boeing 727/100.

Sometimes, when he felt like putting on the dog for a chief of state, Khashoggi descended on a country with all three planes.

Usually, however, Khashoggi took the stretched Boeing 727, registered as N111-AK, while his brother Essam used the standard 727, registered as N111-EK. The children were supposed to use the DC-9.

But one afternoon in New York, Khashoggi told Shaheen to get the stretch ready to fly. Shaheen told him that his eldest son, Mohamed, had taken it; he had an appointment in Boston to be photographed by Bachrach for a magazine layout.

"He's supposed to have the DC-9," Khashoggi said.

Round and round they went. The people with them in the Olympic Tower apartment just grunted or kept silent. They didn't want to get involved in a family argument.

For his copilot Renegar hired Jerry Soderstrom, a former charter pilot, who took over as chief pilot when Renegar retired in 1979. In the first six months, the two men and a flight engineer were on call twenty-four hours a day, 365 days a year. They never got a chance to go home. Later, Renegar hired a second crew for each plane.

The pay was just under $100,000 a year, comparable to what many international commercial pilots make. The scope of the experience could not be duplicated.

Very few companies or individuals do that kind of global flying. Most corporate pilots fly to Paris or Rome. If they go to remote places like Gabon or the Sudan, they have plenty of advance warning. Commercial pilots have flight departments that tell them where to fly, how to get there, and how much fuel to take.

Renegar had to learn to fly to dozens of countries most people have never heard of, as well as to deal with the customs and immigration requirements, the routes, and the special permissions that are sometimes needed.

Saudi Arabia, for example, doesn't allow any plane to enter its territory without special government clearance. Sometimes that took weeks, but Khashoggi could speed up the process. Eventually, he obtained permanent permission to enter.

The Sudan had one railroad line that brought in jet fuel, and when the railroad didn't work, fuel was in short supply. Khashoggi got the government to arrange for special allotments.

Eventually, Khashoggi's air force consisted of thirty-four people, including twelve pilots—four per plane—plus four flight engineers, a ground handling agent, and twelve stewards.

It was Renegar's decision to hire stewards. Living together, there were enough possible sources of friction among the crew without introducing women flight attendants.

He tried to alternate crews every two weeks, but it was hard to know where to change crews. First, they had to find the plane. Khashoggi would not be pinned down to any schedule, so the relief crew flew out to a likely city and waited. If the plane didn't show up, the crew went home.

The entire operation comes under the umbrella of Handlingair Ltd., a company based in Dana Point, California. Handlingair, in effect, is Khashoggi's airline. It owns the planes, hires the crew, pays for the fuel, maintenance, phone bills, and insurance, and provides routing information.

Halfway between Los Angeles and San Diego, it is owned by AK Holdings Ltd., a Khashoggi company based in the Cayman Islands.

Every 120 hours of flight time, each plane gets a routine maintenance check by Eastern Airlines. A more extensive check is done every 200 hours. The checks can be done at any airport serviced by Eastern but are usually done at La Guardia in New York.

Every eighteen months, in Miami, Eastern does a complete "C" check, which entails a check of every part. This requires twenty men working twenty-four hours a day in three shifts for five days. United Airlines services Khashoggi's newest plane.

Each plane flies roughly 60,000 miles a month. In a year, the three planes fly more than 2 million miles—enough to circle the globe eighty times.

The total annual bill for Khashoggi's air force—excluding acquisition costs and depreciation—is $12 million. Depending on the plane, the hourly cost to operate it ranges from $3,800 to more than $6,000. With that and a passport, you could circumnavigate the globe three times on TWA.

The pilots gave up making reservations at hotels. Invariably, Khashoggi changed destinations. Ending up at any place that had space, they stayed in some of the best hotels in the world and some of the worst.

In case a pilot became incapacitated, the pilots who were off or on vacation were expected to be able to fly to anywhere in the world within forty-eight hours. When they traveled with

Khashoggi, they had to stay near a telephone in case he suddenly decided to fly.

Khashoggi's life-style aggravated the stress. The pilots saw the young girls trooping on board, the movie actresses, the princes, the champagne, and the extravagant parties on the ground. They were expected to tip generously to ensure good service at airports, and they were constantly surrounded by sumptuous food and unimaginable wealth.

It was a milieu that could wreak havoc with anybody's value system. When they got home to their wives and their lawns, they had to separate themselves mentally from Khashoggi's world. The dishes needed to be done, and the kids wanted to be taken to Knott's Berry Farm.

Renegar tried to choose pilots who were stable and sober. He wanted them to have complete confidence in their flying ability yet not be aggressive on the ground. He expected them to do their jobs and not mix with the entourage.

"You're not paid to have excitement; you're paid to avoid it," he told them.

When several pilots joined in the partying, Renegar fired them.

The policy paid off. The only problems they encountered were mechanical. The worst one occurred in Riyadh, when a fifty-pound bird flew into an engine and forced a plane to turn back to the airport, its three other engines unharmed.

If Renegar had to keep his pilots in line, he also had to contain Khashoggi's exuberance. When he first began working for him, they flew for twenty-five hours in a thirty-six-hour period. After conferring with Raytheon Co. executives in Boston, Khashoggi told Renegar to fly back to Los Angeles.

"We can't do that. This is as far as it goes," Renegar said.

Khashoggi didn't object.

One of Renegar's more pleasant problems was Soraya Khashoggi's fear of flying. She was what pilots refer to as a "white knuckle" passenger. Thunderstorms and bad weather terrified her, and she often rode in the cockpit with him to calm her fears. He explained what he was doing with the instruments and how he would avoid the clouds.

Khashoggi's second wife, Lamia, was just the opposite. She relaxed, and flying didn't bother her. But she had a healthy appetite. All of the exotic food could not substitute for Baskin-Robbins ice cream, a McDonald's hamburger, or a good pizza. When she or Khashoggi craved one of these items, they dispatched one of the planes from Spain or Nice to London to bring back takeout.

The guest books on board the planes were filled with the names of Hollywood celebrities and political and business leaders. But part of the unwritten agreement was that the pilots would keep their mouths shut about the guests they flew.

After he left the presidency, Jimmy Carter met with Khashoggi on board the plane for an hour on Santa Maria Island in the Azores. In October 1984, the pilots called for Chrysler Chairman Lee A. Iacocca in Milan to take him to a Khashoggi bash in Vienna.

Until he was deposed as president of the Sudan, Gaafar Nimeri borrowed the plane for trips to the U.S. and other countries. King Hussein of Jordan rode the plane, as did King Constantine of Greece. The Saudi princes were frequent flyers. The list went on and on.

Nowhere in the guest book does Howard Hughes' name appear, but he flew on the DC-9 from London to Freeport in the early morning hours of December 20, 1973. The flight was one of Hughes' infrequent changes of locale, accompanied by fanatical secrecy and never-ending mystery.

Hughes had his own fleet of planes, but they would be recognized, and Hughes prized secrecy. He owned the Sands Hotel, where Khashoggi often gambled, and Khashoggi's longtime friend Eugene R. Warner knew him. Through Warner, Khashoggi had dealt with Hughes' top lieutenant, F. William Gay, on business deals. Gay regarded Khashoggi as a man who understood money and power even better than did his own boss.

Eventually, Khashoggi met with Hughes himself, and when he learned that Hughes wanted to change his base of operations, he offered to make his plane available for the trip.

When Hughes appeared at Heathrow Airport in a wheelchair, his aides and bodyguards insisted on locking the cockpit door of the DC-9 so Khashoggi's people couldn't see him. Peering through a peephole in the cockpit door, the pilots noticed that Hughes looked scraggly but didn't have the long fingernails of a recluse.

Later in the flight, the Hughes people hung a blanket over the peephole.

Before he died on April 5, 1976, Hughes had moved again from Freeport to Mexico, where the billionaire wasted away. He died on a flight to Houston.

In December 1973, a year after the DC-9 flew Hughes to the Bahamas, Khashoggi used the plane for another secret mission—a visit to Pope Paul VI.

The visit was the idea of Khashoggi and Salim Issa, a Lebanese Catholic who was a Khashoggi associate and an adviser to Sudanese President Gaafar Nimeri. One day, Issa came up with a plan to try to return to the Arabs a measure of control over East Jerusalem.

Jerusalem has religious significance for Moslems as well as for Christians and Jews. Initially, Mohamed patterned many of his teachings on Jewish practices, and he ordained that his followers face Jerusalem when praying. After he fled from Mecca to Medina to avoid persecution, he directed the believers to face Mecca.

Since 1967, East Jerusalem had been under Israeli control. Even though the Israelis allowed Arabs to enter the city, the idea that they no longer controlled the holy city infuriated them. With tensions high between the Arabs and Israel just after the Yom Kippur War, Issa suggested to Khashoggi that Nimeri enlist Moslem and Christian leaders to seek the Pope's help in restoring the holy places to the Arabs.

But first, Issa said, King Faisal would have to be persuaded to drop his fierce opposition to any compromise over Jerusalem. Khashoggi said he might be able to get the blessing of the king, and both men convinced Nimeri to support the plan.

Khashoggi decided the best way to win the Pope's support was for the chiefs of state to meet with him. To represent Christians, they got Ethiopian President Haile Selassie, a Coptic Christian, to go along. Khashoggi offered his DC-9 for the trip and accompanied the delegation to the Vatican, where he knelt before the Pope.

Nothing came of the trip, but Khashoggi knew that his generosity would pay off someday. Besides, he had made an invaluable contact. Motioning to the picture of himself with the Pope that hung on the wall of his dark-paneled office in Beirut, Khashoggi told an aide, "You never know when you might need the Pope."

An individual flying his own commercial airplane automatically aroused the suspicions of customs officers. They thought it would be a perfect vehicle for massive smuggling.

On the plane, Khashoggi always kept an ample supply of new custom-made Sulka shirts, packed in boxes of a dozen. On a flight to Paris, a French customs officer noticed the shirts and became convinced that Khashoggi was in the shirt business. Even the monogrammed "AK" on the shirt pockets did not convince him that anyone would possess so many shirts for his own use.

Later, Khashoggi ran into an Italian customs officer who became enraged at Khashoggi. As Khashoggi entered the country from Switzerland to board his plane at the Milan airport, the customs officer asked him if he had any money.

"Yes," Khashoggi said.

"How much?" the customs officer asked.

"Well, I don't know," Khashoggi said. "I'll open my briefcase, and you can count it."

He opened the case, and the customs officer looked inside. It was filled with Italian lire worth at least $100,000.

Khashoggi explained that he won the money gambling at a casino in Lausanne.

"You were supposed to declare that at the border post," the officer said. "Did you?"

"No, nobody asked me," Khashoggi answered.

The officer called over other inspectors; in whispers, they began arguing among themselves.

Khashoggi said, "If you want it, keep it."

"Please," the customs officer said, "just close the briefcase and leave."

Usually Khashoggi carries no cash himself. Shaheen carries it for him.

Like the bedouin, who pack their possessions on their camels, Shaheen keeps Khashoggi's corporate documents and cash in twenty-seven steel suitcases. He takes at least ten of them wherever Khashoggi goes. When he needs them all, he has them shipped to him from New York, Paris, or wherever they might be. Each is labeled with a letter—A through Z. After Z, he uses double letters.

Khashoggi uses a standard green American Express Co. card as well. Kept by Shaheen, it's for charging meals and hotel accommodations.

Shaheen switched to American Express after Carte Blanche refused to accept a charge. Before the credit card company knew better, American Express one day yanked Khashoggi's card when the unpaid balance reached $500,000.

Now the balance due exceeds $1 million and sometimes $5 million without a threatening letter.

• • •

Robert Evans was traveling to New York on Khashoggi's stretched Boeing 727 when an extraordinarily beautiful woman appeared from nowhere.

Evans, who looks like a model himself, had just had dinner in Las Vegas with Khashoggi. The two talked about Khashoggi's financing of Evans' new movie *The Cotton Club*.

Fresh from successes as Paramount Pictures' production chief, Evans had presided over *Rosemary's Baby*, *The Odd Couple*, and *Love Story*. Then he took an option on the film rights to a book called *The Godfather*. The movie made a fortune.

Yet he was not the producer; he was an executive. Evans wanted to be closer to the action, to obtain credit in his own right, and he decided to become an independent producer. For $15,000, he bought an option on the film rights to a nonfiction work, *The Cotton Club*, a saga of Harlem in the jazz age. By all tenets that Hollywood holds dear, it couldn't lose. It had gangsters, sex, and music. Yet Evans was having a hard time raising cash.

He mentioned the idea to Melissa Prophet, a former Miss California who portrayed a tennis groupie in his 1977 movie *Players.*

Evans knew that she was good friends with Khashoggi. Her father, Las Vegas entertainer Johnny Prophet, had introduced them in Las Vegas in 1967. Melissa, twenty-seven, often traveled with Khashoggi and attended parties on his yacht.

With long curly hair, she was a perpetually tanned flower child who said outrageous things and got away with it. Khashoggi liked her California good looks and her impish sense of humor.

She recalled that Khashoggi had once said to her, "Well, Melissa, let us produce a movie for you."

Khashoggi had dabbled in movies several times, once as a backer of the ill-fated film *Mohamed—Messenger of God.* Later shortened to *The Message*, the movie starred Anthony Quinn and was meant to enlighten the world about Mohamed and Islam. Once it had been cleared by religious scholars, critics found it crudely reverential toward its subject and oddly uninspiring.

Ironically, it was banned in the Moslem world and, in March 1977, helped spark acts of terrorism by Hanafi Moslems in Washington, D.C. It is blasphemy to portray Mohamed, and the protesters believed the movie had done so by having Mohamed's followers address the movie camera as if it were their leader.

When Melissa Prophet heard Evans describe his plans for *The Cotton Club*, she decided this was the right movie for her collaboration with Khashoggi. She pitched it to him in Las Vegas. The next morning, an aide woke her with instructions to fly to Los Angeles on the Boeing 727 and bring Evans back for dinner.

My God, she thought, I couldn't be any luckier—Bob Evans and AK.

But Evans, fifty-three, was in no mood to drop everything and fly to Las Vegas. Prophet wondered how she was going to get this prima donna on the plane. Finally, he agreed to go if Khashoggi would fly him to New York after dinner.

During the dinner, Khashoggi offered to give Evans seed money, but Evans wanted more than that. As he rode off to the airport in a limousine, she and Khashoggi stood in the driveway.

"He'll come back, Melissa. They always do," Khashoggi said.

She thought it was like a scene from a movie.

When Evans boarded the plane, a strikingly beautiful woman served him champagne. In all his years in Hollywood, Evans had rarely seen such a gorgeous face and form.

Then the woman changed into a diaphanous negligee and yawned.

"Let's go to bed," she said, beckoning toward the flying bedroom.

"Good night," Evans said, his legs shaking.

"Aren't you going to come in?" she asked.

"No," he replied.

After they landed in New York, Melissa phoned Evans and giggled. She said she had heard a tape recording of the entire conversation.

A few days later, Evans called Khashoggi and accepted Khashoggi's original offer. It was just as Khashoggi said: They always come back.

Khashoggi agreed to put $750,000 into the film immediately and another $1,250,000 once Evans secured other backers. Melissa Prophet was to be given a credit as associate producer.

With the money, Evans hired Mario Puzo to write the script.

Khashoggi threw a party for both of them at the Dunes Hotel in Las Vegas. At a private casino there, Evans saw Khashoggi drop $250,000 on a single roll of the dice.

Later, their deal fell apart. Khashoggi wanted to invest another $10 million in the movie, but he wanted to own more than half of it. Evans wanted to retain control and considered Khashoggi's demand out of the question.

In fact, Khashoggi had just received an adviser's opinion against investing in the film.

To buy out Khashoggi, Evans had to give him back his $750,000 plus another $250,000 in interest.

Eventually, the film cost $47 million and was a financial failure. Evans returned to Paramount as a producer. But Melissa Prophet got her credit line. And Khashoggi, in a year, had made a profit on his investment of 33 percent.

To Melissa, the incident on the plane was but another of Khashoggi's jokes, a prank to amuse himself and his friends, who included the woman on the plane.

On one occasion, Jan Stenbeck, a Morgan Stanley & Co. vice-president, was to meet Khashoggi at a hotel in Cairo. Checking in late, he found Khashoggi had not yet arrived. He left word with the operator that he was going to sleep and wanted no calls put through to his room.

When Khashoggi arrived and was ushered into his suite, it was long after midnight. Told that Stenbeck wanted no calls, Khashoggi dialed him directly on a house phone. Posing as a male operator, he told Stenbeck, "There's an overseas call from [Stenbeck's boss at Morgan Stanley]. Please stay on the line."

Khashoggi then put down the phone in his suite and enjoyed a late dinner. From time to time, he would come on the line to repeat the message, while Stenbeck tried to stay awake holding the receiver.

Eventually, Stenbeck fell asleep, the receiver still cradled to his ear.

For more than a year, a model of a McDonnell-Douglas DC-8 sat on Shaheen's table at his office in Khashoggi's Olympic Tower apartment in New York.

"This is our next plane," he told visitors proudly, as if pointing out a car he was about to acquire. "It goes from Los Angeles to Riyadh without refueling."

Khashoggi always wanted to outdo himself, and the plane— known as a DC-8/73—fit the pattern. It was one of eighty-nine DC-8s reengined by California's Cammacorp Inc., and then converted into a luxury craft for Khashoggi at a total cost of $31 million.

As long as a jumbo jet and as wide as the Boeing 727, the plane weighed 358,000 pounds fully loaded. More than twice the size of the DC-9, the plane carried 24,000 gallons of fuel and could fly forty passengers and their baggage for fifteen hours without refueling. Its four GE/Snecma fan jet, fuel-efficient engines cruised at eight-tenths the speed of sound.

To customize the interior, Khashoggi again hired Ai-Research, which brought in a separate designer, Michael Reese of Reese Design Inc. in Austin, Texas. To suggest what he had in mind, Khashoggi set up a meeting on his yacht, the *Nabila*, as it floated off the coast of Martinique.

Taking AiResearch's Graser and Reese on a tour of the boat, he showed them the discotheque, the advanced communications equipment, the swimming pool on deck, the movie theater, and even the engine room.

In the lounge, he discussed the new plane and told them what he wanted: "Make it way out—avant-garde," he said.

At lunch with twenty associates and family members on board, both men realized they would have to surpass the sumptuous interior of the *Nabila*.

Reese created two lush main salons lined with couches of soft leather and silk, built-in end tables, silk and leather wall coverings and trim, and hand-woven, platinum-colored carpeting made of silk. Between the two salons curves an arch of holographic art forms; with lights perceived as three-dimensional images, the display changes color and seethes like a galaxy of darting comets.

In the center of one of the salons, a gold-trimmed ottomanlike cocktail table contains a color video monitor that shows the ground below and the view the pilots see. Besides takeoffs and landings, the guests can watch sunrises and sunsets on the monitor.

Constantly changing electronic maps show the position of the plane as it flies across the earth, and can display close-ups of any area of the globe.

One end table holds a gold gimballike device—a representation of the solar system calibrated in accordance with the Moslem calendar. A holographic light emanates from a huge mirror on the wall of one of the salons. On the end tables are specially designed white matchbooks with "AK" done in silver encircled in gold.

The aircraft has six video machines for playing movies, which Khashoggi often obtains before they are previewed. The entire interior of the plane can be closed to outside light with electronically operated panels.

Usually, Khashoggi travels with these panels closed. That way, he has total control of his environment and can choose to sleep or stay up according to his own time schedule.

As big as a conventional kitchen, the galley has all the accoutrements of Julia Child's kitchen, including a rotisserie and Jennair convection oven.

Food on the new plane is usually cooked on board. While flying from Kenya on Thanksgiving in 1984, Khashoggi's chefs roasted a twenty-one-pound turkey in the plane's kitchen.

Done in vibrant maroon tones, the dining area uses settings of triangular-shaped chinaware. The total cost for the custom-made pattern, with sixty-five settings to allow for breakage, was $600,000 including flatware and crystal—on top of the $11-million cost of the interior. After the chinaware was made, the mold was broken.

Khashoggi's bedroom has the obligatory ten-foot-wide bed, closets, and dressers lined with recessed lights that give the room an ethereal quality. Above the bed, a firmament of stars appears to be a porthole to the night skies.

Several times while the DC-8 was being designed, Reese took models of the plane with various options to Khashoggi to ask his preferences. One of the items was specially designed crystal with a streamlined, tapered form.

Reese showed Khashoggi how the crystal portion fitted into a sterling-silver base. Demonstrating the goblet further, he poured Dom Pérignon into the glass.

As the bubbles quickly rose to the surface, Khashoggi asked, "Now can you light the bubbles for me?"

"Sir?" Reese said.

"Can you light the bubbles?" Khashoggi repeated.

Reese went back to his drawing board in Austin. He tried batteries, switches, light bulbs. Finally, he hit upon cold light, emitted when two chemicals react. Kids use tubes of it at Halloween.

Reese had the lights made specially in Japan and brought them to show Khashoggi. He broke the membrane, separating the two chemicals, and dropped the tube into the silver base. Then he placed the crystal bowl on its base.

As he poured champagne into the goblet, the tube shot darts of greenish-yellow light through the champagne, complementing the golden hue of the bubbles.

As the plane was being finished, friends of Khashoggi's came to see it in Long Beach, California, where AiResearch, now Garrett General Aviation Services Co., is based. Among them were Farrah Fawcett and Ryan O'Neal.

Meanwhile, Khashoggi sold his stretched Boeing 727 to Muda Hassanal Bolkiah, the sultan of Brunei, for $19 million. The thirty-eight-year-old pleasure-loving sultan presides over a newly independent kingdom of 200,000 subjects on Borneo's north coast. The price was $8 million more than Khashoggi originally paid for the plane.

As part of the deal, Khashoggi agreed to temporarily lease his yacht, the *Nabila*, to the sultan for $800,000 a month in 1984.

Just before the DC-8 was ready to be delivered in August 1984, Khashoggi's ravishing twenty-three-year-old daughter, Nabila, looked it over.

A refreshingly direct woman with long black hair and warm brown eyes, she lives in her own villa in Cannes, complete with its own ten-foot-wide bed for her father.

She has taken the presidency of one of Khashoggi's subsidiaries. On the side, she is developing a computerized service called Infolex that lists entertainment, shopping, and restaurant possibilities for hotel guests in eight different languages. The system was launched at New York's Waldorf-Astoria in early 1985.

"Frankly, I'm a young girl, and I have got to prove myself," she told one interviewer.

When she saw the DC-8 for the first time, she remarked, "What we need is a ribbon."

So Reese designed a ribbon that would wrap around the fuselage of the giant airplane when Khashoggi took possession of it in Nice. Using red nylon sailcloth measuring eight feet wide and weighing twenty-five pounds, he fastened it with a fourteen-foot bow.

The ribbon was in place when Khashoggi asked his chief pilot, Soderstrom, for a pair of scissors.

Contemplating the plane he was about to fly, Soderstrom said, "Scissors, sir?"

"Yes, I need to cut the ribbon," Khashoggi said.

The plane was like the convertible Khashoggi bought to impress the girls while attending Chico State University. Nobody turned down an invitation to ride on it.

It was his dream machine.

# The Investigators

The prince must . . . avoid those things which will make him
hated or despised; and whenever he succeeds in this, he will
have done his part, and will find no danger in other vices.

—*Niccolò Machiavelli, The Prince*

**W**HEN Jerome I. Levinson heard a knock on the door
of his suite at the Sands Hotel in Las Vegas, he thought it was
the bellboy with more of his baggage. The chief counsel of the
Senate Foreign Relations subcommittee on multinational corporations, Levinson had just checked into the hotel after being
met at the airport by Eugene R. Warner.

Warner was one of Khashoggi's closest buddies. Levinson
had heard he was disaffected and might spill the beans about
Khashoggi and his secret dealings with Richard M. Nixon.

As they drove to the Sands in a chauffeured limousine,
Warner told Levinson he had a few friends he would like him
to meet. Warner would see him at dinner.

Hearing the knock, the white-haired Levinson opened the
door. There was a shapely blonde, about twenty-seven years
old, dressed in a gray pants suit.

"Mr. Warner asked me to see you," she said softly. "I'm here for your pleasure."

Levinson did not know whether to laugh or slam the door shut. He did neither.

As the highly attractive woman edged toward the bedroom, she suggested that a drink might relax him.

Levinson could not believe that Khashoggi would be so blatant. Perhaps a beautiful woman could brush against him in the lobby, but sending one to knock on his door? Levinson was not so stupid that he would fall for that, and he did not need to be relaxed.

Reaching for his wallet, he displayed his U.S. Senate credentials, a plastic card with his picture on it.

"I'm not sure if you're aware of it, but I'm employed by the U.S. Senate Committee on Foreign Relations," he told her. "Your being here could be construed as an attempt to interfere with a congressional investigation, and that's a federal crime."

The woman blanched and became agitated.

"I know nothing about this," she said. "I'm here as a friend of Mr. Warner's. He said you're a friend of his and wanted some company. I don't want to get in the middle of this. If you want me to leave, I'll leave."

As the woman turned toward the door, she asked, "Can I tell Mr. Warner that you had a good time?"

"You can tell him anything you want," Levinson barked as he closed the door.

When he returned to Washington, Levinson told his boss about the incident. In August 1975, just after the first disclosure of Khashoggi's mammoth fees from Northrop Corp., Senator Frank Church was besieged by Wall Street powers to can his investigation. Church was aware that the slightest mistake could ruin him politically. He did not need another headache.

"It's dangerous to go out on interviews like this solo," the Idaho Democrat told Levinson. "Really, two people should go because of the possibility of entrapment."

It was one of the more amusing episodes in the Church committee's three-year investigation of Khashoggi. Taking them to London, Paris, and Germany, it required grueling seven-day weeks and fortitude against attacks from within the committee and without.

In the end, it produced hearings that revealed for the first time the magnitude of Khashoggi's commissions. Together with many other disclosures of foreign payments by U.S. companies, the hearings led to passage of the Corrupt Practices Act of 1977.

So much was Church Khashoggi's nemesis that Khashoggi's staff came to refer to events as "B.C." and "A.C."—before Church and after Church. Church put Khashoggi on the map. He transformed the clipping files in newspaper morgues from thin envelopes with a few items on Khashoggi's investments to massive packets overflowing with stories of alleged bribes and fees in the tens of millions of dollars.

Ten years later, Shaheen mutters at the mention of Church, as if he had heard the name of a war criminal.

Why did he do that to the chief? Shaheen wants to know. The answer begins on the West Coast, with the Watergate hearings.

Herbert W. Kalmbach, the former personal attorney to President Nixon, was making his historic admission that he collected funds for the Watergate burglars, and John R. Phillips, one of three founders of the Center for Law in the Public Interest, was following the story closely.

Bathed in television lights, Kalmbach told how he raised $219,000 for the men who broke into Democratic National Committee headquarters on June 17, 1972. It required clandestine meetings, calls from telephone booths—and a big boost from Thomas V. Jones, chairman of Northrop Corp.

Watching on a set in his Los Angeles office, Phillips sat up a little straighter in his chair—a castoff donated by another law firm. Northrop's headquarters were just three hundred yards from the law center's offices on Santa Monica Boulevard.

Kalmbach said he told Jones only that he needed money for "a special assignment." Jones was happy to oblige. It's not every day that the President's personal attorney comes calling.

Jones gave Kalmbach $50,000 on July 31, 1972. The money was in hundred-dollar bills. Kalmbach said he thought it was to help the Watergate defendants with legal bills.

Switching off the set, Phillips strode into the adjoining office, where Brent N. Rushforth, one of his partners, had been watching on his own set.

"That's got to be shareholders' money," Phillips said.

Rushforth agreed, and they talked about filing a stockholders' derivative suit to recover the money. After Jones and

Northrop pleaded guilty in U.S. District Court in Washington
to felony charges of making illegal donations of $150,000, Jay
Springer, a New York lawyer and Northrop stockholder, called
Phillips. He was outraged and wanted the center to sue.

At the end of May, the lawyers filed a class action suit in
federal court in Los Angeles, charging that Jones and others
had illegally used shareholders' money for the contributions.
They got their first break when the case was assigned to U.S.
District Court Judge Warren J. Ferguson, a strong judge. Northrop wanted to limit the questions that could be asked of Jones
in depositions, but Ferguson would have none of that.

In October 1974, at their threadbare offices, the center
lawyers took Jones' deposition in the presence of Northrop
lawyers, a phalanx of the Los Angeles legal establishment. To
form a conference table, the lawyers moved some smaller tables together. Removed from its hinges for some renovation
work, a door leaned precariously against a wall. No chairs in
the turquoise-carpeted room matched.

After Jones was sworn, Rushforth asked him to recite his
background and responsibilities. Slowly, Rushforth edged into
the matter at hand. An hour into the deposition, he asked how
Jones had managed to come up with $50,000 in hundred-dollar
bills and whether he had made such payments before.

Rushforth noticed that Jones was going pale. When he had
pleaded guilty, there was no need to say just how he arranged
to secure so much cash. Without a trial, the details had never
come out. Now Jones was about to reveal secrets he had kept
hidden so well.

As the court reporter's fingers danced over the keys of
the transcribing machine, Jones began telling of secret slush
funds, cash in attaché cases, Swiss and Luxembourg bank accounts, off-the-books disbursements, and payments to shadowy foreign agents, including Khashoggi.

The center lawyers were stunned. They had expected to
hear of more payments to politicians in the U.S. Nobody had
ever heard of the practice of paying bribes overseas—foreign
payments, they were called euphemistically.

Later, the Securities and Exchange Commission would move
against household names like 3M, Gulf Oil, Phillips Petroleum,
and United Brands. A former Japanese prime minister, Kakuei
Tanaka, would be charged with corruption and jailed for accepting $1.6 million from Lockheed Corp. Prince Bernhard of
the Netherlands would be stripped of his job in the armed

forces. Interior Minister Luigi Gui of Italy would resign amid charges he received $50,000 from Lockheed while defense minister. It would be revealed that William Franz Josef Bach, a former member of the lower House of the West German Parliament, was supplied with Northrop money through a Swiss consulting firm.

The suicide of a Lockheed treasurer would follow, and the mysterious death in Paris of a former French air force chief of staff who was secretly on the Northrop payroll.

Rushforth asked Jones where he had gotten the idea for making foreign payments.

"I was only following the Lockheed model," he said.

After learning of Jones' payment to Kalmbach, Northrop's outside directors ordered a special investigation. The board hired an outside law firm—Wilmer, Cutler & Pickering from Washington, D.C.—and commissioned an investigative audit by the accounting firm of Ernst & Ernst.

By November 1974, the auditors had prepared some initial findings, and Judge Ferguson ordered Northrop to give the center lawyers a copy of the report. It was a navigator's chart to rivulets of secret cash payments all over the world.

The report traced Northrop's practice of paying off government officials to the early 1960s. Ever looking for new markets, Jones had hired William A. Savy as Northrop's "window" on West Germany. He was a Paris-based attorney and former intelligence officer. In the next three or four years, he became a conduit for political payments as well.

By interviewing Northrop executives and consultants, the auditors and Wilmer, Cutler lawyers learned that many of the intended recipients of these and other funds were government officials, including President Nixon through his campaign committee and Generals Hashim and Zuhair of the Saudi Royal Air Force.

The disclosures were sensational and would soon be political dynamite in countries all over the world. But Northrop had managed to keep them secret and wanted no public release of the information. At Northrop's request, the judge ordered the report kept under seal, along with Jones' deposition. The SEC got a copy, but it lay on a pile of papers, unread.

If big corporations hate litigation about sensitive matters, they loathe publicity about them. The outside Northrop directors were conducting their own investigation. As Northrop management saw it, there was no need for the SEC to become involved.

That was the message Northrop and the outside directors wanted to convey to the SEC. So Wilmer, Cutler arranged a meeting with Stanley Sporkin, the chief of enforcement of the SEC. Manny Cohen, a senior partner of the law firm, knew him. As a former SEC chairman, Cohen had been his boss.

Together with Howard P. Willens and Michael R. Klein of the law firm, Cohen visited Sporkin at his office at 500 North Capitol Street in Washington. Forty-four years old, he was a Philadelphia native who graduated Phi Beta Kappa from Pennsylvania State University. In 1957, he graduated from Yale School of Law.

Sporkin spent most of his professional career at the SEC, becoming director of the division of enforcement in 1974. He was instrumental in transforming a sleepy regulatory agency focused on securities trading into a highly aggressive watchdog on corporate conduct.

Trained both as a lawyer and an accountant, Sporkin was the chief policeman of the industry, and he took the job seriously. The SEC's role was to make sure investors had accurate and timely information about the stocks they were buying.

Sporkin had a quick, forceful way of talking and always had a frazzled look, enhanced by the furnishings in his office. He had purchased a sofa with his own funds, for sixty-nine dollars—marked down because an arm was missing.

Cohen explained that the internal investigation had things well in hand. Reforms would be recommended and carried out. There was nothing to worry about.

The center lawyers were also at the meeting. They had developed a good relationship with Klein and thought he could be trusted to carry out the probe impartially. But they did not think Northrop would change without outside pressure.

From the comments by Sporkin and his staff, it was clear they had not read the auditor's report. Rushforth said they would be amazed when they did.

Sporkin had already seen signs of foreign payments made by two other companies. But his concern had been with payments to U.S. politicians. He had felt foreign payments were beyond the jurisdiction of the SEC. Now, as he focused on this new animal, he wasn't so sure.

At the end of the one-hour meeting, Sporkin turned to Cohen.

"What-am-I-buying, Manny?" he said, stringing the words together. "I don't know what-I'm-buying."

Everyone in the room knew the nickel had dropped. Sporkin wanted to determine for himself whether Northrop was cleaning its own house.

Instead of cooling the fire, the meeting had fanned the flames. Now Sporkin was beginning to see that foreign payments could corrupt an entire company and its accounting system. After the meeting, the center lawyers went over the report with Sporkin's staff.

It was too late to turn back.

In February 1972, columnist Jack Anderson reported that internal documents of International Telephone & Telegraph Co. showed ITT had collaborated with the Central Intelligence Agency to prevent Salvador Allende from becoming president of Chile. For Frank Forrester Church, it was the match that ignited his interest in multinational corporations.

Thin, with black hair and brown eyes, Church had an incandescent smile and was entertaining with friends. But he developed a reputation for being cold, humorless, and publicity-hungry.

In his view, multinational companies had become a fifth column in international politics, using their home governments to destroy regimes not to their liking. Church called them by the initials MNC, suggesting a new disease.

A member of the Senate Foreign Relations Committee, he got the committee to form the subcommittee on multinational corporations. Thus began one of the most controversial investigations ever undertaken by the Congress.

Church hired Levinson as chief counsel. Levinson was special adviser to the president of the Inter-American Development Bank, which makes development loans to Latin American countries. As he began developing sources, Levinson became a telephone acquaintance of Sporkin, who gave him hints on where to look.

In April 1975, Sporkin called.

"There's something here that bears looking into and may go beyond our jurisdiction," he said. It involved overseas payments by Northrop and by Gulf, which alone paid nearly $5 million in bribes to political parties in South Korea, Bolivia, and other countries.

"You ought to look into it," Sporkin said.

• • •

The Watergate Special Prosecution Force already knew about Khashoggi and began telling Levinson about him, too. The prosecutors were trying to trace Khashoggi's relationship with Nixon and zillions he supposedly donated to Nixon's first or second run for the presidency. There were rumors that he knew Nixon, but they could not be pinned down.

In fact, Khashoggi had known Nixon since March 1967, when they had dinner together at the Rasputin Restaurant in Paris. John Pochna, a mutual friend and a consultant to oilman J. Paul Getty, arranged the meeting. Besides Nixon, Pochna, and Khashoggi, those present were Hassan Yassin, Khashoggi's cousin and a former associate, and Morton P. MacLeod, Khashoggi's chief of staff.

In the summer of 1967, when Nixon was preparing to run for the presidency, Khashoggi met with him again, this time in Nixon's apartment in New York. They discussed the Arab–Israeli war and the prospect of Nixon's making a trip to the Middle East.

In January 1968, Pochna introduced Khashoggi to Nixon's close friend Charles G. (Bebe) Rebozo at Khashoggi's suite at the Waldorf-Astoria in New York. The next month, Khashoggi directed Eugene Warner in Las Vegas to open an account at Rebozo's Key Biscayne Bank in Florida.

As described in a letter to Warner, the account was to provide for Khashoggi's personal expenses when he visited the Sands Hotel and to fund business opportunities developed through Rebozo. Warner was appointed trustee on the account.

In October 1968, to aid in the campaign, Khashoggi agreed to give Pochna $43,000 to finance the production of records of Nixon's speeches.

After Nixon was elected, Khashoggi sent him a letter of congratulations. In December, Khashoggi, Yassin, and Warner met with Rebozo at Rebozo's home in Key Biscayne. There, they discussed possible business ventures. Near the end of the meeting, Nixon joined the group.

In January 1969, Khashoggi attended Nixon's inauguration with London playgirl Viviane Ventura. ("He's incredible, a wonderful human being," the beautiful, mysterious-looking woman later told the *Washington Post*.)

Once Nixon became President, Khashoggi met with him again at Nixon's Key Biscayne compound in early 1969. They discussed Middle East diplomacy and the need for economic development in Saudi Arabia.

Later, they exchanged letters concerning the social and economic problems of the Middle East, and Khashoggi discussed with Rebozo the possibility of purchasing a home in Key Biscayne through him.

At Khashoggi's request, Rebozo gave Nixon a prospectus prepared by Khashoggi on Petrosat, a joint Saudi–U.S. energy venture. This was the idea dreamed up by MacLeod—the one that Khashoggi's staff could not understand.

Much to Khashoggi's disappointment, the administration showed no interest in the project.

If Nixon took no interest in Petrosat, he took a deep interest in Khashoggi's points about Saudi Arabia and its strategic importance to the U.S. Almost as soon as he was in the White House, he began a series of exchanges and visits between the two countries.

In October 1969, Nixon invited Prince Fahd, then second deputy premier, to meet with him at the White House. In May 1971, Nixon invited King Faisal for a visit, and they discussed an Arab–Israeli peace settlement. The following year, Prince Sultan saw Nixon again at the White House. In June 1974, Prince Fahd visited with Nixon to discuss military and economic relations. Later that month, Nixon flew to Saudi Arabia to meet with King Faisal.

On each occasion, Khashoggi was part of the unofficial party, preparing position papers, arranging entertainment, and offering suggestions.

During much of this time, Khashoggi was transferring several million dollars from Swiss Bank Corp. in Geneva into his account at Rebozo's Key Biscayne Bank. Through Warner, he withdrew all but $200,000 of it in the form of checks written to "cash" and signed over to the Sands Hotel.

Khashoggi said he used the $200,000 for yachting and other personal expenses. The rest he used to pay gambling debts run up at the casino. He often played with executives he wanted to influence. If he lost to them, it was only another T&E (travel and entertainment) expense.

By making the checks out to "cash," Khashoggi hoped to conceal the fact that the money was spent for gambling. It would not enhance his reputation among government officials or business executives in the U.S.—or among the populace in Saudi Arabia, for that matter—if one of his favorite pastimes became public knowledge. The Koran takes a dim view of games of chance.

When Charles F. C. Ruff took over as special prosecutor, he read the memos scattered throughout File No. 806—"Arab Money."

There were numerous allegations in the file about contributions by Khashoggi to Nixon. The numbers were always different—$1 million, or $800,000, or $80,000. And it was either the first or the second Nixon campaign, but never both.

Ruff wanted a thorough investigation.

The prosecutors interviewed Warner; Rose Mary Woods, Nixon's personal secretary; Shaheen; Yassin; and later Soraya Khashoggi. Finally, on April 25, 1975, just before the first public disclosure of the size of Khashoggi's fees, Paul R. Michel of Ruff's staff interviewed Khashoggi himself.

The interview began at 3 P.M. at the low-slung Marriott Hotel at Washington's Dulles International Airport. Khashoggi ran through his dealings with Nixon and showed Michel copies of correspondence with him.

When asked why he placed his account at Key Biscayne Bank, Khashoggi answered with typical bravado. He said he hoped to "curry favor" with the President's best friend, so he would convey his ideas to the President. And he hoped Rebozo would act as a "finder" for business opportunities in southern Florida. He said the relationship never developed to that point.

Khashoggi knew it was just what the prosecutors wanted to hear—that he churned millions through the tiny bank to win favor with the President. But once the prosecutors heard it, there was little they could do with it. Other than having Rebozo forward some written material to Nixon, Khashoggi did not, in fact, win any significant favors. He could have sent the material directly to Nixon, and later did.

If the talks with Khashoggi influenced Nixon to improve relations with the Saudis, that could not be traced back to money placed at the Key Biscayne Bank. The meetings boosted Khashoggi's prestige among the Saudi princes, but that was hardly a criminal offense. In any event, the prosecutors did not think to ask about the visits of Saudi princes.

Khashoggi had consented to be interviewed with the understanding he would not be prosecuted if he told the truth. After the two-hour interview, Michel decided Khashoggi was telling the truth.

A year later, Ruff himself interviewed Soraya Khashoggi at her Eaton Square town house in the Belgravia section of London. She served tea to the man who, crippled by a form of polio while teaching law in Liberia as a Peace Corps volunteer, appeared in court in a wheelchair.

The two had a pleasant chat. But Ruff learned nothing more than he could have learned from reading the newspapers.

It is always frustrating to pursue an investigation and find that it leads nowhere, Ruff thought as he closed out the case.

While the Watergate prosecutors were pursuing their investigation, Jerome Levinson at the Church subcommittee was developing his own sources who said that Khashoggi used sex to win over U.S. executives. One person suggested that Eugene Warner was disaffected and would be worth interviewing.

Warner was a character from a Damon Runyon novel. Perpetually tanned, with an expansive chest, he was a Hungarian Jew who wore sunglasses day and night and spoke in a raspy voice. His assertiveness alienated many of the people around Khashoggi, but Warner's directness could also be endearing. Khashoggi liked him because he was smart and knew how to have a good time.

The two met in 1955, when Khashoggi was attending Stanford University and traveling to Las Vegas with Roy Eidal, who made vehicles for desert travel, first in Seattle and later in Albuquerque, New Mexico.

A real estate broker, Warner lived in a penthouse of the Sands Hotel, where he was a consultant to the casino and entertained high rollers. When Khashoggi visited in the U.S., Warner made hotel and limousine reservations, introduced him to politicians, and filled him in on political developments. A man who knew Hebrew and Arabic and quoted liberally from the Koran and the Talmud, he was a good storyteller and could elicit belly laughs.

Never married, Warner valued his creature comforts. He kept a book listing the numbers of the loveliest girls in Las Vegas. Jokingly, he explained sending a woman to Jerry Levinson's hotel suite as an effort to extend the "hospitality of the hotel" by giving him a "massage, or something like that."

When service was not up to Warner's standards, he complained like a baby. His bleating gave rise to the impression he was disaffected.

One evening in May 1985, Khashoggi invited Warner and

more than a hundred other guests to the Ballet West production of *Abdallah* at the John F. Kennedy Center for the Performing Arts in Washington. Because the ballet company is located in Salt Lake City, where Triad is a major force, Khashoggi has been a backer of the performers.

Warner tried to stay awake as the dancers bounded across the stage. Set in Basra, Iraq, *Abdallah* tells a tale in the genre of *Arabian Nights*—of a shoemaker who becomes wealthy through wishing but then loses it all after wishing for too much.

The other guests included Nizar Hamdoon, the Iraqi ambassador to the U.S., Nevada Senator Orrin G. Hatch, a clutch of aides from the Reagan White House, and a deeply tanned Jane Seymour. As Khashoggi's executive assistant, Shaheen had arranged for twenty-six-dollar seats in the first row of the first balcony, arguably the best location for a ballet.

Afterward, limousines shuttled Warner and other guests across the street to the Watergate, where Khashoggi's brother Essam hosted a spectacular Middle Eastern buffet.

Arrayed on both sides of a long table were a whole roasted lamb carved to order, on a bed of rice pilaf; chicken and lamb shish kebabs; dark green grape leaves stuffed with ground lamb; tiny Arabian sausages flavored with coriander; a salad laden with huge green and black olives; and meatballs made with lamb in a delicate tomato and pignolia sauce.

There was also an assortment of Middle Eastern dips served with Syrian pita bread—flat, round coarse loaves with hollow insides: *hummos bi'tahini*, made with mashed chick-peas, ground sesame paste, fresh lemon juice, and garlic; *baba ghanouj*, a similar dip using mashed, roasted eggplant; and *tabbouleh*, an aromatic mixture of cracked wheat, chopped onions and tomatoes, lemon juice, and fresh mint leaves.

Waiters served two kinds of wine throughout the midnight meal.

For dessert, there was baklava, cut in triangles and made with paper-thin phyllo dough, chopped walnuts, and honey, and fresh fruit.

But Warner took aside a Khashoggi aide and harangued him mercilessly because there was no well-done lamb.

"You know I like my meat well done," he hammered at the man, who made helpless movements with his arms.

• • •

Hoping that Warner would open up about Khashoggi, Levinson arranged to interview him in Las Vegas. At dinner at the Sands, Levinson quickly realized Warner was not going to discuss anything unless he thought Levinson already knew about it.

Levinson wanted to find out if Khashoggi actually had met Nixon. According to his source, Khashoggi passed a message to Nixon from King Faisal during the Yom Kippur War of October 6, 1973.

The war started when Syrian and Egyptian forces attacked Israeli positions in the Golan Heights and along the Suez Canal. Israel recovered and pushed the Syrians beyond the 1967 cease-fire lines, recrossing the canal and taking part of the West Bank. The fact that the U.S. backed Israel led King Faisal to impose a total embargo on oil shipments to the U.S., raising oil prices.

According to what Levinson had been told, Khashoggi informed Nixon that Faisal wanted Nixon to stop the war and end the supply of jets to Israel. But Levinson did not know if the story was true. In Washington, it was not uncommon for lobbyists to use mirrors to launch such rumors to give the appearance of having access to key politicians. In telling their home offices of a dinner with Senator X, they might imply an intimate meeting when, in fact, the dinner was a charity affair open to the public.

Perhaps Khashoggi himself had generated the stories that he knew Nixon to magnify his own importance, Levinson thought. He had no tangible evidence that Khashoggi really operated on such exalted levels.

Using his most confident tone of voice, Levinson told Warner at dinner that he knew all about the message conveyed by Khashoggi to Nixon.

He was surprised that Warner confirmed what he had heard—that Khashoggi passed such a message through Rose Mary Woods, Nixon's personal secretary.

Warner said he first met Woods when he invited her to a Shoreham Hotel luncheon in Washington for a visiting Saudi. Later, he arranged for Khashoggi to meet with her at her Watergate apartment one Saturday. She and Khashoggi had a private talk while Warner remained in another room.

Famous for her strained efforts to show how she might have erased a key portion of the White House tapes, Woods could recall very little of the conversation, except that Warner told her she would have to "meet the prince" one of these days.

Following the meeting, on October 29, 1973, Nixon wrote to Faisal, saying that the points he conveyed through their "mutual friend [Khashoggi] concerning the war were given serious consideration."

Diplomatic middleman was a role Khashoggi often played. It was an uninhibited parallel line of communication not affected by the official line. If one or the other side wanted to convey a message that might create a negative reaction, Khashoggi could do it without embarrassing repercussions.

The role only enhanced his access, enabling him later to propose business deals directly to heads of state.

After their dinner at the Sands, Warner and Levinson walked through the lobby of the hotel as another girl, even more attractive than the first, began walking alongside them.

"She's a player," Warner said to Levinson.

As they reached Levinson's room, Levinson opened the door and held on to it.

"Eugene, good night," he said firmly. "I enjoyed our evening. See you in the morning."

Warner laughed and walked off with the girl.

In April 1975, Sporkin called Levinson to tell him about an expanded version of the Ernst & Ernst report on Northrop's foreign payments. The subcommittee immediately subpoenaed the report and the backup documents from Ernst & Ernst in Los Angeles.

As the subcommittee decided to make public many of the documents, some of the details were already trickling out in the press. At the request of the State Department, the names of recipients of bribes were deleted.

On Friday, June 6, 1975, the subcommittee staff tossed packets of 530 pages of the documents on the press table in the full committee's hearing room. The unprecedented disclosure was part of Levinson's penchant for documenting fully the committee's charges.

Like hungry lions, reporters descended on the tables and carried off the packets under their arms. They barely had time to digest their kill before that night's deadline. But they got the essential points: Through Khashoggi, Northrop paid $450,000 in bribes earmarked for two unnamed Saudi generals.

The headlines circled the globe.

•  •  •

Three days later, the subcommittee convened to hear testimony from Northrop officials. The hearing was held in room 4221 of the Dirksen Senate Office Building, a blond-paneled room.

The senators sat behind a mahogany horseshoe-shaped dais. Each of the two press tables was crowded with reporters, and the seventy seats in the hearing room were filled.

The gold-faced clock at the rear of the high-ceilinged room read 10:05 A.M.

Looking like a fresh-faced choirboy, Church said the documents "lay out in excruciating detail a sordid tale of bribery and of shadowy figures operating behind the scenes...." It was, he said, a cast of characters "out of a novel of international intrigue." However, he said, "we are not dealing with fiction but with real life: deliberate deception, for example, of our own officials in the Department of Defense as to the full scope of services performed by Northrop's agent in Saudi Arabia, Mr. Khashoggi."

As the first witness, Church called Richard W. Millar, chairman of Northrop's executive committee. Like the other committee witnesses, Millar had already participated in a mock hearing with the subcommittee staff. It was to give him an idea of the questions that would be asked and to give the staff an idea of the answers. Levinson wanted no surprises.

A stolid individual, Millar gave the impression as he sat at the witness table of someone who felt out of place and wanted everyone to know it. He did not join the Northrop board to become involved in investigations of bribes.

In broad outline, he told the subcommittee how Khashoggi had requested the money for the Saudi generals.

"So this was really a form of blackmail, was it not?" Church said of the $450,000 payment.

"I would not argue with the..." he started to say.

"You would not argue with that, would you?" Church cut in.

"No, sir," Millar said.

The next day, Jones testified. Saying he took full responsibility for Northrop's actions, the Northrop chairman promised, "The mistakes we have made will not be repeated."

Senator Charles H. Percy asked Jones if he thought a law should be passed to prohibit such payments.

"I agree with that 100 percent," Jones said.

It was one of the few acknowledgments that the Church committee was dealing in a gray area—payments that are prohibited when made in the U.S. but tolerated, if not condoned, in most countries overseas.

Three months later, on September 12, 1975, D. J. Haughton, Lockheed's chairman, appeared in the same hearing room. He revealed that Lockheed had paid Khashoggi an astounding $106 million in the five years ending in 1975.

Under fire from Lockheed directors, Haughton, together with Lockheed's president, A. C. Kotchian, resigned six months later.

By now, Church was inundated by pressure from Wall Street and the full committee. David Rockefeller was making calls to express concern. Members of Congress were hearing from defense manufacturers in their districts. Businessmen were saying these people are wild men.

Even Pat M. Holt, the full committee's staff director who helped hire Levinson, turned on him. Levinson had developed a close relationship with Church; the two often drove to work together down River Road in suburban Bethesda, Maryland. Holt thought Levinson and his people were beyond his control, and he resented it. They were aggressive and abrasive—fine qualities in investigators but not in his titular subordinates. They had failed to do a broader, academic study that was supposed to be part of their mandate.

While Church bathed in the publicity, he had ambitions to run for the presidency. This was not necessarily the way to get there.

"You're making all kinds of friends for me in the corporate community," he ribbed Levinson. "We tackled ITT, the banks, and now you've gotten the oil companies mad. With friends like you, I don't need enemies."

In 1976, Holt and others mentioned to the Senate Rules Committee that the subcommittee was only supposed to be in existence four years. It was now beyond its mandate.

At a meeting of the full committee, the subcommittee was abolished. It was done routinely and without emotion. The subcommittee had exhausted its political capital. The senators had a million other things on their minds.

The following year, Congress passed the Foreign Corrupt Practices Act, an outgrowth of the committee's investigation. It banned any payments to foreign officials for the purpose of

influencing a decision. It also banned payments to any person
with knowledge that he might make such a payoff.

The law immediately improved the bookkeeping practices
of U.S. corporations; clandestine cash funds and off-the-books
payments became a thing of the past. But the companies, faced
with a different environment overseas, either lost lucrative
contracts or came up with ways around the law.

A favorite method was to set up joint ventures in other
countries with their former agents. To ensure that the ventures
succeeded, the foreign partners greased the right palms. Seeing
no evil and hearing none, the American companies insulated
themselves from the payments. The Justice Department rarely
enforced the law as it stood.

As part of Wilmer, Cutler's investigation of the Northrop
payments, Michael Klein met with Khashoggi in June 1975. He
invited him to bungalow number 10 on the immaculate, verdant
grounds of the Beverly Hills Hotel. There, Khashoggi offered
Klein caviar, champagne, and canapes.

It was the peak of the publicity about his payments, yet
Khashoggi seemed unperturbed. If the U.S. government decided
he was a scummy bagman and the Saudis refused to deal with
him, his entire world would have fallen apart. Yet Klein thought
he maintained grace under pressure.

Klein remembered that. Much like a jury that acquits a
defendant because he seems to be without guile, Klein was
willing to give Khashoggi the benefit of a doubt. In Klein's
opinion, Khashoggi had either bribed the Saudi generals or
embezzled $450,000 from Northrop. The facts might be against
the man, yet Klein, a Harvard Law School graduate and leading
securities lawyer, liked Khashoggi.

Every language has at least one word for it—payoff, bribe,
grease, kickback, *baksheesh*, *dash*, *shmeer*. Who are we to
pass judgment on other societies? Klein thought.

Meanwhile, Jones had to step down as president of Northrop, but he continued as chairman and chief executive officer.
Later, he was reinstated as president, too.

Northrop directors explained to Judge Ferguson that
Northrop's business would suffer grievous damage in Iran
and other parts of the world if Jones were no longer with the
company.

It was the ultimate recognition that having friends in high
places overseas counts after all.

The richest man in the world.

The men who opened Khashoggi's path to wealth: King Faisal of Saudi Arabia (second from left) with his successor, Prince Khalid. Fahd, now king, and Abdullah, now crown prince, are to Faisal's left. (*Gamma-Liaison*)

Powerful friends of Khashoggi are Saudi Arabia's King Fahd and, at left, Prince Sultan. (*Gamma-Liaison*)

Robert Shaheen and his wife, Patricia. As executive assistant, he is the most powerful man in Khashoggi's empire.

Wrap it up and send it airmail; Khashoggi's present to himself—a $31 million DC-8, able to fly 15 hours without refueling. (*AiResearch Aviation*)

Originally designed to carry 259 passengers Khashoggi's DC-8 was custom converted to become a billionaire's dream machine. (*AiResearch Aviation*)

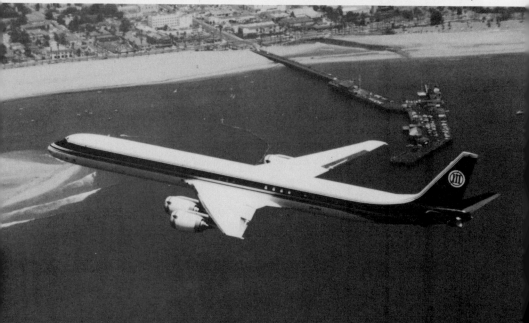

The cockpit of the DC-8 is state-of-the-art—the envy of commercial airlines. (*AiResearch Aviation*)

In-flight meals are served in the dining area. Triangular, for Triad, the specially made chinaware cost $600,000 with crystal and gold flatware thrown in. (*AiResearch Aviation*)

Lounge area of the DC-8. Guests on Khashoggi's private aircraft have included Howard Hughes, Jimmy Carter, Lee Iacocca, and King Fahd. (*AiResearch Aviation*)

In the galley of the DC-8 Khashoggi's chefs prepare gourmet meals on equipment worthy of Julia Child. (*AiResearch Aviation*)

Caroline Kennedy's photo of Khashoggi meeting with Anwar Sadat, who gave his approval for a $1 billion project to rival the pyramids. (*AP/Wide World Photos*)

Among Khashoggi's twelve homes is this villa in Marbella, Spain. Set on 5,000 acres overlooking the Rock of Gibraltar it comes with its own rifle range, disco, bowling alley and helipad, 20 Arabian stallions and 70,000 pheasants. Nearby neighbors: Baron Guy de Rothschild and King Fahd of Saudi Arabia. (*Juan Carlos Teuma*)

One of Khashoggi's Third World investments, the Mount Kenya Safari Club is reflected in the pool.

Khashoggi dines at the Sands Hotel in November, 1961, with Soraya and friends just after they were married. At left is Eugene Warner.

Photographers were standing by when Marvin Mitchelson, prosecuting her $2.5 billion divorce suit, arrived with Soraya Khashoggi for a private session with the SEC. (*AP/Wide World Photos*)

Called by Time-Life Books "the most opulent modern yacht afloat" the $70 million *Nabila* is manned by a crew of 40 and equipped with its own helicopter, screening room, globe-spanning radio communications, and master

staterooms decorated with paintings by Picasso and Léger. Hollywood
borrowed the *Nabila* for the James Bond movie, *Never Say Never Again*.
(*Rudy Maxa*)

With American University
president Richard E. Berendzen
in 1985 at the ground-breaking
ceremonies for the $14 million
Adnan Khashoggi Sports Center.
(*Rhoda Baer*)

Belly dancers entertain at Harold Robbins' party in 1974 for Khashoggi,
who may have modeled for the main character in Robbins' novel, *The Pirate*.
(*Peter C. Borsari*)

Architect's drawing of the 43-story office tower to be built as part of Khashoggi's Triad Center project in Salt Lake City, Utah.

Khashoggi and wife, Lamia, with Cary Grant at the MGM Studio tribute to the actor in Culver City, 1984. (*Peter C. Borsari*)

Nabila and her stepmother, Lamia, pull up in a carriage for the 21st birthday party of Mohamed Khashoggi at Auersberg Palace in Vienna. (*Udo Schreiber, Gamma-Liaison*)

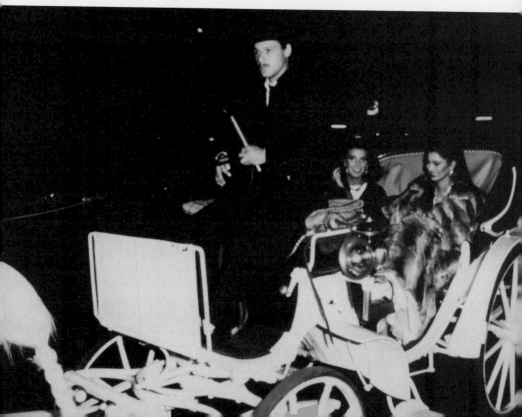

A superstar in the world of jet set celebrities, Khashoggi greets *Dynasty's* Joan Collins. (*Peter C. Borsari*)

Brooke Shields tries not to tower over her dancing partner at his 50th birthday party in Marbella. (*Hola!*)

In sumptuous party dress, Lamia and Adnan greet guests to the 50th birthday celebration outside their villa in Marbella. (*Hola!*)

# The
# Incident at
# the Sands

He who is patient is rewarded.

—*Arabic saying*

**H**ILLEL J. Cohn and Larry J. Jacobs were anxious. The day before, they had been given an urgent assignment. Stanley Sporkin, the SEC's chief of enforcement, wanted them to serve a subpoena on Khashoggi in Las Vegas.

Now that the Church subcommittee and the Watergate prosecutors had each taken their turns investigating Khashoggi, Sporkin wanted to obtain his testimony.

Clearly, Khashoggi was the granddaddy of the foreign agents. All the commissions collected by all the other agents investigated by the SEC didn't come close to matching the sums Khashoggi had managed to squeeze from American firms. Sporkin wanted to know what he had done to earn so much money.

He had long ago decided that foreign payments merited his attention. If an official who was bribed lost power, or the bribes became publicly known, the contracts could be canceled, depressing earnings. On the other hand, if an investor wanted to buy shares of the company knowing these risks, that was his business, he felt.

Sporkin was not impressed by Khashoggi's charm. He wanted him, and wanted him badly.

The SEC tried to get Khashoggi to appear voluntarily, without success. And serving a subpoena on him was like trying to swat a fly with a rubber band. You never knew where he was going to fly to next.

Stuart R. Allen, a special investigator with the SEC and a former employee of Intertel, a private investigative agency, had the job of trying to locate him.

Laboriously, he pored over newspaper clippings on Khashoggi and kept notes in longhand on his whereabouts. "Residence: Box 6, Riyadh, Saudi Arabia," he wrote. "Principal business address: Gefinor Center, Beirut, Lebanon."

Allen had sources in a raft of investigative agencies, from the FBI to the Defense Intelligence Agency. His SEC superiors were always impressed when he came to them with tales of Mafia chieftains and their mistresses, learned in the course of his work. Allen put out the word that he wanted Khashoggi, and tips began coming in. Once, following a report that Khashoggi's plane was due in to a certain airport, Allen fruitlessly spent the night in a control tower.

On Wednesday, March 2, 1976, the Immigration and Naturalization Service gave Allen the first definite word that Khashoggi was in the country. He had flown in from South Korea a few days earler. Khashoggi's stretched Boeing 727 was parked on the tarmac at McCarran International Airport in Las Vegas.

From other sources, Allen learned that Khashoggi had already lost a quarter of a million dollars gambling at the Sands Hotel & Casino.

Allen passed the word to Michael F. Perlis, an assistant director in the SEC's enforcement division who was in charge of the Khashoggi investigation. Perlis immediately called Cohn, an attorney in the SEC's Los Angeles office. Perlis told him to catch the next plane to Las Vegas and carry lots of blank subpoenas.

The twenty-six-year-old Cohn chose Jacobs, his friend in the Los Angeles office, to come along because of what Cohn called his "street smarts."

Neither man had heard of Khashoggi, but they soon got a

fill-in from Washington. What impressed them most was that Khashoggi always traveled with two Korean bodyguards.

The bodyguards—named Keel and Lee—were both skilled in the Korean martial art of tae kwon do. Formerly assigned to President Park Chung Hee of South Korea, they would demonstrate their skill at parties by making a lightning 360-degree turn, kicking a cigarette from the mouth of a startled guest with a heel.

Once, when Khashoggi was the guest of the South Korean government, they challenged six karate experts from the Korean Academy. One of the experts had to be carried out on a stretcher.

After hopping on a plane to Las Vegas, Cohn and Jacobs had drinks at Las Vegas' Union Plaza Hotel. Cohn joked nervously with Jacobs: "What if they think we're Israeli hit men?"

Anticipating the possibility of violence, SEC officials in Washington had tried to arrange to have U.S. marshals accompany them. Because of bureaucratic wrangling, the help never came.

At 8 A.M. the next day, the two men got in a scruffy-looking General Services Administration car and headed toward the Sands. They discussed the fact that they didn't even know what Khashoggi looked like. They had a photocopy of a *Business Week* article with his picture, but it was hard to make out.

They parked the car behind the eighteen-story cylindrical tower that sits over the hotel lobby. The color of sand, the building looks like a remnant from the World's Fair circa 1960. Like neglected poor cousins at a family reunion, low-slung buildings lie behind the main building, bordered by pools and greenery.

As they approached the main entrance, Cohn and Jacobs shivered in the 42-degree air. A twenty-eight-year-old accountant making $20,000 a year, Jacobs was feeling the salary was not enough.

Not having Khashoggi's room number, the two men first tried to get it by calling the hotel operator on a pay phone outside the building. When that failed, they entered the lobby, which was deserted at that hour.

Striding to the front desk, Cohn flipped open his wallet and displayed his SEC credentials. He asked for Khashoggi's room number.

"I'm sorry, we do not give that information out," the clerk said.

Trying to look nonchalant, the two men strolled around the lobby and wrote on a subpoena, "Records indicating the room or rooms where Adnan Khashoggi is located."

Back to the front desk they went and handed the subpoena to the clerk.

Now they had his attention; he called for assistance. Several managers hustled Cohn and Jacobs into an executive suite, where they assured them they would comply if the government men wouldn't make a scene.

During the meeting, William C. Turner, an assistant U.S. attorney in Las Vegas, showed up with two Drug Enforcement Administration agents. Looking like Starsky and Hutch, the DEA agents were dressed in jeans and wide belts with .38 revolvers stuck in their back pockets.

A former SEC employee, Turner had been involved in the negotiations to obtain the marshals' help. When he couldn't get it, he asked the two DEA agents, as a personal favor, to help out. As he looked at Cohn and Jacobs, he was glad he had. They looked scared.

By 11 A.M., Cohn and Jacobs had Khashoggi's room number, and they strode toward the buildings in the back, where Khashoggi was staying. With the two DEA agents trailing behind, they located the Aqueduct Building, where he had rented fifteen rooms.

Cohn knocked on the door of Khashoggi's suite. An Oriental man dressed in a tight black suit opened it.

"We're from the SEC and would like to see Mr. Khashoggi," Cohn said.

There was a look on the bodyguard's face that made it clear it would be dangerous to try to enter.

"I'll get back to you," he said, closing the door on them.

"Let's break down the door and get this fat Arab," one of the DEA men said.

But Cohn decided they had no authority to enter forcefully. They tried the doorknob. It was locked. So they camped out in a hallway outside the room. Eventually, Khashoggi would have to come out, and they would serve him.

Soon, Shaheen came bustling down the hall and introduced himself as Khashoggi's executive assistant. Shaheen was used to smoothing the way for Khashoggi. For the purpose, he always carried a two-inch roll of crisp hundred-dollar bills. He was quick to extend invitations to dinner or trips, or to drop the names of the dignitaries and celebrities who traveled in Khashoggi's orbit.

Shaheen bantered with the two SEC men, offering them tickets to a floor show that night. He offered to bring them lunch, but Cohn and Jacobs declined. They accepted coffee instead.

"We want to be cleaner than Caesar's wife," Cohn earnestly told Jacobs, thinking of how they would explain to Sporkin that they had accepted lunch from Khashoggi.

As they sat waiting on a bench in an anteroom, Shaheen emerged a number of times. Each time, it seemed he was dressed in a different suit, each more elegant than the last. During one such visit, Shaheen told them that one of the bodyguards had to buy special shoes so he could go to a party and still be able to practice his art.

At 4 P.M., a man with a high forehead and academic appearance strode down the corridor and introduced himself as Ralph E. Erickson, Khashoggi's lawyer. Erickson handed his card to Cohn, who recognized the name. Three years earlier, Erickson had been deputy attorney general in the Nixon administration. Now he represented Khashoggi through his Los Angeles law firm.

He already knew the SEC wanted to talk with Khashoggi. The SEC had mailed a subpoena to Clark M. Clifford, thinking the former secretary of defense represented him. When he said he didn't, the SEC turned to Erickson, who responded by telling the SEC in a letter that he was not authorized by Khashoggi to accept service of a subpoena.

As a foreign citizen, Erickson argued, Khashoggi was not subject to the SEC's jurisdiction. But Erickson said he was willing to work out an arrangement to have his client testify under proper safeguards.

As Erickson went to meet Cohn and Jacobs, he had a clear purpose in mind: He would continue the negotiations he had tried to start six months earlier. At the same time, he would avoid saying anything definitive about the subpoena.

With the subpoena lying on a table, Erickson asked Cohn and Jacobs what they wanted. Erickson took the subpoena, but what was said is subject to differing interpretations.

Although Erickson seemed to be couching his language carefully, Cohn and Jacobs were sure they heard him say he accepted service. But Erickson was just as sure he didn't.

Later, he told Khashoggi, "I didn't accept service."

The SEC representatives felt they had successfully completed their task. Now they could return to Los Angeles. They found a pay telephone and called Perlis at home in Potomac, Maryland.

"We served it on Erickson," Cohn announced when Perlis came on the line.

"Wait a minute," Perlis said. "Ralph Erickson has written a letter saying he's not authorized to accept service."

Cohn said they would go back and make sure they got his acceptance in writing. Erickson refused, but to Cohn and Jacobs, it seemed he again accepted service on Khashoggi's behalf.

"If there is any defect in the subpoena, it is not in the service," he intoned.

Flying back to Los Angeles, Erickson smiled. He had noticed that the subpoena called for Khashoggi to appear at 10 A.M. the next day, March 4, 1976, at SEC offices in Washington, bringing all his corporate records. Even by the SEC's normally aggressive methods, it was an outlandish demand that would later come back to haunt the agency.

That evening, Shaheen gave the word to Khashoggi's chief pilot, Harold G. Renegar, to have the plane ready for a 1:30 A.M. takeoff. As Renegar and his copilot, Jerry Soderstrom, began running the more than three hundred checks required, the pilot thought to himself that he didn't really expect to leave at 1:30. Invariably, he got instructions to fly at 10 A.M. from Las Vegas to London. Khashoggi would show up at 10, but at night, and they would go to Beirut instead of London.

This time, Khashoggi was on time.

Telling Soderstrom to start the first engine, Renegar pulled the fuel lever with his right hand and brought the engine up to 35 percent of power. He repeated the procedure with the other two engines. Then he brought the engines up to 55 percent of power and taxied to the runway.

Releasing the brakes, he turned the aircraft into a head wind and gave the turbofan engines full power. The plane roared down the runway. As the plane reached 160 knots, it lifted off the ground.

The plane flew first to New York's John F. Kennedy International Airport, where it refueled, then to Barbados. An effort by the Federal Aviation Administration to stop the plane in New York failed.

When they got back to the Los Angeles SEC office, Cohn and Jacobs learned that Khashoggi was gone.

Sporkin was furious. He never expected Khashoggi to appear at 10 A.M. with all his corporate documents, but he expected that Khashoggi's lawyers would call to arrange a more suitable day.

Instead, Khashoggi had flown away.

Almost daily, Sporkin asked for progress reports from Perlis on finding him. Perlis thought about an unfortunate SEC staffer in Los Angeles named Ralph Erickson. Maybe he should change his name.

One afternoon, Perlis walked into Sporkin's cluttered office on the fourth floor of SEC headquarters. Tongsun Park, the Korean influence peddler, was big in the news. Thinking he would break the tension, Perlis said, "Stan, there's a big new influence peddler in town."

"What's his name?" Sporkin said.

"Rock Creek Park," Perlis answered.

"Serve him!" Sporkin shouted.

Sporkin paused, thought a minute, and realized Rock Creek Park is the name of a ravine that runs through Washington.

"Ah, s---. Get the hell out of here!" Sporkin yelled.

On hearing of the fiasco in Las Vegas, Sporkin referred the case to the Justice Department. He wanted Khashoggi indicted under an SEC law punishing willful evasion of a subpoena.

On May 6, 1976, Earl J. Silbert, the U.S. attorney in Washington, began a grand jury investigation. Robert W. Ogren, the assistant U.S. attorney who got the case, had never heard of Khashoggi, nor was he sure he wanted to.

Six feet three inches tall, he had blond hair, smooth skin, and broad shoulders. After working for a Wall Street law firm, he joined the Justice Department in 1967.

As the word spread that Ogren had charge of the investigation, he began getting calls from some of the classiest lawyers in Washington. They were not the sort of lawyers Ogren would expect to find representing a foreign client on a matter involving the service of a subpoena.

The law that Sporkin hoped to invoke carried a misdemeanor penalty. It had been used by the SEC only three times. Only once had it produced a conviction. Yet some of the finest and most highly paid lawyers in Washington were calling. At one point, Ogren thought that Khashoggi must have hired half the Washington bar. He had never seen anything like it.

"Maybe we should give them a baton that the real lawyer could produce to show he represents Khashoggi," Ogren joked to Robert G. Clark, a lawyer from Justice Department headquarters who worked with him on the case.

Clark hesitated to pick up the phone. It seemed there was always a new lawyer on the line.

The two prosecutors could almost smell the money being made, and they tried to guess how much each lawyer was charging. They figured Dennis G. Lyons, an Arnold & Porter partner, must be making the most because of his polished demeanor and the tomes of material he filed. Immaculately dressed and silvery-voiced, he seemed to take notes on everything that was said.

In part, the swarm of lawyers arose from Khashoggi's habit of obtaining advice from many quarters and going with his own instincts. It was an outgrowth of the Arab practice of "coffeehousing." They would confer and meet and haggle with many different parties before they came to a decision.

In this case, Khashoggi hired even more advisers than usual because of a suggestion by Edward K. Moss, his public affairs consultant. Moss was appalled at the public relations damage done when Khashoggi left the country. He blamed Daniel G. Zerfas, vice-president and general counsel of a Triad subsidiary, for Khashoggi's decision to avoid the subpoena.

A former special assistant to the deputy attorney general in the Justice Department, Zerfas thought the SEC was out to get Khashoggi and had no right to compel a foreign national to testify. But Moss felt that was beside the point. Even if Zerfas was right on the legal issues, the harm to Khashoggi's image was not worth whatever legal principle might be at stake.

One day, while flying over Europe with Khashoggi, Moss urged him to consult other lawyers recommended by him, and Khashoggi agreed to do it. Because he couldn't enter the U.S., Khashoggi set up the meeting on his yacht in the Caribbean. He invited Zerfas, who got to invite his own lawyer, Donald E. Santarelli, a chum who had been associate deputy attorney general in the Nixon administration and formerly headed the Law Enforcement Assistance Administration.

The trip to the yacht was set for a Friday evening, when the lawyers were to meet on board Khashoggi's stretched Boeing 727 at Dulles International Airport.

The first to arrive, Santarelli thought he had never seen anything so opulent in his life.

Offering caviar, a steward said, "Mr. Khashoggi would like you to have some of this."

"What would Mr. Khashoggi like me to drink with this?" Santarelli asked.

The steward proffered a bottle of Dom Pérignon and popped it open, saying, "Mr. Khashoggi would want you to drink this."

At forty-nine dollars a bottle, Santarelli thought the champagne grossly overrated.

Turning the label toward Santarelli, the steward said, "You should take note that it's a 1959."

After Santarelli indicated he was duly awed, the steward added, "I believe Mr. Khashoggi has most of the 1959."

As Santarelli sipped his champagne, Jerris Leonard and Brian P. Gettings boarded the plane. Leonard had been assistant attorney general in charge of the civil rights division of the Justice Department, then headed the LEAA before Santarelli took it over. Gettings had just finished a term as the U.S. attorney in northern Virginia.

Moss showed up next, along with Willis Armstrong, a former assistant secretary of state for economic affairs. He consulted for Khashoggi on economic and political problems. Then came Charles R. McCarthy, Jr., a former SEC lawyer invited by Moss.

When they got off the plane, they realized they were in Antigua.

Arriving on Khashoggi's yacht at 12:30 P.M., the lawyers entered a room where a lavish buffet was waiting. There was a whole roasted lamb, its head still on, standing on its legs on a frame. There was a large quantity of cold lobster, along with Arabian food and smoked salmon.

Introducing himself, Khashoggi joked, "We catch these lobsters with our sonar."

With Zerfas, who was already on the yacht, and the others, Khashoggi held court like King Arthur at a large round table. He said he felt humiliated by the way the SEC had treated him and considered it a matter of principle that foreign businessmen should not be at the beck and call of the commission.

"I send my lawyers in good faith to negotiate with them, and then they try to hit me with a subpoena when I am in the U.S., telling me to appear—this subpoena appears at 4 P.M.," Khashoggi said. "At ten o'clock in the morning, I should be in Washington with all my records and papers from Saudi Arabia. This is harassment. It's not good faith."

Round and round they went, the lawyers giving advice that circled the compass. They said Khashoggi should come to terms with Sporkin and testify, or Khashoggi should challenge the SEC's authority in court, or Khashoggi should testify only overseas, or he should reply only to written questions.

The meeting was conducted the way he ran all his business meetings—like a three-ring circus. Quite often, he had six meetings going at the same time, frequently with the chief executive officers of major corporations. Usually, he moved from one group to another. Upon returning to the first group, he picked up exactly where he had left off, recalling everything that was said previously.

On the yacht, the mood chilled as Gettings lectured Khashoggi—some thought too sternly—on the possibility that he might go to prison if he returned to the U.S. without honoring the subpoena.

"If you have been served and fail to respond and are reachable, you can go to jail if you are in the jurisdiction of the SEC," Gettings intoned.

Gettings considered the legal mumbo jumbo a standard warning that he gave many other clients, before and since. He didn't notice a negative reaction by Khashoggi or the other lawyers.

But some thought they detected a trace of annoyance on Khashoggi's round face, and later the word filtered back that Khashoggi had been irritated by what he considered Gettings' lack of tact.

Lawyers tend to tread a fine line between telling their clients the facts and offending them—particularly if they are wealthy and could enhance their practices. Often, clients want to feel comforted, not threatened.

The next day, there were more meetings on the yacht, including a private twenty-minute conversation with Maxwell M. Rabb. Rabb had once been an aide to Senator Henry Cabot Lodge of Massachusetts, then secretary to the cabinet of President Eisenhower. In 1981, President Reagan appointed him to be ambassador to Italy.

Moss wanted to counteract a feeling by some of Khashoggi's American advisers that the SEC investigation was part of a Jewish conspiracy against Arabs. After all, several of them had said, Sporkin and several others involved in the investigation were Jewish.

Khashoggi himself felt no animosity toward Jews. Everyone around him knew of his remark that he would be the first to do business in Israel when peace comes. Yet he distinguished between Jews and Zionists.

"A Jew is a man who believes in his religion, and we believe in his religion," he told the *Institutional Investor* magazine in July 1975. "We pray to Moses in our prayers; we pray to Jesus.... But Zionism is another matter.... It's a political organization. They have their own ambitions, their own desires. To us, they are aggressively trying to destroy the Arab relationship with the Western world."

The Jewish issue would not go away, and Moss thought that bringing in Rabb—then president of Temple Emanu-El in New York—would help to defuse it. Besides, what was one more lawyer among the multitude already at the feed trough?

Rabb agreed to meet Khashoggi but would not charge for his services. Arriving separately, he was intrigued by the man but never formally represented him.

Each of the other lawyers hoped Khashoggi would choose him for the counsel he so obviously needed. To his surprise, Leonard was chosen. In his stateroom later that day, Khashoggi told him, "I want you to develop a global legal strategy and implement it."

When he got off the boat on Saturday night, Leonard thought he had been placed in charge of Khashoggi's worldwide litigation. Exhausted, he spent the next two days in bed.

Over the next month, he and Gettings did additional research for Khashoggi, but Khashoggi had come to realize that Leonard was a partner of Gettings. Leonard never heard from him again.

Like a spider, Khashoggi had woven a web of dreams around the lawyers and then disappeared to weave a new one, leaving them with the limp remnants of their own expectations.

Back at the U.S. Attorney's office, Ogren had decided that he couldn't charge Khashoggi with a crime. Even if Erickson had said he accepted service, there was no evidence that Khashoggi had, in fact, authorized Erickson to accept the subpoena on his behalf.

Instead, Ogren decided to focus on whether Erickson lied to the grand jury when he said he never accepted service.

The new investigation brought another lawyer to the fore—
Plato Cacheris, a former Justice Department official who was
retained by Khashoggi to represent Erickson.

Cacheris met with Khashoggi five times in Cannes, Paris,
and other European cities. Each time, Khashoggi instructed
him to take the Concorde, and each time he was put "on hold"
for two to four days while waiting to see him.

This was standard Khashoggi practice. All his lawyers and
employees were used to it. While they waited, they stayed at
the Hôtel George V and ate pressed duck or *loup de mer*, a
French version of sea bass. All the while, they billed Khashoggi
for their time.

Outsiders never knew if the delays were a polite way of
saying Khashoggi didn't want to see them, or were just attributable to Khashoggi's disregard for other people's schedules. Once he saw them, Khashoggi was always gracious and
hospitable. He apologized profusely for the delay. Some sus-
pected he did it purposely to make his presence that much
more sought after.

In Washington, Cacheris made presentations to Ogren and
Clark. Both knew him and trusted him. They felt he touched
on all the weak points of the case.

Criminal law requires a high standard of proof. To warrant
putting someone in jail, perjury must involve blatant false-
hoods that are clear and provable. Ogren was not going to
recommend that the grand jury indict someone based on a
possibly ambiguous statement in a hotel corridor.

In the end, if Erickson were indicted, a jury would have to
decide who was more believable, Erickson or the two SEC men.
While the SEC representatives were nice guys and sincere, Ogren
thought a jury would be swayed by Erickson's demonstrated
experience.

What's more, the SEC's demand that Khashoggi appear
the next morning with all his records created the appearance
of a witch-hunt, in the view of Brian W. Shaughnessy, an assistant U.S. attorney who also worked on the case.

To Ogren, the bottom line was that Sporkin did not want
Erickson anyway. Even if Erickson were hung from a tree in
broad daylight, it would not appease Sporkin, who wanted
Khashoggi.

•  •  •

Through his connection with Zerfas, Santarelli continued to represent Khashoggi. One afternoon, after the usual delay of several days, he met with him for an hour in Cannes.

As dinnertime approached, Khashoggi said, "I feel like having spaghetti."

"Great," Santarelli said. "I'd like to join you."

So Khashoggi summoned his Mercedes limousines, which took them and the entourage to the airport. There, they boarded Khashoggi's DC-9 and flew to Venice, where they had spaghetti at a superb restaurant.

Several gorgeous women came along, including a vibrant twenty-one-year-old from Torino, Italy. She had long dark hair, dazzling blue eyes, tan silky skin, and a Nefertiti profile. But Santarelli thought her luscious good looks were icing on the cake. She was intelligent, witty, and vivacious as well. Her questions showed tremendous perception. He delighted in talking with her in Italian.

"How can you be so sophisticated and so young?" he asked.

The woman, Laura Biancolini, later took the Arabic name Lamia and became Khashoggi's second wife.

Returning to Cannes that night, Santarelli was soon back in the steaming Washington heat. His idea of good legal representation included knowing all the facts. It became clear to him that Khashoggi's entourage resented his probing questions.

As Santarelli faded from the picture, Edward P. Morgan, a former General Accounting Office auditor and Federal Bureau of Investigation inspector, emerged.

Morgan knew how to handle wealthy clients. From his Washington office in an unimposing building on the corner of 17th and I Streets Northwest, Morgan represented billionaire recluse Howard R. Hughes.

Morgan often bemused himself thinking about the differences between the two men. In contrast to Khashoggi, during the few years that Morgan represented him, Hughes never left the ninth floor of the Dunes Hotel in Las Vegas. Khashoggi, on the other hand, lived all over the world and hated to be alone.

Morgan knew that clients and issues come and go, but the powers in Washington remain largely unchanged. These are the survivors—government investigators, prosecutors, congressional aides, and government bureaucrats whose positions shift with different administrations but who remain in government forever.

It is not wise to alienate them with brashness or arrogance, and he felt some of Khashoggi's advisers had been guilty of that.

When the publicity about foreign payments died down, Morgan was one of the lawyers who recommended that Khashoggi testify before the SEC.

Yet, in the end, it was Kenneth J. Bialkin who brought the baton home.

Bialkin was a New York lawyer who knew the SEC as well as he knew his home on Central Park West. Unlike the other lawyers Khashoggi had hired, he specialized in securities law. As the chairman of the American Bar Association's committee on federal regulation of securities, he was considered one of the best at it in the country.

In Khashoggi's sumptuous Paris home, Bialkin listened to his story—the Keystone Kops scene at the Sands, and then Khashoggi's lawyers demanding terms he knew the SEC would never agree to. In Bialkin's view, there was nothing unusual about Sporkin's desire to have Khashoggi testify. If Khashoggi was telling the truth, he could not be charged with any offense and should tell the SEC what it wanted to know, Bialkin told him.

Khashoggi agreed to go, and Bialkin set up an appointment with Sporkin.

Sporkin knew Bialkin and admired his unerring ability to strike deals that satisfied both sides.

"I'll make a deal with you," Bialkin said to Sporkin. "I will bring Mr. Khashoggi in here, and you can interview him like any other witness. You can do it under oath, subject to the penalties of perjury. I want two things from you: I'll bring him in, but not under subpoena. And I want an understanding that if there is any question you ask that he's not willing to answer, you give him twenty-four hours to clear the country."

"Fine," Sporkin said. But he doubted whether Bialkin really could bring Khashoggi in.

In early October 1978, two and a half years after Khashoggi's plane lifted off the runway in Las Vegas, Khashoggi sat in Perlis' fifth-floor office and testified for four days. He brought with him a sheaf of documents requested by the SEC.

At the end of the testimony, Perlis was satisfied that Khashoggi had answered all his questions without being evasive. Yet he did not think Khashoggi was telling him the entire truth.

Notations on some of the documents suggested that his financial relationships with Saudi princes ought to be pursued. But Perlis never focused on the Swiss bank accounts used by Khashoggi for funneling payments to the princes. This was the way Khashoggi diverted millions of dollars back to the people who made it all possible—his partners who were members of the royal family and helped approve his contracts.

Even if he had focused on them, Perlis was in no mood to start an entirely new investigation that might lead all over the world and produce nothing. The Lockheed and Northrop cases were already settled. The Raytheon case was about to be closed with no action taken. Perlis had been working foreign payments cases for several years and was personally bored.

He recommended to Sporkin that they close their investigation, and Sporkin reluctantly agreed.

Yet the episode continued to haunt Khashoggi. When he offered to donate money to universities or colleges, there were always nagging questions about his evasion of a subpoena, and he had to address them.

The incident left imprints on many of the other players as well.

Ralph Erickson felt left out in the cold. He hoped to continue to represent Khashoggi but learned he was considered a liability.

Kenneth Bialkin wound up representing Khashoggi on other cases, as did Edward Morgan, who hired other attorneys to litigate specific cases for him.

Daniel Zerfas, tired of traveling all over the world, left Khashoggi, expressing frustration with the way he consulted multitudes of lawyers without coordinating their efforts.

Khashoggi had been forced to testify, but only when the investigators had lost interest because of the passage of time. No charges were ever brought against him. Once again, he could come and go as he pleased, and he soon returned to the gambling tables of Las Vegas and his businesses in the United States.

To Robert Ogren, who later became chief of the Justice Department's fraud section, what happened was quite simple.

Khashoggi had outsmarted the SEC.

NINE

# The
# Homes

"Master, ask what you will," said the jinni, as he appeared
before him.

"I have an important task to set you," Aladdin replied. "I wish
you to build me, with the least possible delay, a palace—a
marvel of a building. Let it be furnished magnificently and
fitted with every comfort."

*—Aladdin and the Enchanted Lamp*

JUST after Khashoggi testified before the Securities and Exchange Commission, he moved into his Olympic Tower apartment in New York. On the mock Monopoly game based on
Khashoggi's assets, this, his twelfth home, is designated
"Boardwalk."

Spread over two full floors of a fifty-two-story building,
the home was a Garden of Eden in the center of Manhattan. It
had its own Olympic-size swimming pool, its own Jacuzzi, and
an interior so sumptuous that *House & Garden* magazine devoted eighteen full-color pages to it in 1984. The most spectacular feature was the view of Manhattan's skyscrapers
through windows that began on the forty-fifth floor and ended
on the forty-sixth.

Estimated to be worth $25 million, the New York home at
51st Street and Fifth Avenue is Khashoggi's most expensive

residence, yet each of the others has its charm—along with the requisite swimming pool, sauna, barber chair, and bed ten feet wide by seven feet long.

Located in Paris, Monte Carlo, Cannes, Madrid, Kenya, Cairo, Riyadh, Jeddah, New York, the Canary Islands, Beirut, and Marbella, they range from a penthouse on the Mediterranean to a ranch at the foot of Mount Kenya. The locations are constantly shifting; previously, he had homes in London and Sardinia.

Khashoggi's $30-million art collection is displayed in all the homes, with the greatest works in his spectacular Paris duplex.

Alain Cavro, Khashoggi's own architect, designed the interiors of many of the homes. A bearded Frenchman, he headed Triad Condas, a Triad subsidiary that also designed the interiors of palaces and lesser homes, under Khashoggi's direction, for heads of state and Saudi princes. One, a palace in Jeddah for King Faisal, had twenty buildings for servants, kitchens, and guests.

Like Khashoggi's planes and yachts, his homes had a dual purpose: They eased his frenetic comings and goings, and they served as chits. Fully staffed at all times, they could be offered as a *pied-à-terre* for heads of state—people whose help might be needed in some future deal.

Khashoggi's custom-designed Monopoly set suggests the pattern. Along with the jackpot at Monte Carlo, the Chance cards include one that is good for a free stay at the Olympic Tower apartment.

Khashoggi began house-hunting in Marbella in 1973. He did it on his DC-9, flying over the territory to scout the best terrain. Along for the ride was the jowly Prince Fahd, then the Saudi interior minister and now king.

Just sixty miles across the Mediterranean from Morocco, at the southern tip of Spain, the village of Marbella was not exactly foreign territory. Over the centuries, it had attracted invaders ranging from the Phoenicians and Visigoths to the Romans, the Greeks, and—until the late 1400s—the Arabs.

The old portion of the city is still surrounded by an Arab wall, a relic of the Moorish occupation of Spain from the eighth century until its final conquest by King Ferdinand and Queen Isabella.

Shortly after dispatching Christopher Columbus in quest

of a passage to India, the queen visited Marbella on Spain's Costa del Sol and remarked, "What a beautiful sea!"

Protected from winter winds by the 6,000-foot Sierra Blanca, Marbella has a subtropical clime and spectacular scenery. Reminiscent of the coast of Southern California, the mountains, sometimes masked in purple haze, reach down to white beaches, where waves of silver, turquoise, and intense blue wash in from North Africa.

In recent years, Marbella has become a playland for Europe's aristocracy, who are attracted both to its isolated location and to the trendy Marbella Club and Regine's, the discotheque at the Puente Romano Hotel.

Among those with homes are the Baroness Hubert van Pantz, heiress to the Avon fortune; Prince Alphonso von Hohenlohe, who built the Marbella Club Hotel; Luis Miguel Dominguin, the former bullfighter; Italian millionaire Bastiano Berghese; Spanish socialite Anna Pliego; French recording tycoon Jean Bonfantin; and Baron Guy de Rothschild.

King Juan Carlos visits periodically, as have most of the dukes and duchesses of Spain, Prince Bernhard of the Netherlands, Princess Margaret of England, Queen Fabiola of Belgium, Liza Minnelli, and the late Richard Burton, not to mention Christina Onassis, who weighs in at a fat farm.

Khashoggi decided Marbella would be the perfect vacation spot for himself and for the royal family—a place where they could avoid the scorn they sometimes felt in London and Paris.

As crown prince, Fahd in 1981 built himself a gleaming white marble palace in Marbella that could be mistaken for the White House. Overlooking the Mediterranean, it is surrounded by palm trees, jasmine, and bougainvillea.

Down the road on the way to the ancient town of Ronda, Khashoggi bought a home on five thousand rolling acres of land. It had been owned by a friend, French pharmaceutical tycoon Henry Roussel. Several miles from the berth for Khashoggi's yacht, the home has a reserve of seventy thousand pheasants for hunting and thoroughbred Arabian stallions that are shampooed every day. Done in a Moorish motif, the home has mirrored ceilings and walls, lavender pillows, and gold sofas. Each of the ten bathrooms is done in a different marble.

With smaller villas for some of Khashoggi's children, the Marbella home is where Khashoggi is most likely to spend time with his family.

When Khashoggi feels the urge to gamble, he piles into his limousines with his entourage and heads for the casino in town.

Recently, the proprietor had a look of terror on his face as he saw the entourage approach, but he relaxed when Khashoggi passed the word that he would set a limit to the evening's stakes.

The roulette wheel rolled and Khashoggi began winning. He smiled and slid chips worth five hundred dollars to each of two girls at the table.

"You can't take that. Do you know how much it's worth?" one of the girls whispered to the other.

"He's just sharing his luck, and he'll be offended if we don't," replied her girlfriend, giggling.

In 1976, Olympic Tower opened in New York with little fanfare. That was the way the prospective residents wanted it.

Built by Aristotle Onassis, the building at 641 Fifth Avenue was one of the most exclusive residences in Manhattan, and one of the most secretive.

"Nobody," one resident told *Newsweek* at the time, "wants anybody to know we're here."

When hairstylist Ian Harrington opened his salon there, he asked for a list of the other tenants so he could send them announcements. The answer came back from management: The list is secret, even to other tenants.

Many of the residents bought their apartments outright for cash—no questions asked—and put them in corporate names for tax or security reasons.

"They're deathly afraid of kidnapings," observed Greek artist Vassili Lambrinos, who bought a $180,000 one-bedroom apartment on the thirtieth floor.

The residents included counts, duchesses, and heiresses, along with designer Halston and Maurizio Gucci, chairman of the renowned accessory house and grandson of its founder.

But the talk of the tower was Khashoggi's residence, which occupied sixteen normal-size apartments priced originally at $150,000 to $650,000 each.

Khashoggi's apartment serves as office and home, separated, in the traditional Arab way, into guest and family areas. There is a large suite for Shaheen and an office for the secretaries, who answer the phone when it isn't the butler's turn.

As the tower was being completed, Khashoggi hired Alessandro Pianon, a designer from Venice, to do the apartment's interior. The ceilings would be too low, Pianon decided, and ordered that the concrete slab between the forty-fifth and forty-sixth floors be removed. Instead, a swimming pool would occupy the lower floor of the duplex.

The bottom of the pool is painted in a leaf motif by artist Fabrizio Plessi, reflecting in his design the lush greenness of the tropical plants in the surrounding atrium. He painted more leaves on the mirrored ceiling above the pool. It is an oasis in the middle of midtown Manhattan, which is visible from the pool and just about everywhere else in the apartment.

Something of a bird's-eye view of the Empire State Building can be had while sitting at the dining room table, inlaid with lapis lazuli. Through sheer architectural strength, the views outmuscle the early twentieth-century art in the apartment—a Léger painting here and a Kandinsky there.

Tasteful and dignified, the duplex is done in tawny gold tones—pale yellow and golden beige, with sable brown accents—from the yellow tile poolside and the brown king-size lounges there, to the floor of the main entry hall, whose parquet pattern is accomplished with three shades of marble. In the living room of palest lemon, a pair of elephant tusks curves before a window. The room is accented with antique Chinese vases and a clock with a face made of a single enormous topaz.

Worthy of a potentate, Khashoggi's bedroom is paneled in polished brass, with a $200,000 Russian sable spread on the ten-foot-wide bed. Off the bedroom in his dressing room stands his "throne"—actually, a royal-looking barber's chair. The dressing room holds four closets: one for suits, one for jackets and sweaters, one for coats, and one for sport shirts and ties, purchased at $150 each from Bijan, just down the street and open by appointment only. In drawers, handmade cotton dress shirts are lined up by color, as are socks.

Lamia's bedroom is as feminine as her husband's is masculine. An exception to the gold color scheme, her room is done entirely in white. Piled at the foot of her bed is a mound of small lace pillows. Completing the virginal decor, two small dolls perch there—one dressed in pink, the other in purple.

But the jewels that she collects and keeps here in her room are anything but childish. Enough to fill Tiffany's windows, her diamonds, emeralds, and rubies are valued at millions of dollars and rival the Russian crown jewels. Her everyday ring alone—the one she always wears—is a 40-carat diamond the size and shape of a sugar cube.

There are the little touches to the apartment that make a house a home—in her bathroom, gilded faucets copied from the Waldorf-Astoria, circa 1930. Off his bedroom a sauna.

And then there are the five guest rooms.

For the construction firm that did the work, Khashoggi's apartment posed problems never faced in Manhattan, before or since. First, the sixteen existing, unoccupied apartments on both floors had to be ripped out. Then, to support the weight of the water in the pool, special concrete and steel reinforcements had to be installed below. This meant lowering the height of the ceilings beneath the pool and compensating the tenants for surrendering some of their space. Likewise, tenants above Khashoggi had to be compensated for permitting thicker walls to accommodate the flue for his fireplace on their way to the roof.

The smoke from the fireplaces would asphyxiate the occupants, and the moisture from the pool would fog the windows in the apartment. So a powerful air conditioning system had to be installed on the roof, just for Khashoggi's apartment.

Not satisfied with the private staircase built between the two levels of his apartment, Khashoggi wanted his own private elevator as well. A two-story safe was installed to store cash and valuables, and a separate room was built just for the security men who monitor video cameras that pan the apartment's 46,782 square feet—equal to 20 average-size houses. A security firm rigged up alarm devices that were so secret even the construction men were not told where they were or how they worked.

Pianon wanted no paint to touch the walls, so he used plaster mixed with glistening ground marble. Then a worker flown from Milan buffed the walls with beeswax applied with a lamb's wool mitt.

To install the gold-plated plumbing fixtures, workers used special tools so they wouldn't mar the surfaces. And they installed alarms that would sound were water to leak from the welded, stainless steel pool or from the waterfall that appears to cascade from the windows facing St. Patrick's Cathedral.

The construction work alone cost $10 million.

On his first day back in the U.S. after testifying before the SEC, Khashoggi threw a cocktail party at the Olympic Tower apartment for sixty friends and associates. Serving drinks and answering the door was a white-haired butler with a ruddy complexion and watery blue eyes.

"Mr. James," as he was called, had been hired by Khashoggi's brother Essam as soon as the apartment opened.

Typical of the first-class household help Khashoggi hired all over the world, James Flannery had erect posture and a commanding voice. He could have passed for the chairman of Chase Manhattan Bank. Even though a butler, he read widely and conversed easily about the works of Chaucer, Beethoven, or Van Gogh, switching from politics to foreign policy to nuclear war without missing a beat.

"The genius of man to make this world livable is infinite, yet we're always in danger of being smashed," he mused to one guest in his Scotch burr. "Now we have the ultimate smasher."

Born in Scotland, Flannery became a purser in the British navy. In 1949, he emigrated to the U.S. Having worked for an heir to the Mellon fortune and other aristocrats, Flannery was used to opulent surroundings and knew more about fine wines, clothes, and art than most of his employers.

His wife, a maid, also worked for Khashoggi. The two lived in the apartment full-time. When Khashoggi was away—as he was most of the time—the Flannerys lived regally, lighting a fire in the fireplace and eating smoked salmon delivered by Zabar's.

Flannery learned that money meant nothing to Khashoggi. A typical grocery bill was $10,000—frequently padded by 10 percent to cover a kickback to whoever placed the order. An order from First Avenue Wines and Spirits usually totaled $8,000—a bargain price for sixteen cases of Dom Pérignon champagne.

As the senior member of the staff, Flannery held himself aloof from the six chefs, waiters, and maids who made the apartment work. He had a sense of his own importance. To the staff, as to everyone else, he was "Mr. James," always dressed in one of his ten tuxedos.

Flannery considered his most important duty to be guarding access to Khashoggi—answering the door and phone. In this role, he was unassailable. The door was sacrosanct. If a bigwig thought he would give his name to Flannery and walk on in, he was mistaken. Flannery would make him wait while he checked with Khashoggi.

• • •

Flannery had never been impressed by authority, not since he was a child and his mother took him to a parade. Pointing to the prince riding by on a horse, she told her son, "A prince has a nose like everybody else."

That homegrown philosophy, combined with his strict Presbyterian upbringing, had endowed Flannery with a judgmental quality that knew no bounds. Walking down the street, he would remark on the stupidity of Citibank for its building design, or on the latest foibles of President Carter or Reagan, or the secrecy of the Catholic Church, or Marvin M. Mitchelson's penchant for publicity.

So it was hardly surprising, when Flannery began working for Khashoggi, that he decided he had no use for him either. Flannery found Khashoggi's taste in art nonexistent and his eating habits deplorable—taking cake for breakfast or munching on some of those primitive Arab delicacies.

He disapproved of the racy films he found lying around. Khashoggi's habit of rising from his chair and heading for the airport, without any warning, annoyed him as well.

He had no use, either, for Khashoggi's hangers-on—the people who came with hands out looking for a piece of the Rock. While some were quite smart, many had difficulty carrying on a thought-provoking conversation, Flannery decided.

From morning until night, the only subject ever discussed in the apartment was money. It was Khashoggi's whole reason for being, Flannery thought, and it sickened him.

When Khashoggi bought a half dozen suede and leather jackets lined with fur and cashmere at $2,000 a jacket, he shook his head. When he bought a black suede jacket for himself with a black mink collar and lining for $6,500, Flannery muttered to his wife about the man's self-indulgence.

"I wonder if he is all right mentally?" Flannery said softly to his wife, sounding like Alfred Hitchcock examining a corpse.

But it was the call girls who made Flannery a nervous wreck. At least once a month, Khashoggi would import eight girls at a time. Flannery knew when they would be arriving because he was told to prepare the bedrooms for them.

They came in from California or Texas, or from France on the Concorde. As if handing out Tootsie Rolls, Khashoggi always gave them gold bracelets.

Flannery had no idea what Khashoggi did with so many girls. It seemed he believed in numbers. He saw him pad from one bedroom to another, visiting each of them in turn, or two or three at a time. Perhaps they had a jamboree. Flannery didn't care to know.

He had a clear sense of his professional duties; preparing rooms for prostitutes was not one of them.

Sometimes in the morning, Flannery was confronted with a girl demanding her pay. When he was asked to throw two of the girls out, apparently because they were of poor quality, he refused.

"Get rid of them yourself," he told a Khashoggi aide.

Flannery turned on his heels. His voice and carriage pointedly betrayed his annoyance.

In March 1980, he gave notice.

All the homes were guarded with electronic and audio sensors and video cameras. Always, there were people posing as members of Khashoggi's family or his employees, trying to sell something or worm their way into the inner circle. Sometimes, they would claim to have just had breakfast with Khashoggi, or flash business cards they had had printed with the name Triad on them.

Sometimes, the poseurs took a more serious turn, as when Ashit Patel rented limousines, stayed in the best hotels, and generally warmed the winter of 1979 posing as Khashoggi's son.

A Londoner of Indian descent, the twenty-one-year-old Patel got the idea from a chance encounter with a Khashoggi relative in Los Angeles. To carry it out, he needed a paper that would identify him as a Khashoggi. So he applied for a telephone for his nonexistent limousine, telling the telephone company to charge it to "Khashoggi Enterprises."

Then he telephoned American Express Co. in Phoenix, saying he was Khashoggi's son and needed a credit card. Eager to please so illustrious a client, the credit card company said the plastic would be waiting in twenty-four hours at its agency in London's Piccadilly. There, the clerk asked for identification, and Patel pulled out the slip of paper saying he had applied for a limousine phone.

With the card, he moved into a plush London hotel, bought himself a princely wardrobe, and phoned a real estate broker on the Riviera to ask about buying a few villas in Antibes.

Mesmerized by the Khashoggi name, the broker flew to London, then flew back with Patel to show him properties in

France. Not knowing it is one of the hotels used by Khashoggi, Patel next checked into the Hôtel de la Croisette in Cannes.

Whispering the omnipotent Khashoggi name, he handed the reception clerk his card, only to be met with a frown.

"Could I see your passport?" asked the clerk.

Unflappable as ever, Patel pulled out his passport showing his real name. He told the clerk he traveled under an assumed name for security reasons.

Discreetly, the clerk asked a Khashoggi employee registered at the hotel to check out the young man. He took one look at him and called the police.

Patel was brought before a judge and charged with fraud and illegal impersonation.

In 1980, Khashoggi bought a home in the Canary Islands, a Spanish possession off the west coast of Africa. With only three bedrooms, it was his smallest home, yet he considered it one of his loveliest. Sitting on a hillside on Gran Canaria Island, it overlooked the ocean and was done in simple Scandinavian style.

When he saw the home, Khashoggi fell in love with it, but there was a problem: It was not for sale, and the owner, Swedish developer Rolf Par Hedenberg, refused to sell it.

It happened that Hedenberg had been negotiating with Khashoggi and Khashoggi's friend Prince Talal to obtain financing for a hotel that Hedenberg wanted to build on the island.

To be called the Aquamarina, the hotel would be built on land owned by Hedenberg, who would organize the construction. He wanted Talal and Khashoggi to contribute $15 million toward the project. In return, they would get a 60 percent interest.

By the account of David J. Greenslade, Khashoggi's and Talal's financial consultant on the project, all the parties signed an agreement to go ahead with it at Khashoggi's Olympic Tower apartment on April 10, 1980.

"It is always an honor to sign an agreement with Your Royal Highness," Khashoggi said.

But then Talal said he wanted to put his interest in a corporate name, and he took the signature page.

"You will see this next week in Riyadh," he said.

Instead of signing the agreement again in Riyadh, Talal

had his Saudi lawyer look it over. The lawyer decided that changes needed to be made.

More meetings were held, and the agreement was redrafted fifteen times. Beside himself because of the delays, Hedenberg found that Talal would not take his calls. Meanwhile, the Spanish government's approvals for the project ran out after being extended once.

Hedenberg sued both Khashoggi and Talal in New York State Supreme Court for $47 million.

Process server Neal J. Sroka and his partner tried to serve the complaint on Talal on September 23, 1982, at his farm near Leesburg, Virginia. Called Beacon Hill, it had once been owned by Arthur Godfrey.

By Sroka's account, armed security guards confronted them at the farm, and one of them fired a shot at the ground three feet in front of Sroka's partner. Jumping two feet in the air, the man yelled, "I'm on the job; I'm on the job"—lingo used by undercover police to avoid being shot by their own men.

By the account of Talal's employees, the process servers had misrepresented themselves by claiming to work for Talal's lawyers.

The next day, the indefatigable Sroka and his men staked out the lobby of the Waldorf-Astoria Hotel in New York, where Talal was to speak at a United Nations conference. When a hotel clerk addressed Talal as "Your Highness," Sroka handed Talal the summons.

One of Talal's bodyguards jammed a gun in Sroka's belly, but the gutsy Sroka left unscathed.

Talal later maintained he never agreed to invest in the project.

If the hotel was never built, Khashoggi got another home out of it. Early on, he had insisted that he would not help finance the project if Hedenberg didn't sell him his home high on a hill as part of the package. By the time the hotel deal fell apart, Khashoggi already owned the new home.

Now he had an even dozen.

# The Public Relations War

*Thenceforth Aladdin went out in the city every day, his slaves scattering gold before him as he rode along.*

*—Aladdin and the Enchanted Lamp*

FOR months, Karen G. Lerner, a National Broadcasting Co. producer, had been after Khashoggi to let her film his world-wide odysseys for her *Weekend* television show. Nothing came of her calls until she learned that he was staying at the Dorchester Hotel in London, where she had checked in on her way to Sweden.

Lerner sent Khashoggi a note, and he agreed to meet her in the lobby the next day. When Lerner told him that seventeen-year-old Caroline Kennedy was with her, helping lug cameras and plan schedules as part of a school project, Khashoggi's interest was piqued.

He was attracted to celebrities almost as much as he was to money. Like planes and homes and yachts, they were assets he used to cultivate business leaders and chiefs of state— key players in his quest to accumulate even more money. And celebrities attracted publicity, which he found he could manipulate to his own advantage.

After hearing that a Kennedy was along, Khashoggi agreed to take the NBC crew on one of his global missions, beginning later in the week. It was February 1975, and Lerner didn't know how long she would be gone or where she was going. She told her executive producer, Reuven Frank, that she would call when she could.

Since they were on their way to Sweden, the TV people had brought warm clothes, and Kennedy worried that they would end up in the desert wearing ski pants.

After they met him in Paris, Khashoggi flew them on his DC-9 to Khartoum, where Lerner filmed Khashoggi meeting with President Gaafar Nimeri of the Sudan. She stayed in Nimeri's guest house. Then they flew to Jeddah, to Riyadh, and back to Beirut, where Khashoggi disappeared.

After five days with no sign of him, Lerner returned to Paris, where she ran into Shaheen in the lobby of the Plaza Athenée Hotel, a few doors down the street from Khashoggi's Paris home at 11 Avenue Montaigne.

After the chance meeting, the filming resumed, this time at Khashoggi's home. Jacqueline Kennedy Onassis was in town, and she dropped by to see how her daughter was doing. While Lerner filmed an interview with Khashoggi, Onassis sat on the floor and watched.

Then on to Cannes, where Khashoggi threw a birthday party on his yacht for his girlfriend, Laura Biancolini. Attended by Regine Choukroun and other Parisian celebrities, the party was on the *Khalidia*, now relegated to second-yacht status.

The next stop was Cairo, where the crew filmed Egyptian President Anwar Sadat giving his blessing to Khashoggi's plan for a vast development project next to the Pyramids.

During the sixteen-day trip, Shaheen circled around Lerner like a moth around a light, constantly making suggestions and worrying about the way Khashoggi would be portrayed.

"We get to see it before it airs," he said on a number of occasions. Each time, Lerner avoided the subject.

It was awkward enough that the crew was dependent on Khashoggi for food, lodging, and—because it would be difficult to change currency in each country—even spending money. Lerner didn't want to create the appearance that Khashoggi had any control over the program. Besides, it was against NBC policy to show a film to the subject before it airs.

Shaheen seemed convinced that Lerner, who had just been divorced from librettist Alan Jay Lerner, was going to do a hatchet job. At other times, Shaheen seemed surprisingly sensitive to her logistical needs. Lerner learned to love him and hate him at the same time.

Shaheen was getting nowhere with his demands, and he discussed them with Edward K. Moss, Khashoggi's public affairs consultant, at Moss' office in Washington.

Moss told him to lay off the NBC producer. To Moss, the demands were typical of Shaheen's theatrical style. It was his way to yell and scream at times. But if someone told him, "Bob, you're full of s---," he would smile and say, "You're right."

The program aired on March 15, 1975, and was the first to portray Khashoggi's glamorous life-style. Like a kid watching his father on television for the first time, Khashoggi swelled with pride when he saw it. Shaheen ordered twenty-five copies of the tape.

Khashoggi couldn't have paid for all the publicity he got out of it. He was like Texas billionaire Sid Richardson Bass, who until recently listed his home telephone number with information in Fort Worth because he didn't want to miss a deal. Publicity meant more people would come to Khashoggi with more business proposals. Bankers would vie for his business and give him concessions. And more celebrities would be attracted to him and attract still more deals.

Awakened from a sound sleep by his ringing telephone, Moss heard the ethereal sounds of an international hookup and a deep, stentorian, cultured voice at the other end.

"Good morning. This is Isa Sabbagh calling from Beirut," the voice said.

As an international public affairs and economic development adviser, Moss already knew Sabbagh, a Palestinian who was regional adviser on public affairs to the United States Information Agency. Sabbagh had previously been an Arabic language commentator for the British Broadcasting Corp. and later became chief of the Arabic service of Voice of America. On some of Henry Kissinger's trips to the Middle East, he acted as interpreter.

"There's someone sitting at my desk here," Sabbagh was saying, "and I've told him you're the only person who can do the job he wants. I'll put him on."

Moss heard a flat Ohio accent, formal rather than friendly, as Shaheen introduced himself, saying he was Khashoggi's executive assistant.

It was 7 A.M. Little did Moss realize that he was about to begin one of the most challenging and frustrating jobs in his thirty-year career.

"A Saudi Arabian government official will be visiting the United States in three weeks," Shaheen said, "and we would like you to help get the widest possible attention on it so the U.S. will recognize his importance."

Shaheen had an overpowering voice that made the snottiest headwaiters cower. But Moss hesitated.

"I'd like to help out, but it's only three weeks until he arrives," Moss said. "Is there someone here I can talk to about it? It isn't the sort of thing you can talk about on the phone."

"I'll meet you tomorrow," Shaheen said.

Shaheen flew to Washington and met with Moss at his office in downtown Washington. It was a beautiful spring day in late May 1972.

Shaheen told Moss that the Saudi official was Prince Sultan, the minister of defense and aviation. It would be the prince's first visit in his own right, rather than as part of the king's party, and Khashoggi wanted a media campaign to introduce him to America. He had a private meeting scheduled with President Nixon in the White House, and Defense Secretary Melvin R. Laird would be greeting him. In addition, Sultan would be seeing Thomas V. Jones, chairman of Northrop Corp.

Moss had never heard of Khashoggi, and he knew nothing about Prince Sultan. What's more, Shaheen's request puzzled him. If Sultan wanted him, why didn't he hire him himself?

"I don't do a job like this for someone I haven't met," Moss told Shaheen. "Unless he agrees, I can't do it."

Shaheen assured him that he could meet with the prince and obtain his approval. He asked how much he would charge. When Moss named a figure, an associate sitting in on the meeting began coughing. Moss took him to get some water.

When they were alone, the man told Moss he should not underprice his services.

"Double that figure," he said. "They'll think you're cheap and no good otherwise."

So Moss went back and quoted a higher figure. Shaheen said he would arrange for him to see Sultan in New York.

Meanwhile, Moss checked out Khashoggi with the State Department. He didn't want to represent a client whose interests were at odds with those of the United States.

Then fifty-five, Moss was a Yale man and lieutenant commander in the navy during World War II. He began his career as a reporter for the *Atlantic City* (N.J.) *Press*, the Associated Press, and the *Philadelphia Bulletin.* He became an assistant to the president of the American Management Association and, during the Korean Conflict, was loaned to the government to help oversee defense production programs.

In 1954, he started Moss International Inc., which has advised nineteen countries, helped the Democratic National Committee organize conventions, and represented the National Coffee Association and the Bank of America.

Moss asked Rodger P. Davies, deputy undersecretary for the Near East and Southeast Asia, about Khashoggi. After consulting the Saudi desk, Davies reported that he was in bad graces with the Saudi government.

"Their advice to you is don't touch that man with a ten-foot pole," Davies said. "He has a bad reputation, and they don't think Sultan would be caught dead with him."

On the off chance the State Department was wrong, Moss met with Sultan anyway at the Waldorf. The prince couldn't have given Khashoggi a better reference.

"He gives good advice," the bearded prince said. "His word is his bond."

Moss' staff arranged for publicity and briefed Sultan on things to say and not say during his ten-day visit. On June 15, 1972, the prince met for forty minutes with Nixon, then went on to Los Angeles to see Jones at Northrop headquarters in Beverly Hills.

During his stay, Moss noticed, the prince had dinner with Khashoggi every day except two.

After the trip, Khashoggi asked to see Moss in the presidential suite at the Waldorf-Astoria. Until he bought his Olympic Tower residence, this suite—big enough for a reception for one hundred people—was where Khashoggi always stayed in New York.

Khashoggi asked him to prepare a memorandum outlining a public relations program that the Saudi government could undertake.

"I think my country needs your kind of work," he said.

A few months later, Khashoggi asked to meet with him

again. This time, he showed Moss a clipping from a Paris newspaper. Based on a report in a Lebanese newspaper, it called Khashoggi an arms dealer who traveled with an entourage of pretty women and worked for any country that would hire him.

Khashoggi was not angry. He almost never seemed angry. Yet the "arms dealer" label was a description reporters were beginning to attach to him like butter smeared on bread. He resented the label. It implied there was something wrong with selling defense weapons. If that were true, why were Lockheed, Northrop, and Raytheon in the business?

"We don't deal in guns or ammunition," he told Moss. "What we are involved in is high technology sales with big corporations that employ thousands of people and whose products are a factor in the balance of payments in their countries."

Nor was he a hired gun who sold arms to any country, he insisted. As a Saudi patriot, he only sold to his own country.

"You can't stop stories like this," Moss told him, "but what you can do is start telling the world what you are doing. If you let everyone call you names and try to hunker down until it goes away, it won't."

Moss said he could introduce him to editors and reporters and try to interest them in doing stories about his positive side—a man who was bringing jobs to the United States by arranging major contracts with U.S. defense manufacturers.

"I don't want publicity. I don't like it," Khashoggi said. "But if you think it's good for business, okay."

Khashoggi was being only half truthful. He liked publicity if it was favorable. When he was twenty-six, Khashoggi noticed an article in *Time* magazine on a wealthy Kuwaiti businessman.

To Ansbert G. Skina, the president of Commonwealth International Services Inc., one of his American clients, he confided, "I'd like to have an article like that done on me."

Over the years, Khashoggi has insisted he has nothing to hide and has periodically submitted to press interviews. But the publications and reporters were carefully selected. For the most part, they were friends of his friends and interested in his life-style rather than in his business transactions. When authors wanted to include chapters on him in their books, Shaheen usually tried, in return for granting an interview, to get the right to correct the manuscript.

All the while, Khashoggi complained that the press was only interested in trivia.

Moss later marveled at the irony. When Khashoggi told him he didn't like publicity, no major stories had appeared on him, either in the U.S. or in Europe. Khashoggi had not yet learned how to orchestrate stories about his life-style, and the derogatory stories about his fabulous commissions had not yet appeared.

As the publicity about Khashoggi mounted, Moss began subscribing to a clipping service that eventually sent him hundreds of stories every week about his client. In 1975 alone, the *New York Times* ran twenty-eight stories about Khashoggi, many on page one. Yet in 1972, he was virtually unknown.

As Khashoggi's public relations consultant, Moss reported to Shaheen or to Khashoggi. Because there were few clear lines of authority in Khashoggi's operations, Moss often tangled with other Khashoggi executives who were guarding their own turf or resentful of what he did. Many thought he made fat fees for doing work they didn't feel was needed.

Generally Republican and conservative, the executives who reported to Morton P. MacLeod, Khashoggi's staff director, didn't trust the press and looked askance at Moss, who was a Democrat. They didn't know what he was doing and didn't care to know. The schism was best illustrated by Moss' attempt to override their advice that Khashoggi avoid testifying before the SEC.

Moss spent much of his time trying to explain to Khashoggi and Triad executives how an independent press works. When Prince Fahd, then second deputy premier of Saudi Arabia, got bad publicity for losing $6 million at the Monte Carlo gambling tables in 1974, Khashoggi showed Moss a favorable cover story on Fahd in a French magazine.

"We have to do something like this with *Time* magazine," he said.

"Adnan, it doesn't work that way in this country," Moss said.

"Don't you have friends at *Time*?" Khashoggi said.

"Yes, but the kinds of publications in this country that will do that sort of thing aren't worth talking to," Moss said.

"Yes, but this is so embarrassing," Khashoggi said.

"Do you know what he should do?" Moss said, laughing. "He should stop going to Monte Carlo."

When Moss needed to talk with Khashoggi to clear a response to some new charge, he often had to call all over the world. He kept a list of phone numbers and telex numbers for each of Khashoggi's homes, offices, yachts, planes, and friends.

On top of these difficulties, Moss' work included trying to counteract prejudice against Arabs. Often stereotyped as shiftless traders or gun-toting terrorists, Arabs have faced bias so pervasive that *Roget's International Thesaurus* lists as synonyms for Arab *drifter, vagrant,* and *tramp.*

Despite the problems, Moss liked and admired Khashoggi. Somehow, the vast wealth never seemed to go to his head. Unlike other Saudis, for example, he declined to adopt the honorific title of "sheikh," a meaningless designation used when addressing any person of stature.

It seemed to Moss that Khashoggi liked stories that dwelled on his life-style, while he was indifferent to other stories. In the U.S., *Business Week* ran the first major national story about him in its August 11, 1973, issue. The two-page article focused on his plans for Petrosat, the ill-fated oil venture dreamed up by MacLeod.

While going over press policy with Moss and his assistant, Joan G. Boros, Khashoggi drew attention to the paragraph in the article that said he flew his own DC-9, kept a yacht moored off the French Riviera at Cannes, and cruised London streets in a Rolls-Royce licensed as AK-1.

Referring to the license tag number, Khashoggi said, "That's not true." Then he turned to Shaheen and laughed. "Now, Bob, why isn't it? Do something!"

Shaheen soon arranged for an AK-1 license tag.

Ultimately, it was Shaheen who made the final decisions about press. As long as he had some control over it, Shaheen liked the press, glorying in publicity that magnified the importance of his boss and, by extension, himself.

His idea of what constituted good press was sometimes curious. At times he seemed to revel in stories emphasizing Khashoggi's life-style, while at other times he denounced journalists who ignored the more serious, business side of Khashoggi.

Shaheen told Moss that he should read Harold Robbins' *The Pirate*, which some took to be based on Khashoggi. Later, he drew attention to a scene near the end when Baydr, the globe-trotting protagonist in the novel, orders Jabir, his executive assistant, to push a man over a cliff with his car.

"Did you see the way he murdered the guy?" Shaheen asked Moss exuberantly.

As the publicity about Khashoggi's commissions mounted, Moss responded to the charges and tried to devise ways to improve his image: a panel discussion at the College of William and Mary School of Business; an interview with Gilbert E. Kaplan, editor in chief of *Institutional Investor*; and meetings with editors of the *New York Times* and *Time* magazine.

When Prince Fahd, as crown prince, and other Saudi princes visited the U.S., Moss again handled many of the arrangements, including filming of ceremonies.

At one point, Khashoggi was paying the salaries of a network of Moss assistants in New York, Paris, London, Hong Kong, Beirut, Washington, and the Sudan.

On occasion, in addition to handling the press, Moss or his assistants arranged sight-seeing trips for the Khashoggi children or bought the latest American toys for them or designer jeans for Soraya Khashoggi.

One day, Shaheen called to ask if Joan Boros, Moss' assistant, could look after a twelve-year-old prince for a few days. A son of Sattam ibn Abdul-Aziz, the deputy governor of Riyadh, the prince had a long name but was called simply Prince Abdul-Aziz. He was on a tour of the U.S., and Khashoggi wanted him exposed to the American life-style.

Boros had a son and daughter of about the same age, and she agreed to take the prince for several weeks. Soon after he arrived, Boros took him to a friend's house in Silver Spring, Maryland.

"Your house is smaller than my family's servants' quarters!" the prince exclaimed to the friend.

Later, Boros took the prince aside. "This is what she has," she said. "People don't feel good when you point out you have more."

The prince took the criticism gracefully, and occasionally showed consideration beyond what might be expected of a twelve-year-old.

During Ramadan, which marks the revealing of the Koran, he fasted. Observing the fast is the fourth pillar of Islam and entails refraining from food, drink, sex, and other sensory pleasures during the daylight hours for an entire lunar month in the spring.

At the end of the fast, a Moslem family in Washington invited Boros and the prince to celebrate Eid al-Fitr, or breaking of the fast. Boros was sick and couldn't go, but the prince walked home from the affair with a piece of cake for her.

Moss recommended other consultants to work for Khashoggi, including Erle Cocke, Jr., a Washington political adviser. Cocke had been a U.S. representative to the World Bank and a U.S. alternate representative to the United Nations. Three times, Cocke had been a prisoner of war, and he was former national commander of the American Legion. On his office wall, he kept pictures of all the presidents going back to Franklin D. Roosevelt—almost every one with a personal inscription.

"To Erle Cocke, from his friend," said the one from Roosevelt.

Cocke's job was to keep Khashoggi abreast of political developments in Washington. If he heard that Henry Kissinger was about to be given a new job, or Billy Graham was planning to visit the Soviet Union, he passed the tidbits on to Moss in written reports. Then Moss told Khashoggi.

The information helped Khashoggi plan strategy and magnified his importance to the Saudi princes. He was their eyes and ears on the United States.

Cocke told Khashoggi he should get to know ten to fifteen senators from the areas where he had businesses. Yet Cocke could never get Khashoggi to sit still long enough to arrange any significant meetings.

He'd say he would be in town on a Monday and would arrive on a Friday—of the following week.

To bolster his client's image and broaden his contacts, Cocke, on Khashoggi's behalf, in 1975 arranged a reception for United Nations delegates. Cocke knew all the right people and already had acceptances from the permanent representatives from Saudi Arabia, Korea, Egypt, and the Sudan. Then Khashoggi said he would not be in town that day.

Again in 1976, Cocke put his prestige on the line, this time to arrange a breakfast for World Bank delegates in Manila. Khashoggi was trying to establish himself as a banker, and Cocke felt this would enhance his reputation.

On Khashoggi's behalf, Cocke invited all the World Bank delegates and the treasury secretaries or finance ministers of each member country. The engraved invitations had already been sent out when Khashoggi told Cocke through Moss to cancel the event. The wires for canceling the invitations cost $20,000.

Cocke was so embarrassed that he stayed away from the Manila conference that year.

As Moss began traveling with Khashoggi, he noticed that he was constantly besieged by people seeking to invest with him or to get handouts—acquaintances bumping into him in hotel lobbies, for example. Quite often, Khashoggi agreed to the requests from people he hardly knew.

In addition, he was sending ten to twenty people to college in America—mostly relatives of people who had been working for him as chauffeurs or bookkeepers. Anyone who could show a blood tie to him would be put on the payroll. And he continued to retain nearly all the executives who had worked for him in the early days, even if they had long ago retired, feeling that it was bad luck to cut them off.

*Zakat*, a tax for the needy, is the third pillar of Islam, and Moss figured Khashoggi was discharging his obligation to the tune of $300,000 to $500,000 a year outside of Saudi Arabia. Inside his homeland, Khashoggi made additional grants in the hundreds of thousands of dollars.

To Moss, it seemed a disorganized and desultory approach. There was no screening of the requests to determine how worthy they were. Supplicants were wasting Khashoggi's time. They were one reason he was invariably late. Besides, if Khashoggi was being portrayed in the press as an evil force on the international scene, why shouldn't he take credit for his philanthropy?

Moss talked it over with Shaheen, who suggested that Khashoggi establish a foundation. The idea was not to obtain tax-exempt status: Khashoggi never paid any personal taxes. Because of its plentiful revenue from oil, Saudi Arabia levied no taxes. As a Saudi citizen, Khashoggi was exempt from U.S. personal income taxes. Rather, the foundation would provide a vehicle for evaluating requests and publicizing his contributions.

Khashoggi approved the idea, and the Triad Foundation was established in Washington on December 12, 1975. Moss became executive director at a salary of $25,000 a year, while Willis C. Armstrong, Khashoggi's adviser on political and economic trends, became secretary and treasurer.

As the word spread, requests for money came pouring in from universities and institutes that study the Middle East.

Within a month, Moss got the Associated Press interested

in one of the projects. It was an archaeological dig at Petra in Jordan.

Often referred to as a "rose red city half as old as time" because of the reddish sandstone cliffs that surround it, the city lies south of the Dead Sea in Jordan's Wadi Musa, or Valley of Moses.

Some two thousand years ago, it was the home of the Nabataeans, a Nomadic tribe of Arabs who got their start in commerce as pirates in the Red Sea. Later, they controlled the great caravan routes that crisscrossed the Middle East. The tribe chose Petra as its base because the city commands the only convenient pass through the mountains that blocked travel between the ancient civilizations of the Nile and the Tigris and Euphrates rivers.

Levying a duty on gold, spices, cotton, myrrh, and ivory passing through, the Nabataeans used the money in part to sculpt magnificent temples with graceful columns, garlands, flowers, and friezes. The ruins now line the road to Petra.

"Rich Arab Aids Petra 'Dig'" was the headline over a *Washington Post* story on the project. It said Khashoggi was helping to fund a trip to look for remnants of the ancient civilization by Professor Philip C. Hammond of the University of Utah with his students. Hundreds of papers picked it up, from the *Shreveport Times* to the *Fresno Bee.*

Other projects ranged from trips to the Middle East for U.S. students to creation of an International Institute of Banking and Finance specializing in training students from Third World countries. Set up twenty miles east of San Francisco at St. Mary's College of California, the institute was the idea of John E. Thompson, a Triad executive in charge of Khashoggi's U.S. banks. Thompson knew that Khashoggi wanted to encourage consumer banking in Saudi Arabia, where banks only made loans to businesses. This was a way to transport U.S. banking methods back to Saudi Arabia.

The foundation launched the institute with a gift of $115,000 and also contributed $50,000 toward scholarships.

Armstrong, meanwhile, decided the foundation should fund courses in Middle East studies at universities. In a memo to Moss, he wrote that the dearth of courses focusing on this part of the world has "a parallel to the 1930s, when school and college curricula in the U.S. focused on American and western European studies to the exclusion of other areas of the world."

Armstrong broached the idea to Swarthmore College, his

alma mater, and to Haverford and Bryn Mawr. Since they were near each other in the Philadelphia suburbs, the three universities often undertook joint programs.

In July 1977, the colleges invited Armstrong to lunch. He told their representatives the foundation could either fund courses or pay for books on the Middle East.

Harris L. Wofford, Jr., the president of Bryn Mawr, seemed the most receptive. A former special assistant to President Kennedy, Wofford was a lawyer with a background in civil rights issues. At Bryn Mawr, he had been trying to court foreign students and send American students overseas for special programs.

But Wofford knew something about Khashoggi's reputation and realized a public relations nightmare could ensue. At the luncheon, Armstrong distributed copies of a June 1977 *Fortune* magazine article on Khashoggi. Entitled "Super-Connector from Saudi Arabia," it outlined Khashoggi's problems with the SEC and said a subpoena for him was then outstanding.

With his staff and trustees, Wofford thrashed out the question of who should or should not be allowed to put up money for special programs. Clearly, the Mafia should not. But Khashoggi had not been charged with anything, not even indicted. One should be wary when money is coming from a government—Arab, Israeli, or communist—or from a corporation in the thick of controversy, Wofford thought.

But Wofford had, in the past, sought and received money from Jewish groups for Israeli scholars at Bryn Mawr. So long as the donor did not influence the program, the source of the money should not be a big consideration, he felt.

Bryn Mawr and the other two colleges decided to apply for a scholarship fund for Middle East students, for library funds, and for a program to hire professors. Already, the foundation had successfully distributed books on the Middle East to dozens of college libraries.

Before the foundation formally considered the application, the story that Khashoggi might contribute hit the college newspapers. A representative of the American Jewish Committee in Philadelphia met with Wofford and expressed concern that the courses might take the Arab point of view. Other Jewish leaders, faculty members, and alumni fired off blasts of alarm.

Within twenty-four hours, Haverford and Swarthmore withdrew their application. Hanging tough, Wofford issued a terse comment saying only that Bryn Mawr was reviewing the matter.

Armstrong was stung. Jewish groups had every right to raise objections, he felt, but the net effect was to discourage learning about an important area of the world—a result out of keeping with the traditional Jewish emphasis on learning.

"A university should be free to study whatever it wants to study, and there's nothing wrong with studying about Arabs," Armstrong complained to Amr Khashoggi, Khashoggi's half brother, a director of the foundation.

Eventually, Bryn Mawr opted to apply for scholarships for Middle East women and for books on Middle East culture, but not for funding of academic programs.

By then, it was too late.

Shaheen had tried to get Moss to clear all requests for money with him, but Moss had refused, saying he had legal responsibilities to the directors. Now Shaheen went to Khashoggi and said the foundation was driving him back into the headlines.

Khashoggi needed little persuading. He moved the foundation to London and changed its name to Khashoggi Foundation. Bryn Mawr never got a response to its application. And the institute at St. Mary's College was dissolved.

In its only full year of operation, the foundation had disbursed $696,500.

Despite the establishment of the foundation and the elaborate procedures for reviewing requests, the bulk of the funds disbursed came first from Khashoggi's checkbook. Later, the foundation reimbursed him.

In 1976, for example, he wrote checks for $15,000 to a mosque building fund in Manila; $100,000 to the Medina Mosque and School; $100,000 for a mosque in Beirut; $30,000 for flood relief in Manila; $25,000 to the Arab Press Association; $10,000 to the Sydney Yachting Club for International Racing; $5,000 for the French Orphan Society in Paris; and $1,500 for the Mayor's Christmas Tree Fund in Nairobi, according to the foundation's confidential records.

Khashoggi liked to give money with flair, the way he did in 1967, to celebrate his son Mohamed's fourth birthday: After hiring three gondolas in Venice, one laden with musicians, he threw a party for several hundred Italian orphans.

After the fiasco with the Pennsylvania colleges, Khashoggi put his daughter, Nabila, on the board of the new foundation and brought it more directly under his control. Now he was free to give away money as he saw fit—as he did in October 1983, when Carleton Varney was looking for contributions to finance a black-tie preview of an auction to raise money for the Carter Presidential Library.

Knowing that Khashoggi was a major donor to the library, Varney asked if Khashoggi would underwrite some of the cost of the reception.

The preview, held at New York's Sotheby Parke-Bernet Building, was expected to cost $50,000 on top of the $50 charge for each guest.

To Varney's amazement, Khashoggi agreed to pick up the entire bill.

Then in November 1985, Khashoggi paid $50,000 for two tickets to a charity dinner arranged by industrialist Armand Hammer for Prince Charles and Princess Diana in Palm Beach, Florida.

Khashoggi never intended to go and sent his daughter, Nabila, instead.

Richard E. Berendzen was flipping through a copy of *Leaders* magazine, the ultimate upscale publication that features interviews with chief executive officers of major international corporations.

The mild-mannered, scholarly president of American University in Washington was an astronomer who had taught at Harvard University, Boston University, and American University before deciding that administering held more challenge.

As college president, he was trying to do what all college presidents try to do—cultivate wealthy businessmen and alumni. It occurred to him that Henry O. Dormann, president and editor in chief of the stiff, glossy *Leaders* magazine, could help.

He called Dormann, who invited him to lunch in New York. After a year, Berendzen invited him to join the board of the university.

Dormann had interviewed Khashoggi for his magazine, and he introduced Berendzen to him by letter. In February 1983, Berendzen was in New York and called Shaheen at the Olympic Tower apartment.

"I had a cancellation, and I'd like to meet you," Berendzen said.

He didn't know that the Olympic Tower office also was Khashoggi's residence.

"Why don't you come by our offices on the forty-sixth floor?" Shaheen asked.

Berendzen found Shaheen to be engaging and easygoing. After half an hour, Shaheen asked what Berendzen would like for lunch.

"What do you have?" Berendzen asked.

"Anything you want," came the crisp reply.

Berendzen, who looks like an intellectual choirboy, ordered a hamburger, but Shaheen said to the waiter, "Bring him a steak."

That night, Shaheen invited Berendzen to dinner—a French and Chinese buffet with fifteen dishes—with Khashoggi and his wife, Lamia, and Shaheen and his wife, Patricia.

Patricia Shaheen has beautiful, mysterious brown saucers for eyes and a model's figure. She knows five dead languages (Sumerian, Akkadian, Neo-Syrian, Aramaic, and Middle Babylonian), in addition to French, Spanish, and Arabic. She is at home quoting from the Koran or discussing the editorial policies of the *New York Times*, where her stepfather, Roger Starr, is a member of the editorial board.

She got her striking good looks from her mother, Jodi, once a senior editor at Macmillan Inc. and a descendant of Joshua Ward, founder of the city of Newark, New Jersey.

Because of her background, Patricia is looked to for advice on the literary world. When she didn't like one version of a script for the movie *The Cotton Club*, Khashoggi decided against investing more money in the movie.

Patricia is indulged by Shaheen. When they are in New York, he drops her off at Rockefeller Center so she can ice-skate. While they have homes in Paris and New York, they move with Khashoggi, their clothes transported on racks, from Cannes and Marbella in the summer to New York in the fall, then to Kenya, Saudi Arabia, and Paris by spring.

Berendzen thought Khashoggi was a blend of cultures—Middle Eastern but with a dash of Paris, New York, and Monte Carlo. Soon, he invited Khashoggi to become a trustee of American University.

In October 1983, Khashoggi attended his first board meeting. After the meeting, he examined the photos of far-off galaxies in Berendzen's office. On the way to National Airport, Shaheen called Berendzen from a limousine.

"The chief is really up on astronomy," he said. "Do you think you could come up tomorrow night to talk about it?"

Without looking at his calendar, Berendzen said yes.

A few minutes later, Shaheen called back. "Why don't you bring some other trustees?" he suggested.

When Shaheen told him that Khashoggi's plane would fly them to New York, Berendzen expressed concern. He visualized a small corporate jet. His wife's father had died in a plane crash.

"Don't worry," Shaheen said.

Berendzen rounded up a crew that included Agriculture Secretary John R. Block; Carolyn Deaver, wife of the White House deputy chief of staff; and television journalist Nancy Dickerson.

At the airport, Berendzen was amazed to see a Boeing 727, with three in the cockpit. When they got to Newark Airport, he expected taxis to take them to Khashoggi's home. Instead, five limousines pulled up to the rear exit of the plane.

At the Olympic Tower apartment, Khashoggi greeted them at the elevator on the forty-sixth floor.

After a buffet of French, American, and Arabian cuisine, Berendzen and Khashoggi fumbled together in a closet for an extension cord so Berendzen could plug in a slide projector.

Even though he is older than Berendzen, Khashoggi always called him "professor."

Here is the richest man in the world, looking for an extension cord so the son of a hardware store owner can show his slides, Berendzen thought.

The lecture on the stars began at 1 A.M. By then, everyone was exhausted, and Berendzen kept it to half an hour. Later, Khashoggi put them up at the Helmsley Palace Hotel.

During the lecture, Khashoggi asked questions about the possibility of life on other planets and the birth of the universe. Berendzen thought he was like a little boy. He punctuated every declarative sentence with a question: "How do scientific findings fit with the Koran or the Bible? ... Do you really believe all this? ... What will happen in the year 2000?"

But above all, Khashoggi was taken with the black hole concept: that anything could disappear and yet be so dense. Maybe it's because it's one of the few things he can't buy, Berendzen thought.

Several months later, Khashoggi agreed to donate $5 million to American University. It was to help build a $14-million sports center which will include a basketball court with seating for 4,500 spectators.

The split was typical of the way Khashoggi invested and donated. He preferred to have partners who contributed capital and shared in the risk. He put as little of his own money in as possible, leveraging his deals. If he could, he would secure any government guarantees he could legally obtain—as he did in 1985 when obtaining a $75-million loan to build an alcohol fuels plant in Louisiana. But he also tried to have at least 50 percent control and his name on the project.

In contrast to the presidents of Haverford and Swarthmore, Berendzen didn't hesitate to take Khashoggi's money. The center, to be called the Adnan Khashoggi Center, had been on the university's "wish list" for forty years, and as ground was broken in the fall of 1985, it became a reality.

When faculty members and students questioned Berendzen about Khashoggi's background, the articulate Harvard alumnus had all the answers.

"He is controversial," he told them. "So is President Reagan and Jesus Christ. Most of the major builders of the U.S.—the Fords, the Vanderbilts, the Rockefellers—were controversial."

Then he paused for effect.

Referring to the inventor of dynamite, Berendzen said, "We all value the Nobel Prize. Is Khashoggi any more controversial than Alfred Nobel?"

Nothing more would be said.

# Africa

*Every day he works as if he is going to live for ever;*
*And plays as if he is going to die tomorrow.*

       *—James R. Mancham, Paradise Raped: Life, Love, and*
       *Power in the Seychelles*

JAMES R. Mancham, the genial chief minister of the Seychelles, was relaxing in his London hotel room when the phone rang.

As the leader of the British Crown Colony in the Indian Ocean, the bearded, dashing Mancham had established a reputation as a playboy—the "Trudeau of the East," one newspaper called him—because of his affinity for long-haired blondes.

In fact, he had just met a German blonde while visiting with the real Pierre Trudeau in Canada. Over poached Nova Scotia salmon, the two chiefs of state had discussed the meaning of love and life while Mancham made a pitch for more aid for his ninety-nine-island vacation spot a thousand miles east of Kenya.

As the phone rang on this lazy summer day in 1974, Mancham was looking forward to a weekend fling with his new-found German girlfriend.

"Chief minister, my name is Gerard Boissier," the caller said. "I am the Geneva representative of the Triad Corp. Our chairman would like to invite you to Cannes for the weekend."

"And who is your chairman?" Mancham asked.

"He is Mr. Adnan Khashoggi," Boissier said.

Mancham knew of Khashoggi by reputation. Articles in the press always tagged him as "the super-salesman," the "Arab Rockefeller," or the "top wheeler-dealer."

"But it's Friday evening," Mancham said. "How does Mr. Khashoggi expect me to get to Cannes by tomorrow morning?"

"Sir," Boissier said, "our chairman will send his plane for you."

Mancham was intrigued. The superpowers wanted the Seychelles in their camp because it could be used as a military base. But Mancham's nation had a population of just 65,000 and shared a U.S. ambassador with Kenya. Even today, its gross national product is just $95 million. No one had ever sent a plane for him.

Much as he wanted to say yes, Mancham already had plans to have dinner Saturday with his new girlfriend and three other friends.

When he explained to Boissier why he couldn't make it, the Triad executive said without pausing, "Sir, your friends will be the welcome guests of Mr. Khashoggi."

Thus began Khashoggi's relationship with the Seychelles and later Kenya, a relationship that included major investments in cattle ranching, construction of still another of Khashoggi's homes, and acquisition of the world-famous Mount Kenya Safari Club, founded by actor William Holden.

Like his investments in dozens of other countries, Khashoggi's involvement here turned out to have a political as well as a moneymaking motive. Ever-watchful Saudi Arabia was looking to make new friends among strategically located countries. To Saudi Arabia, any country in the world met the test.

Increasingly, the countries around Kenya and the Seychelles were becoming anticapitalist. Some had accepted Soviet arms. Kenya, in particular, was the odd man out in Africa and looking for trading partners. For the Arabs, it could be a big prize diplomatically and a source of meat, vegetables, and grain as well.

The morning after Boissier's call, three Rolls-Royce lim-

ousines—with license plates AMK-1, AMK-2, and AMK-3—
pulled up in front of the Churchill Hotel. In walked Boissier and
two Triad executives to escort Mancham and his friends to London's Heathrow Airport, where Khashoggi's DC-9 was waiting.

As they sipped the requisite Dom Pérignon champagne and
ate beluga caviar, a steward played a videocassette of a recent
television documentary on Khashoggi.

Referring to a "new kind of Arab" invading American
shores, the announcer said, "These Arabs are now busy. They
are busy buying our cattle ranches, they are busy buying our
hotel chains, they are even buying our banks. And the most
flamboyant of them all is a forty-year-old Saudi Arabian, Adnan Khashoggi."

At the Nice airport, Shaheen introduced himself as Khashoggi's executive assistant. He escorted Mancham and his
group by Cadillac limousine to the grand Carlton Hotel. There,
a suite filled with fresh flowers was waiting.

"Royalty could not have been better treated," one of Mancham's friends remarked.

Dressed in a black shirt and trousers, Khashoggi appeared
at 12:30 P.M. Around his neck, he wore a gold zodiac sign of
Leo, the unconquerable.

"I have heard a lot about the Seychelles, and I think you
are doing a good job," Khashoggi began.

Already, Mancham was charmed.

"From what I understand, the Seychelles is one of the most
beautiful spots on the earth," he continued.

So that was it, Mancham thought. He wants to vacation in
the Seychelles.

"I would like to contribute something to your islands,"
Khashoggi said.

Mancham's guard went up. Many developers wanted to
exploit the islands.

"I'm flattered by your interest," Mancham said. "But I must
point out that we have a very strict development code. Nothing
can be done which would scar the beauty of the islands."

Khashoggi smiled. "I couldn't agree more," he said. "I have
seen places massacred by uncontrolled development. The nat-
ural beauty and the way of life must be the overriding consideration. In the end, your people must preserve their smiles.
Indeed, if you wish, I could easily find the expertise to help
you achieve this. I leave you to think it over."

Then Khashoggi was gone.

Mancham headed toward the bedroom, where his girl-friend was waiting. The phone rang.

"Mr. Mancham," the caller said, "I am Mr. Khashoggi's personal masseur. After every trip, Mr. Khashoggi enjoys a massage. I would like to offer my services to you."

After the massage, Mancham joined Khashoggi, his companion, Laura Biancolini, and an entourage of forty at dinner. One of the guests was Harold Robbins, whose novel *The Pirate*, the main character of which bore a passing resemblance to Khashoggi, had just been published.

Over the next several years, there would be many more favors, first when Mancham was chief minister and later when he became president of the newly independent Seychelles. Khashoggi loaned Mancham his yachts and his planes, and he paid a French magazine $80,000 to cover the Seychelles' independence from Great Britain on June 29, 1976.

The islands captivated Khashoggi. Except that its foundation is granite and the palm trees lift at odd angles from between huge boulders, the main island, Mahé, is like a small West Indian island—St. Vincent, St. Lucia, or Grenada.

On the west coast spread white-gold beaches. The capital, Victoria, is something out of Graham Greene. Flanked by mango trees and coconut palms, the main shopping thoroughfare passes weathered two-story buildings. Side streets lose themselves in greenery.

On one trip to the Seychelles, Khashoggi brought along his friend, Prince Talal, the twenty-third son of King Abdul-Aziz. Along with other Saudi investors, they bought an option for nearly $1 million for a spectacular new vacation development on a parcel of land in the Mahé group of islands.

At the same time, Khashoggi began orchestrating closer diplomatic relations with Saudi Arabia. King Khalid invited Mancham to visit with him in Riyadh. Then, as a goodwill gesture, Mancham filled Khashoggi's stretched Boeing 727 with fresh fruits and vegetables and sent them to the king.

Mancham was anticipating a shot in the arm to his nation's economy. He envisioned thousands of tourists flocking to the new development. Indeed, a television reporter in the Seychelles asked Khashoggi if he was planning to buy the tiny nation.

Yet when Mancham was in Paris, he received a strange message from Talal asking him to meet him in Austria.

"Mr. President," Talal said at his hotel in Vienna, "I want

to thank you for the welcome you gave me in the Seychelles. It is a beautiful country, and I like your people. As Adnan must have told you, I want to invest a lot of money. But there is a problem."

Talal watched Mancham's reaction.

"Your prime minister," he said. "I don't trust him."

"In what way, Your Highness?" Mancham asked.

He was wondering what kind of trouble his prime minister, France Albert René, had gotten himself into.

"I remember the dinner you gave for me. You put the prime minister's wife to my side. This woman made the point of adapting her voice to the level of the music. When the music was loud, she was loud. When it was low, she whispered."

To himself, Mancham was thinking, So what?

Talal continued, "I think, President, she did not want you to hear what she was telling me. And then there is your prime minister. I didn't like the look in his eyes. He never looked at you straight in the face."

That was the end of the prince's message. He had called Mancham to Vienna to say he didn't like the way the prime minister looked at him.

Mancham wondered if the bedouin, after thousands of years of coping in the desert, had a sixth sense that warned them of danger. But there were no further clues, and Mancham soon forgot about the conversation.

Two months later, in June 1977, Mancham again was out of the country, this time attending the Commonwealth Heads of Government Conference in London. At 3:45 A.M. on June 5, the phone in his hotel room awakened him with incessant ringing. Mancham knew it couldn't be good news at that hour of the morning.

It was Khashoggi calling from Paris. He said his boat, the *Khalidia*, was moored at Victoria. The captain, Peter Lee, had just called him. Listening to the radio, Lee learned that Mancham had been overthrown by his prime minister, René. Already, René had suspended the constitution and disbanded the parliament. Four lives were lost in the coup.

Later, a British diplomat officially gave Mancham the news that he was a deposed ruler.

Khashoggi continued to invite Mancham to his parties, but Khashoggi's development plans for the Seychelles quickly withered. Instead, Khashoggi turned his attention to Kenya, the Seychelles' neighbor and diplomatic partner.

Astride the equator on the east coast of Africa, Kenya is a land of crisp, clear air and striking contrasts. Its beauty has inspired settings for Ernest Hemingway's *Green Hills of Africa* and Joy Adamson's *Born Free.*

Almost the size of Texas, the northern three-fifths of the country is arid and inhabited by nomadic tribes. South of the Tana River, along the coast, is a tropical climate and beautiful beaches. Rolling grasslands fill the southwestern corner. Nairobi, the capital, is temperate and adorned with flowering trees and shrubs. Still other regions north of Nairobi include sweeping plateaus and magnificent peaks. The highest, Mount Kenya, is 17,040 feet above sea level and perpetually capped with snow.

Khashoggi visited Kenya with French pharmaceutical tycoon Henry Roussel and Edward K. Moss, his public affairs consultant. Roussel—whose son, Thierry, later married Christina Onassis—knew of some ranchland for sale near Nanyuki, 125 miles northwest of Nairobi. Moss had done consulting work for the government of Kenyan president Jomo Kenyatta. He went along as an adviser.

A few days after they inspected the ranch, they had lunch at the Mount Kenya Safari Club, where Moss was a member and later chairman.

Founded in 1959 by actor William Holden and three other investors, the club sat on ninety-one acres of magnificent landscape, with Mount Kenya as a backdrop. There were mountain streams, rose gardens, waterfalls flowing into quiet pools, a heated swimming pool, a nine-hole golf course, stables, and vegetable gardens that supplied the kitchens.

Peacocks, storks, ibexes, and exotic birds strolled about. Nearby salt licks attracted big game, including the elephant and the antelope.

The rooms and cottages all had sunken marble tubs, parquet floors, and fireplaces fueled with cedarwood that the staff lighted every afternoon.

Since hunting was banned in Kenya, the club arranged for sight-seeing safaris to look at giraffe, zebra, lion, gazelle, leopard, cheetah, rhinoceros, and buffalo.

Over the years, the club had attracted such regulars as Winston Churchill, the duke of Manchester, Lord Louis Mountbatten, Prince Bernhard of the Netherlands, Princess Ashraf

Pahlavi of Iran, Clark Gable, John Wayne, Trevor Howard, Bing Crosby, and Bob Hope.

Holden, who starred in such films as *Bridge on the River Kwai*, *Network*, *Love Is a Many-Splendored Thing*, and *The World of Suzie Wong*, had a 10 percent interest in the club. He stayed in Cottage No. 7, with a magnificent view of Mount Kenya. Seeking more privacy, he and his longtime companion, actress Stefanie Powers, later stayed in number 12.

For lunch, Khashoggi, Moss, Roussel, and several other guests dined on Kenyan lamb and barbecued beef—some of the finest in the world—several fish dishes, half a dozen salads, pâtés, fruits, and assorted pastries and cakes.

Khashoggi felt the Safari Club was a Shangri-la.

In December 1976, Khashoggi again visited Kenya, this time at the invitation of the government.

The Kenya finance and tourism minister made presentations to Khashoggi about the development possibilities, then took him on a five-day tour of the country.

Near Mombasa, on the Indian Ocean, the government officials showed Khashoggi the area for a planned beach resort and a World Bank study that projected millions of dollars in profits for the area.

"What role can I play?" Khashoggi asked his hosts.

"You can develop one of the hotels," a minister answered.

"How many are there?" Khashoggi asked.

"Twenty-six," he was told.

"I know this is a government project, and quite possibly you can't answer now, but could Triad take on all twenty-six?" Khashoggi asked to an amazed look all around.

"We'll have to see," the minister replied.

But Moss looked into the study and found it was based on a projected annual increase in tourism of 12 to 14 percent.

"Tourism has already begun to level off," Moss told Khashoggi, "and this part of the world has had a surfeit of facilities for five to seven years. They've never had a 12 percent increase in tourism, and they never will."

At the end of the tour, Khashoggi met with President Kenyatta in the State House.

The powerfully built, heavyset Kenyatta was the son of the leader of a small agricultural settlement in Kenya. His grandfather was a *murogi*, or diviner, whose knowledge of medicine and magic set him apart from other people.

Taught to read and write by Scottish missionaries, Kenyatta studied at the London School of Economics. With his gift for oratory, he rose within the government from clerk to president when Kenya won independence from Great Britain in 1963.

Kenyatta's meeting with Khashoggi began stiffly.

"How do you like my country?" Kenyatta asked.

"I think it's a wonderful country," Khashoggi said.

Then Khashoggi gave the eighty-year-old leader a long box wrapped with red velvet.

"This is from the people of Saudi Arabia," he said.

Kenyatta unwrapped the box and took out an elegantly decorated Arabian sword.

Kenyatta's face lit up. To his bodyguards, he said, "Stand clear!" as he whipped the sword through the air.

"Come, let's walk in the rose garden," Kenyatta said.

Fifteen minutes later, they emerged with their arms around each other like old friends.

In the end, Khashoggi bought the ranch, called "Ol Pegeta," with some 114,000 acres of grazing land for 20,000 head of cattle and game. And he started a tourist company.

At the same time, he helped nudge Kenya into a closer relationship with the Arab world, symbolized by the presence of Kenya's then vice-president, Daniel arap Moi, at the March 1977 Cairo Afro–Arab summit conference.

As a result of Khashoggi's visits, Kenya and Saudi Arabia developed plans to build embassies in Nairobi and Jeddah.

Khashoggi spent the 1977 New Year's holiday at the Safari Club with his family.

Seeing that Khashoggi's affection for the club was growing, Moss, as chairman, told him he could buy stock in the club, helping to pay for needed renovations. Eventually, Khashoggi acquired nearly all the outstanding shares. Several years later, he hired Intercontinental Hotels to run the club.

Now Khashoggi ruled a virtual city-state within the jewel-like country—his own personal game ranch, another home with a swimming pool and a pool for pet crocodiles, and one of the most magnificent mountain chalets in the world.

On Khashoggi's mock version of Monopoly, the Safari Club takes the "Park Place" position.

Soon, his Kenya properties became another stopping-off point for the jet set, ranging from Canadian Prime Minister

Trudeau, who spent a weekend with Khashoggi on the ranch in August 1981, to Brooke Shields.

In July 1984, the lithesome eighteen-year-old was visiting Kenya on a safari with her mother, Teri.

Khashoggi's son Mohamed had dated Shields, and later she began dating Khashoggi's nephew Dodi Fayed, executive producer of the Academy Award—winning *Chariots of Fire*. His father, Mohamed al-Fayed, was once Khashoggi's general manager and is now an owner of Harrod's department store in London.

While Shields was visiting Africa, Khashoggi invited her to dinner at the ranch. After natives put on a drum-beating dance, Shields made the first cut into a whole lamb wrapped in herbs and cooked slowly over coals.

As souvenirs, Khashoggi gave Shields and her mother bejeweled bracelets with their initials etched in diamonds.

Brooke Shields as a house guest was but another fringe benefit of being the richest man on earth.

# Khashoggi
# v.
# Khashoggi

*Divorce must be pronounced twice and then a woman must
be retained in honor or released in kindness.*

*—The Koran*

**A**T the Ritz Hotel in London, Soraya Khashoggi was
having dinner with lawyer Marvin M. Mitchelson in April 1979.
As usual, Mitchelson was late, but so was Soraya, and they
wound up arriving about the same time—10 P.M.

Soraya Khashoggi told Mitchelson she wanted to sue her
husband for divorce. It was a story that repeated itself in thousands of lawyers' offices throughout the world, but the husband in this case was Adnan Khashoggi, and the amount sought
would be $2.5 billion—at the time the largest divorce suit in his-
tory.

Soon, the headlines would be coursing around the world
as Mitchelson shrewdly made one sensational disclosure after
another—about Khashoggi and Richard M. Nixon, about
Khashoggi's life-style and call girls, about gambling and payoffs to U.S. executives.

While Khashoggi's name is a household word in Europe, more than any of his ventures, adventures, and misadventures, Khashoggi is known in the U.S. for his wife's divorce suit and its sensational pursuit by Mitchelson.

Meeting her at the Ritz, Mitchelson thought Khashoggi's wife was stunning. Five feet four inches tall, she had a heart-shaped face with large, limpid blue eyes, black hair, a complexion like a cake of white Dove soap, and pale, sensuous lips. Her eyelashes were long and uneven, giving her a wild, exotic look. She peered out from under her eyelids, heightening her sexual appeal.

She walked like a Slinky toy, constantly prancing and moving in unexpected directions. Wearing jeans or an evening gown, Soraya Khashoggi was a knockout. Everything about her, including her chest, seemed larger than life.

For three hours, she held the attention of Mitchelson and her English lawyer, David Joseph Anthony Sarch, who attended the dinner at the Ritz, as she described being married to the richest man in the world.

She was Sandra Patricia Jarvis Daly, the daughter of a London hotel waitress and an unknown father. She grew up in a modest terrace cottage at 90 Lansdowne Road in Leicester, England. After attending Catholic schools, she worked as a telephone operator and volunteered as a nurse's aide in Africa.

When she was nineteen, she met Khashoggi through his cousin, and they were married in Beirut on April 29, 1961. Khashoggi was twenty-five and had just started his gypsum plant in Riyadh. She took the Arab name of Soraya, converted to Islam, and learned Arabic. When in Saudi Arabia, she wore a veil.

They lived in Riyadh and Beirut, where Khashoggi had homes. But money was tight, and one of the hardest things for her to grow accustomed to was the food, which was invariably lamb.

"Everything else began to taste like lamb," she said.

As Khashoggi's wealth grew, their lives changed in storybook fashion. The two flew around the world, acquired more homes, then yachts and planes. In any given month, she visited Paris, Switzerland, Rome, or Cannes, the way other people visit friends down the street.

"We were gypsies," she said.

Instead of her going out to buy clothes, Cardin and Givenchy came to her with their models.

As Khashoggi's business expanded, she saw him less. By 1972, he was spending a third of his time in Saudi Arabia, a quarter of his time in Beirut, and the rest all over the world. Theirs became an open marriage, and she began living in London.

For Khashoggi, the last straw was a report relayed to his London office by the MI-5, the British security agency, that she was having an affair with his friend President Gaafar Nimeri of the Sudan. Meanwhile, he had been dallying with seventeen-year-old Laura Biancolini.

In July 1974, at Cannes, he promised to support Soraya Khashoggi for the rest of her life if she did not hire a lawyer and if she continued to raise the children in the Moslem faith. If she violated the agreement, he told her, he would "declare her blood to be legal," which she took to mean that she could be put to death under Islamic *shariah* law, without judicial process.

On Khashoggi's yacht, Dr. Sabih Deif, who had worked for Khashoggi almost from the beginning of his career, drew up a handwritten agreement. An Egyptian lawyer fluent in English, Arabic, French, and Italian, Dr. Deif had a fine, chiseled head that looked from the side like a profile of the Sphinx.

The agreement was vague about dollar amounts, and she refused to sign it.

In September, Ismet Fouad, Khashoggi's first employee, called her at 11 P.M. in London. Fouad was often Khashoggi's trusted emissary on personal matters. He said he had some papers for her. Khashoggi had told him to present papers to the Cheria Court in Beirut divorcing her under Islamic law.

In Islamic tradition, "I divorce thee" recited by a male three times is sufficient to execute a final divorce. If recited two times, the couple can still change their minds and reunite without having to remarry.

There was no need for Khashoggi to recite the words himself. He sent Fouad to the court as his surrogate.

Soraya took the documents from Fouad and said nothing. He felt she was a very strong woman.

But Khashoggi's manner of divorcing her, through a surrogate and without her knowledge, offended her. For all the pain that had occurred between them, she still loved him. Soon, love turned to anger as the loose financial arrangement began to flounder.

She wanted to be on her own financially, not a chattel in Khashoggi's kingdom. She was trying to establish herself as a professional photographer and was quite good at it. Because of her contacts, she had been able to photograph such celebrities as Sean Connery, Stewart Granger, and a raft of politicians.

But the money could not sustain the life-style to which she had become accustomed, and she would call Khashoggi's London office and scream for money. More often than not, somebody would send it to her. Yet at other times, Khashoggi cut off her credit.

Her difficulty in seeing her children infuriated her. In Islamic tradition, procreation is the primary function of women, and Khashoggi had wasted little time helping her to fulfill her role.

Ten months after they were married, she bore him a daughter, Nabila, followed nine months later by Mohamed. More than two years later, in 1965, Khaled was born, followed by Hussein in 1967 and Omar in 1969.

Because both parents traveled extensively, Susan Hadley, a curly-haired English nanny, played a major role in their upbringing. She was a strict disciplinarian who made sure the children didn't become spoiled like many other Arab children of wealth. When their mother was away, the nanny insisted they write to her and mention her in their prayers.

When civil disturbances in 1975 made life unsafe in Lebanon, the children moved from Beirut to England, where they lived at Gotton House, a seven-bedroom Queen Anne mansion near West Monkton in Somerset. Attending English schools, they saw their mother on weekends.

Soraya lived in an elegant town house at 11 Eaton Square in London's Belgravia section—a cream-colored town house with wrought-iron doors and a swimming pool in the basement. Often, she was seen with handsome men and movie stars. Besides his other homes all over the world, Khashoggi had an apartment in London at Roebuck House, Stag Place.

In 1977, the children, chauffeured by Khashoggi's pilots, began attending boarding school in Lausanne, Switzerland.

When he could, Khashoggi took them on trips with him—on the yacht, on a visit to Finland or the Seychelles. He had custody of them, and Soraya had to arrange through Khashoggi's organization to see them. She would be told to meet them on the yacht, and when she arrived, the yacht had just set sail. At Christmastime, Khashoggi saw the children and she didn't.

Slowly, the anger built up inside her.

When she had a dispute with builders who were working on her home, she consulted Sarch, a big man with a blond curly beard and an impeccable British accent. She had been referred to him by their mutual friend Robin Guild, an interior designer who snapped a photo of her sunbathing topless in South America. Later, the photo found its way, without his knowledge, onto the front page of the *Daily Mirror*, one of London's tabloid newspapers.

Sarch had a lot of celebrity clients, and he knew how to make them feel comfortable. Even though the issues were inconsequential, he took on her case against the builders, and she began consulting him about her marital difficulties. Instead of the loose arrangement then existing, Sarch wanted to work out a more specific monetary agreement with Khashoggi.

"I want madame to be happy," Khashoggi told him expansively one day at the Eaton Square town house. But when Sarch tried to draft an agreement, Shaheen told him to hold off.

Soraya Khashoggi had been reading about Marvin Mitchelson and his successful case against actor Lee Marvin. After they broke up, Mitchelson claimed Marvin owed "palimony" to his live-in girlfriend of six years, Michelle Triola Marvin. (Before the split, she had changed her name to that of her boyfriend.) Mitchelson won $104,000 for his client and established a precedent.

He specialized in divorce, and the names of his clients' husbands lit theater marquees: Mick Jagger, James Mason, Marlon Brando, Bob Dylan, Rod Steiger, Van Johnson, Alan Jay Lerner, Groucho Marx, Richard Pryor, Chevy Chase, Eddie Fisher, and David Bowie. He filed suits against wives by husbands, too: Tony Curtis, Carl Sagan, and Richard Harris.

The more steamy the allegations, the more likely Mitchelson was to be involved. He unsuccessfully handled an appeal by Roxanne Pulitzer, known for her bedtime trumpet-playing, and briefly represented twenty-nine-year-old Vicki Morgan in a suit against her paramour, department store heir Alfred Bloomingdale. In late 1985, he filed suit against the estate of actor Rock Hudson on behalf of his homosexual lover, who claimed Hudson had not told him he had AIDS.

Yet Mitchelson took greatest pride in another case that got only scant attention at the time. It was a Supreme Court case that guaranteed free counsel to the indigent in misdemeanor cases—an extension of the Gideon case that granted free counsel to defendants charged with felonies.

Mitchelson had nightmares in which women were constantly calling to complain about their husbands or boyfriends. He got one call at 2 A.M. from Rhonda Fleming, saying, "He took my bidet!"

Her husband had come into the house and ripped it out.

"For the money we're going to get from him, we'll buy every bidet in Europe," Mitchelson told her.

After that, Mitchelson got an unlisted number.

The son of a Latvian house painter, Mitchelson was born in Detroit. When he was eighteen months old, the family moved to Los Angeles, where his father wound up managing a string of apartments. When Marvin was eighteen and serving as a navy medical corpsman, his father died.

After his two-year enlistment, Mitchelson helped his mother, Sonya, run the apartments. He got to know the tenants while attending what was then Southwestern University Law School. Many were actors and producers who became his clients when he opened a practice.

His first big divorce case, in 1964, was Mrs. James Mason's. There were allegations of adultery on both sides, and California hadn't adopted a no-fault divorce law.

Mitchelson subpoenaed anyone who knew Mason—forty witnesses in all. He didn't know if they knew anything about the case or about any adultery. But when they got their subpoenas, they turned into hornets disturbed in their nest.

Just before the trial began, her husband settled for roughly $2 million—an astounding sum in those days. The headlines read: "PAMELA WINS DIVORCE, SPLITS MILLIONS."

Mitchelson never looked back.

Soraya Khashoggi knew that her British lawyer, Sarch, was friends with Mitchelson. When Sarch told her he was flying to California, she suggested that he consult Mitchelson about her problems.

Sarch still wanted to work out a settlement without filing suit. He knew her chances of winning in the British courts were slim. After all, she was already divorced. The time to litigate is before the divorce, not after.

But Sarch discussed her situation with Mitchelson anyway. When Mitchelson came to London, the three met for dinner at the Ritz. With his prematurely white hair and dark blue Pierre Cardin suit, Mitchelson seemed to belong there.

Now the threesome was scarfing down triple chocolate cake on top of pastries from the pastry cart.

"I wound up talking to the smallest girl in his organization, the switchboard girl, and I, the mother of his children, was in the position of asking her to pay the greengrocer's bill," she complained.

What troubled her most, Soraya said, was the manner in which Khashoggi had divorced her.

"He didn't even give me notice," she said.

Yet the fact was Soraya Khashoggi *was* divorced. By the time she saw Mitchelson, she had been divorced for more than five years. In fact, she had since remarried and had that marriage annulled. Her second marriage, two years earlier, was to Richard J. Coombes, a twenty-five-year-old cartographic draftsman who worked for the British government.

She was thirty-five at the time, and Coombes had been dating her twenty-year-old daughter, Kim Patrick. Before she married Khashoggi, she had had Kim out of wedlock, then gave her up for adoption in Johannesburg. After she lost track of her daughter, Khashoggi hired investigators, who found her in South Africa.

Later, Soraya told Mitchelson about a trip she took with Coombes and Khashoggi two months after her second marriage. It was just after Christmas, and Khashoggi invited them to Kenya.

"When we arrived," she told Mitchelson, "Adnan had Coombes stay in a hotel, and had me stay with him at his ranch, a twenty-minute flight away from the hotel."

On the visit, she said, "Adnan and I slept together."

Mitchelson told her that these problems, while troubling, were not insurmountable. Normally, he said, a divorce settlement cannot be undone. But he said he could challenge the validity of the divorce.

"It was done by a surrogate, without you or Khashoggi being present. I think we can file another divorce action," he said.

If the divorce was not valid, then the marriage to Coombes was invalid, because she was still married to Khashoggi at the time, he pointed out.

Mitchelson told Soraya that the key to winning the suit would be getting the California courts to hear it. The laws in California are among the most liberal in the world and provide for a fifty-fifty split of property acquired during marriage. But they cannot be applied to anyone.

Soraya was a British subject who lived in London. Khashoggi was a Saudi citizen with homes and offices all over the world.

"We have two chances for getting into the California courts," he said. "One is if you establish residence in California. The second is if we can prove that Khashoggi visits California on a systematic basis."

Then Mitchelson asked her if she knew how much Khashoggi was worth.

She hesitated. She didn't know if Mitchelson was fully aware of who this man was.

"It's in the billions, I know that," she said.

As he agreed to represent her, Mitchelson was dividing by two.

Yet Sarch counseled her to hold off suing. He still thought an agreement could be worked out.

In July 1979, she was vacationing in Los Angeles and wanted to take her two youngest sons, Omar and Hussein, along with Sarch's eleven-year-old daughter, to Knott's Berry Farm and Universal Studios.

Khashoggi's organization allowed her only twenty-four hours with the children, then flew them away. Having had to cut the outing short, she flew into a rage.

She instructed Sarch and Mitchelson to file suit against Khashoggi immediately.

Holding an electronic debugging device, Soraya Khashoggi paced in her suite at the Sands Hotel & Casino in Las Vegas. She was meeting with Harold Rhoden, an associate of Mitchelson, who was there to develop the facts needed for her lawsuit.

She told Rhoden the device indicated the suite was bugged. She was sure Khashoggi had arranged it.

Rhoden considered it normal for people involved in bitter litigation to become slightly paranoid.

"Shall we go to the coffee shop?" he asked.

"No, we can talk here," she answered.

Over and over, Rhoden asked her to search her brain to dredge up any times Khashoggi had been in California. The most important task was to get the California courts to accept jurisdiction over her case, issues known as *in personam* jurisdiction and *forum non conveniens*.

She mentioned his stays in California as a college student and his trips to Los Altos to see Morton P. MacLeod, his chief of staff.

"He maintains several bungalows on a full-time basis at

the Beverly Hills Hotel," she offered. He even keeps a full wardrobe at the hotel, she said.

Rhoden took notes, and by the end of his session with her, he knew that they would file two suits on her behalf: one for divorce, and a second one—in case the first failed—for breach of contract, popularly known as palimony. Even if she was divorced, she could share equally in the money Khashoggi acquired while they were married.

Experienced as he was in divorce matters, Mitchelson often turned to Rhoden for help on legal issues when they were unusually intricate.

A litigation lawyer since 1953, Rhoden represented Noah Dietrich when he claimed to be the executor of the estate of Howard R. Hughes under the terms of the "Mormon Will"—a will that was subsequently declared a fraud by a Las Vegas jury.

Later, Rhoden and Mitchelson worked together on a sensational suit brought by the wife of Mohamed al-Fassi, the Moroccan brother-in-law of Prince Turki, who was asked to resign as Saudi vice-minister of defense.

Al-Fassi had met his future wife, sixteen-year-old Diani Bilinelli, in London, where she was working as a salesgirl in a Piccadilly shop. He married her in March 1976, and she became Sheika Dena al-Fassi.

They moved to the gaudy Beverly Hills mansion with its nude statues painted pink and the portrait of al-Fassi on the bottom of the pool. When al-Fassi fell for another woman, he sent Sheika Dena off on a trip, and she hired Mitchelson. By then, she was living in the small guest quarters behind the main house, which had been gutted by fire.

In that case, the two lawyers obtained a judgment of $81 million, some $10 million of which has been paid.

Rhoden wrote the briefs, researched the law, and made oral arguments, while Mitchelson also made oral arguments and handled the press.

That was Mitchelson's forte. He had learned early on that it never hurt to drop by the press room in the courthouse and let reporters know about a case he had filed or was about to file. The reporters appreciated knowing about it, and the publicity sometimes forced defendants to settle without going to trial.

In the days when lawyers couldn't advertise, the publicity helped create Mitchelson's image as an indefatigable lawyer, attracting more clients. He considered the press to be part of the legal process. He called his work in this regard "public relations."

To Rhoden, it was unprofessional to seek press attention. He didn't like it, and he let Mitchelson know that on many occasions. If reporters wanted stories, they could look through the dockets in the public file. If Mitchelson got more clients that way, it was not Rhoden's way.

In many other respects, the two lawyers were the odd couple. Mitchelson had a soft, deferential way of speaking that women liked. Rhoden was direct, if not blunt. Mitchelson wore Pierre Cardin suits fitted in Paris at the designer's studio. Rhoden wore sports jackets and scuffed shoes. Mitchelson was almost always late. Rhoden made it a point to be on time.

The biggest contrast was in their offices. Rhoden originally rented space in Mitchelson's suite but later got himself his own modest office, a blue-carpeted room with oak bookcases. Mitchelson had a sprawling empire at 1801 Century Park East in Century City, the most prized office location in Los Angeles. From the nineteenth floor, it had a view of all of Beverly Hills, Hollywood, and Los Angeles through three floor-to-ceiling windows.

Big brass letters identified his suite, and the reception room, painted pale red, had a light blue sofa with lace-trimmed throw pillows. Turquoise and gold statues stood on the floor and adorned the tables.

The entire suite was done in what Mitchelson grandly called a Renaissance motif from La Belle Epoque, an era of elegance and gaiety that characterized French life just before World War I. He stumbled over the French words, and Rhoden had his own characterization: Transylvania with a touch of Dracula.

Mitchelson was especially fond of *Birth of Venus* by Florentine painter Sandro Botticelli. The painting celebrates the pagan goddess as a pale, chaste, and delicate beauty, standing naked in a clamshell, flanked by angelic beings.

An amateur photographer, Mitchelson snapped a slide of the painting at the Uffizi Gallery in Florence, where the masterpiece is displayed. Then he had it blown up to a three-by-five-foot sepia transparency and mounted it in a rectangular fluorescent light fixture over his desk.

But Mitchelson was proudest of his private bathroom. Complete with bathtub and shower, it was papered with drawings of misty-eyed naked women, their breasts as big as melons.

For all their differences, Rhoden respected Mitchelson for

his guts. When Mitchelson brought the Marvin case in superior court, Rhoden told him, "The case ought to be kicked out of court, and if I were the judge, I'd shove it out. You're going to lose," he told him flatly. "It's silly."

Mitchelson lost and appealed to the Supreme Court. This time Rhoden told him, "A reversal is out of the question. They'll ridicule you."

But Mitchelson won, and Rhoden never forgot how Mitchelson had persevered against the smirks of many of his colleagues.

After Rhoden drafted Soraya Khashoggi's legal complaints as associate counsel, Mitchelson's secretary typed them at the end of July.

"Don't you think there's some mistake?" she asked Mitchelson, bewildered. "There are nine zeroes here."

"No," answered Mitchelson gleefully. "There really are nine zeroes."

Nobody knew for sure what Khashoggi was worth, but Soraya Khashoggi had given Mitchelson some financial statements with big numbers on them, and Mitchelson got estimates from an Arab newspaper editor and others ranging as high as $6 billion. If he wasn't already the richest man in the world, Mitchelson later thought, Khashoggi could thank him for making everyone think he was.

Mitchelson filed the breach-of-contract suit on Friday, August 3, 1979. The allegations in the suit were calculated to grab headlines.

It said that during their marriage, Soraya had advised Khashoggi on business deals, explained contracts written in English, and "engaged in banking transactions in Switzerland and elsewhere for top executives of Khashoggi's American principals, assisted in delivering a gift of expensive jewelry to a daughter of then President Richard M. Nixon, and delivered gifts of cash to one of the princes of Saudi Arabia and to the parties' American principals and their 'ladies.'"

She asked for $2 billion, which she said was half his wealth, plus damages and other payments that brought the total to $2.5 billion.

On Sunday, Mitchelson and Sarch visited Khashoggi's airplanes—the DC-9 and the Boeing 727 used by Khashoggi's brother Essam. Both were at Los Angeles area airports, and newspapers throughout the country ran photos of Mitchelson inspecting them, apparently to try to serve the legal complaint on them.

When Rhoden heard about it, he chuckled. It seemed Mitchelson was trying to emphasize how often Khashoggi was in California. It was good soap opera, Rhoden thought, but would not help the case.

On Monday, Mitchelson filed a separate divorce suit. This was the backup action that covered all bets. If the breach-of-contract suit lost, then she sought a divorce and half his wealth accumulated during their marriage.

Khashoggi was on his yacht the *Nabila* when he heard about the lawsuit. He called Edward P. Morgan, his lawyer in Washington, and asked him to take care of it. Morgan hired Joseph A. Ball, a Los Angeles–based lawyer, to represent Khashoggi.

The former senior counsel to the Warren Commission, Ball was senior partner of Ball, Hunt, Hart, Brown and Baerwitz, which already represented Khashoggi in his arbitration case against Northrop Corp.

In meetings with his lawyers, Khashoggi was adamant that he was not going to be summoned into court in California to respond to a complaint concerning his marital status and obligations to his wife.

In Saudi Arabia, where women exist to have children and accommodate men, it takes the testimony of two women to equal the weight of one man's. While a man needs no grounds to divorce his wife, grounds for a woman to divorce a man are limited and difficult to prove.

At the same time, Khashoggi recognized an obligation to provide for Soraya Khashoggi, as the mother of his children. Islamic tradition was clear on the point: The eldest son takes responsibility for his mother if his father does not.

But Khashoggi was not going to bow to pressure in the form of a public lawsuit.

With friends, Khashoggi tried to put on a brave front: "I couldn't pay for all the publicity I'm getting from this," he told one associate. But the ever-larger headlines that accompanied Mitchelson's disclosures were tearing at him.

Khashoggi blamed Sarch, not Mitchelson, for goading his former wife into suing. He had never liked him, and he liked him even less when he impounded his plane at London's Heathrow Airport.

The incident arose out of a separate lawsuit Sarch filed against Khashoggi in England. It said he failed to pay rent promised to Soraya Khashoggi for the use of her Eaton Square town house after she remarried and moved out. To ensure that the rent would be paid, Sarch got the court to temporarily attach the plane.

One Sunday evening, Samuel M. Evans, the general counsel of Triad Holding Corp., got a call at his London home. It was Shaheen, and he was so livid he could barely speak.

"They've impounded the plane!" he shouted, using his most dramatic delivery.

"What do you mean, Bob?" Evans said.

"They've blocked the DC-9," Shaheen said.

In his role as nanny, Shaheen was supposed to use the DC-9 to take Khashoggi's kids back to school in Lausanne the next day, Shaheen explained.

"Come out here." Shaheen insisted.

Evans knew there was nothing to be accomplished on a Sunday night except to hold Shaheen's hand. But he drove out to the sprawling airport, where a crane was positioned squarely in front of the plane, a hangar blocking the rear.

He boarded the plane that he had been on a hundred times before. Shaheen was still incensed, but Sarch and Mohamed Khashoggi, Khashoggi's eldest son, were seated across from each other over a table. The two were sipping bourbon and playing two-handed poker.

"What are you playing for?" Evans asked.

"The plane," Sarch said, looking up at Evans.

When the SEC's Michael F. Perlis read about Soraya Khashoggi's charges in the *Washington Post*, he picked up the phone and called Mitchelson.

"I'd like to meet with Soraya Khashoggi," he said. "Can we schedule a time in Washington?"

Perlis had largely forgotten about Khashoggi since he testified before him a year earlier at SEC headquarters. But the charges about Nixon and payoffs tantalized him. If Soraya Khashoggi would talk, it might blow the case wide open.

Perlis had heard of Khashoggi paying bribes to foreign officials. But Khashoggi paying bribes to American executives, as she seemed to be claiming, was new. It could be the start of a different ball game.

He arranged to meet with her on Tuesday, August 21, at

10 A.M. Wearing a purple polka-dot dress, Soraya Khashoggi sat at a table that adjoined Perlis' desk at SEC headquarters.

He had heard that she went braless. It seemed to him to be true.

Mitchelson did most of the talking. He said his client feared that if she testified against Khashoggi, he would deprive her of her children.

"Khashoggi is a man with a lot of power," he said. "Saudi law gives the husband the upper hand."

Trying to concentrate on what she was saying instead of her revealing dress, Perlis attempted to find out what Soraya knew. But Mitchelson was not ready to let his client talk and told Perlis less than what he had already read about the suit in the newspapers.

When Mitchelson and Soraya left SEC headquarters, fourteen reporters, photographers, and television cameramen converged on them. Later, an Associated Press shot of Mitchelson escorting Soraya, her purse thrown back over her shoulder, appeared in the *New York Times* and other newspapers throughout the country.

By tipping off the press, Mitchelson had turned up the pressure on Khashoggi. It appeared from the photograph that she must have talked. Why else would she be going to the SEC?

When Mitchelson got back to Los Angeles, Perlis pursued him on the phone. If she testified about Khashoggi, Mitchelson said he wanted his client given immunity from prosecution. But the Justice Department doesn't grant immunity willy-nilly. First, it wants to know what a witness will say. Usually, this is done in the form of a proffer outlining the key points to be discussed.

Mitchelson wouldn't go for it.

To Perlis, it was clear that Mitchelson was trying to put the fear of God in Khashoggi by parading Soraya around and leaking to the press. Every time the SEC talked to her or to him, there was another story in the papers.

Perlis and Sporkin decided to take a tougher approach. They issued a subpoena to force her to testify at the SEC's Los Angeles office.

With a queen's gambit in mind, Mitchelson seized the opportunity to call John R. McDonough, the partner in the Ball firm who did much of the work on the case for Khashoggi. Mitchelson said he would come to McDonough's office, on a side street off Wilshire Boulevard near the Beverly Wilshire Hotel.

Informing him that Soraya had been subpoenaed, Mitchelson told McDonough that she would be forced to testify about Khashoggi's business affairs unless she could claim they were still husband and wife. He suggested that Khashoggi concede that the two were still legally married and that the California courts were the proper forum for the case.

"If you do that," he said, "Soraya Khashoggi will plead the marital privilege when questioned by the SEC."

"You have got no case," declared McDonough, a former Stanford University School of Law professor who had been with the Ball firm since 1970.

Khashoggi wasn't going to be blackmailed.

On October 4, 1979, Soraya appeared at the SEC's Westwood office and invoked her Fifth Amendment privilege against self-incrimination.

This time, when Rhoden accompanied Soraya to the SEC, there were no photographers waiting outside.

The publicity surrounding the divorce action paled before a much larger media event that arose three months later and focused spectacular international attention on Soraya Khashoggi.

It began when she arrived at London's Heathrow airport and noticed $300,000 in jewels missing from her luggage. She accused a porter of taking it, but he was acquitted. Eighteen months later, three Scotland Yard detectives approached her. They demanded $13,200 or they would charge her with perjury for making up the charges against the porter, allegedly to support an insurance claim.

She reported the shakedown attempt to Scotland Yard, which assigned an army of detectives to follow her around while she taped her conversations with the crooked officers.

One evening, she was wearing her concealed tape recorder as one of the detectives drove her around London. The posse of Scotland Yard detectives lost her, and just then, the detective in the car said to her, "If I find you're using a tape recorder, I'll kill you."

Once the officers were charged, they visited Soraya's housekeeper, Ellen Smith, trying to enlist her help in turning up dirt on Soraya. From her, they learned about Soraya's longstanding affair with a world-renowned British politician. Now the officers threatened to expose her if she didn't drop her complaint against them.

At the trial of the detectives, Soraya took the witness stand

and admitted to having the affair, which she said was "common knowledge" in her household. She wrote the name of the politician on a slip of paper, which was handed to the judge and the jury. In the courtroom, the celebrity was referred to only as "Mr. X."

The trial at the Old Bailey Criminal Court in December 1979 enlivened an otherwise cold, damp, and dark British winter. The spectacle of the voluptuous, exotic beauty admitting to having an affair with a mysterious British politician made sensational reading and immediately raised troubling questions about breaches of national security.

Only the previous month, the queen's art adviser, Anthony Blunt, had been revealed to have spied for the Soviets during World War II. He had been allied with Britain's most notorious postwar spies: Guy Burgess, Donald MacLean, and Kim Philby.

The proceedings at the Old Bailey also revived memories of the Profumo affair of 1963, when British War Minister John Profumo resigned after confessing to a sexual relationship with prostitute Christine Keeler, who was dallying with the Soviet naval attaché at the same time.

As the trial of the Scotland Yard detectives proceeded, the word spread that the name on the slip of paper was that of the dashing Winston Churchill, the grandson of the wartime prime minister.

Born at Chequers in 1940, Churchill was named for his grandfather at the insistence of his mother, the daughter of the 11th Baron Digby. After a proper British education at Eton and Oxford, Churchill acquired a small airplane and journeyed to Africa with a friend. His experiences there formed the basis for his first book, *First Journey.* Jobs as a foreign correspondent with a number of British newspapers followed.

His reportage and a second book, *Six Day War*, catapulted him into the public eye, and he made his first race for a seat in the House of Commons in 1967. He lost by 577 votes.

On his second try, in 1970, he was elected from Manchester and rose rapidly to become the opposition spokesman on defense. This made him a likely candidate for a cabinet post in a future Conservative government.

But he opposed Margaret Thatcher when she decided, as Conservative Party leader in Parliament, to support the then Labour government in maintaining British economic sanctions against Ian Smith's former white minority government in

Rhodesia. When Thatcher became prime minister, Churchill's name was absent from the list of government appointments.

Asked once about the advantages of his name, Churchill said, "I've never found it a liability, except when it comes to being bonked over the head in Chicago."

In 1968, he was covering the Democratic Party convention when he asked a police officer for his badge number. The officer had just bopped several anti–Vietnam War demonstrators over the head.

"What's your name?" the officer countered.

"Winston Churchill," he replied.

Recognizing a wise guy when he saw one, the officer and several fellow policemen roughed him up and tossed Churchill over a twelve-foot embankment.

Now two Labour Party members were demanding that Thatcher launch an investigation into the identity of Mr. X to determine if any defense secrets had been compromised.

"Parliament is entitled to the assurance that the politician concerned did not have access to sensitive defense material," thundered opposition Labour legislator James Wellbeloved.

With rumors circulating all over the world that he was Mr. X, Churchill authorized his solicitor, Lord Goodman, to issue a statement to the press.

"To avoid further speculation affecting other members of Parliament," he said, "Mr. Winston Churchill MP has instructed us to state that the name written down in recent criminal proceedings at the Old Bailey—but not published—was that of Mr. Churchill."

"THE NAME WAS THAT OF MR. CHURCHILL," the headlines screamed the next day.

The clean-cut, blue-eyed, blond Churchill was married, with two daughters. He had been a rising political star. Now his reputation was in tatters. He had been having an affair with a sultry jet-setter, married first to a Middle East arms dealer and then to her twenty-year-old daughter's ex-boyfriend.

Churchill's wife issued her own statement, saying her husband had already told her about the affair, which was over. She said the Churchills were now "absolutely happy."

The absolutely happy family then paraded past photographers and reporters at the London Palladium to attend a holiday performance of *The King and I.*

By Christmas, the London tabloids were running their

smiling pictures with the headline: "THE HAPPY CHURCHILLS TO-GETHER."

That same month, Mitchelson and Rhoden took Khashoggi's deposition as part of the fact-finding process required to make their case. Their claim that the lawsuit should be tried in the California courts was tenuous, and they wanted to establish as many contacts between California and Khashoggi as they could.

The lawyers took the deposition at Khashoggi's Olympic Tower residence at 641 Fifth Avenue, where the elevator operator escorted them to Khashoggi's door.

Entering a small foyer, they encountered Khashoggi's two Korean bodyguards, Keel and Lee. They weren't physically big men but they were imposing because of the way they stood— feet apart, eyes down, ready to spring into action. The look on their faces said it all: One false move, and you're dead.

Khashoggi sat the two lawyers at a large round table. Khashoggi mentioned that he was on a diet, but during the testimony, he munched on mixed nuts from a bowl. They were the good kind, with lots of cashews and no peanuts.

Rhoden was a cashew fan, and he wanted some.

During a lunch break, he remarked to Mitchelson, "The guy didn't even offer us any nuts."

Khashoggi answered the questions about his life with Soraya calmly, except when a question came up about his religion. He took it to be a slur, and he said, "You're attacking my religion."

Rhoden thought he was looking for something to get angry about. A man is always right when defending his religion.

On the second day of the testimony, Mitchelson and Rhoden met Khashoggi in the elevator as they were going up to his apartment. He was with a striking, tall blonde who looked about eighteen. She was very pretty and very sweet.

Khashoggi was facing her in the elevator, looking straight at her, which put his eyes on the level of her bosom.

Disguising their resentment, Rhoden and Mitchelson looked at each other and winked. It seemed to them he was enjoying letting them know he was getting a lot of pretty young stuff.

Meanwhile, on the West Coast, Soraya Khashoggi was giving her deposition at the offices of the Ball law firm in Beverly Hills. The secretaries lined up to get a glimpse of her as she walked in, but they were disappointed. She was wearing a shawl and a long dress.

During a break, McDonough asked his secretary what she thought.

"Well, she's pregnant," she said.

"Pregnant!" he exclaimed.

Taking her deposition, he asked Soraya who the father was.

"None of your business," she said.

In July 1980, she gave birth to her seventh child, Petrina Camille Cecilia Khashoggi, a nine-pound eight-ounce blond girl.

She never revealed who the father was.

Now Mitchelson escalated his "public relations" work.

Claiming that it helped show that Khashoggi was a resident of the U.S. and should be tried by the California courts, he told the *New York Daily News* that Khashoggi had fathered a child born at Good Samaritan Hospital in West Palm Beach, Florida.

Born to Laura Biancolini, who later became Khashoggi's second wife, he was a handsome child named Ali.

The fact that Khashoggi had fathered a child born in a U.S. hospital had no connection with the legal issues but made good copy. It was clear to McDonough that Mitchelson hoped to win a settlement of the case by seizing on embarrassing disclosures.

He considered many of the other charges to be irrelevant. Soraya claimed she brought a $60,000 bracelet into the U.S. for one of Nixon's daughters. Ostensibly, the idea was to show that the bracelet was delivered in California, helping to establish Khashoggi's connection with that state.

Once, Khashoggi had remarked that if Nixon had asked him for $1 million, he would have given it to him. But Nixon denied his family had received any such gift from Khashoggi and successfully resisted testifying in the case.

Then Soraya said she opened Swiss bank accounts for some executives of California aerospace companies, that Khashoggi procured prostitutes for these same California executives, and that he gave gifts of up to $25,000 to their mistresses.

The executives weren't named, and the companies said the allegations were too vague for them to give a response.

But some of the material was quite specific. One executive admitted under oath that he had received a $20,000 cash bribe from Khashoggi. Already retired, the man later pleaded with

Rhoden to strike his name from the record because his reputation would be ruined in his last years.

Rhoden agreed to his request, and the testimony of "Mr. Executive," as he was referred to in the proceedings, never got picked up by the press.

Then there was an affidavit of James Flannery, Khashoggi's former butler, who said Khashoggi imported call girls from California to his Olympic Tower apartment in New York.

"I have lived in New York City for approximately the last twenty years," Flannery said in the affidavit. "I previously lived in the United Kingdom, of which I am a subject. My profession for the last twenty years has been that of a gentleman's butler. For approximately the last thirty-three months, I worked for Essam Khashoggi at Olympic Tower at 641 Fifth Avenue."

Flannery said in the affidavit that he and his wife, who worked as a maid at the apartment, decided to terminate their employment in March 1980, mainly because of his "complete disgust with Adnan, because the Olympic Tower residence had been turned into an actual bordello. There was a countless and endless stream of young women being brought in from Europe and from throughout the country, particularly Texas and California.

"These women were brought in to supply the needs of Adnan, and I was asked by Bob Shaheen, Adnan's personal secretary, to throw some of the women out when Adnan tired of them, often on less than five minutes' notice. I resented the imposition of these unprofessional duties and refused to carry them out," Flannery said.

When the affidavit was filed, Mitchelson made sure the press knew about it.

"A British butler, the latest witness to surface in the bitter $2.5 billion divorce case of Adnan and Soraya Khashoggi, says in a sworn affidavit that the Saudi Arabian billionaire ran a house of prostitution," an AP story said.

McDonough immediately moved to have the filings sealed, at least until Khashoggi could respond. Commenting on the butler's allegations, the lawyer said only that Flannery had been "faithless" to his employer because he kept a draft of a contract that had been tossed in a wastebasket.

When another juicy affidavit was filed—this one from a Beverly Hills writer and actor—the press never found out about it.

Sean Walsh, then thirty-one, said in his affidavit that he attended a Beverly Hills party given by a female friend in October 1974. There, he met a man who introduced himself as Samir Traboulsi, an associate of Khashoggi's.

Slim and dashing, Traboulsi was a Lebanese who met Khashoggi in 1964. Ten years younger than Khashoggi, he could obtain sophisticated girls for Khashoggi's parties in as little as thirty minutes.

Over the years, Khashoggi cut him in on business deals, and he became a highly successful businessman. His Paris office, protected by a sliding electronic door, was decorated with paintings by Matisse and cubist Juan Gris.

At the Beverly Hills party, Walsh quoted Traboulsi as saying he was associated with one of the richest men in the world, a man by the name of Khashoggi, who owned jet aircraft and currently was staying at the Beverly Hills Hotel.

He said Khashoggi wanted to "relax for a few days" and asked if Walsh could provide female companions who wanted to have a good time. They would be paid thousands of dollars just for having dinner with Khashoggi and his friends.

Traboulsi denied in an affidavit ever hearing of Walsh.

After calling virtually every woman he knew, Walsh said he rounded up thirty to present later that same evening. At about 11 P.M., Walsh and the women arrived at the hotel and were directed to two bungalows in the back, numbers 3 and 10, where Khashoggi always stayed.

Before introducing the women to Khashoggi, Traboulsi selected fifteen blondes. The rest were dismissed, according to his affidavit.

As the evening progressed, Khashoggi, wearing a *thobe*, became friends with Walsh and asked if he would like to travel with him, along with Traboulsi, Shaheen, and eight other people.

Over the next three days, the group continued to party at the hotel. At the height of it, Traboulsi, with Khashoggi present, showed Walsh two suitcases crammed with $100 and $500 bills. Traboulsi said the suitcases contained money which Khashoggi used for "business dealings in California and gambling in Las Vegas," Walsh said.

Noticing Walsh's surprise, Traboulsi assured him that the money was but "pocket change" to Khashoggi.

Late the second night, two brand-new Porsches arrived. Paid for in cash, they were given to two of the young women.

On the third night, the group went to Au Petit, a Hollywood restaurant, where Walsh met a Hollywood actress and a young foreign woman introduced as "the contessa"—Laura Bianco-lini's nickname.

Later that evening, Walsh related, Shaheen gave him $1,000 in cash, telling him Khashoggi wanted him to buy new clothing with the money. He instructed him to meet the group at the Sands Hotel in Las Vegas.

During the next five days, Walsh was constantly with Khashoggi, Traboulsi, Shaheen, the contessa, and about ten of the original women as they gambled and were entertained.

At one such session, Walsh said Khashoggi gave him more than $20,000 to participate in a crap game at the Tropicana Hotel in Las Vegas.

Then they returned to Beverly Hills, where Khashoggi suddenly departed.

Again in January 1975, Walsh said, Khashoggi invited him for two nights of partying at the Beverly Hills Hotel. A month after that, he got two round-trip, first-class tickets in the mail, with an invitation to come to Paris for a *chemin de fer*, or gambling party.

To Mitchelson, the significance of Walsh's story was not in the girls but in the Porsches, which he said were given for services rendered in California.

McDonough knew from personal experience that Khashoggi surrounded himself with beautiful women. Yet from a legal standpoint, he considered Walsh's affidavit to be fatuous.

For the oral arguments before Superior Court Judge John A. Loomis, Soraya Khashoggi showed up in the bustling Los Angeles courthouse dressed in a bright yellow and red dress and a big, red, full-brimmed hat, with yellow stockings and red shoes. The next day, she wore a purple jump suit with white piping, a big white hat, and white boots.

She looked luscious, if out of place in the dreary courtroom.

The only question before the judge was whether the case should be heard in California. Beyond the two days of arguments, there were no other appearances. All of the evidence—eleven boxes of it—had been presented in writing.

Three months later, on June 7, 1981, the judge issued a thirty-two-page opinion. He ruled against Soraya Khashoggi on every point.

"The court finds that plaintiff ... was not a permanent resident of California when this action was filed," Loomis said.

Rather, she came to California "for the principal purpose of filing and prosecuting actions against the defendant."

Citing her immigration application, the judge said she requested a temporary extension of her stay in the U.S. to "aid litigation under way/give depositions."

The judge also said he had no jurisdiction over Khashoggi, since his contacts in California are neither "wide-ranging" nor "systematic."

"In the interest of substantial justice," he said, the lawsuit should be "heard in an English forum."

After the suit had occupied the front pages of many newspapers for months, the outcome rated only a 404-word AP story.

Mitchelson appealed, but before a record of the proceedings could be sent to the appellate court, Khashoggi agreed to settle the case.

His oldest children, Mohamed and Nabila, had been distraught at the publicity, made even worse by interviews Soraya Khashoggi gave to the *Daily Star* in London about her affair with Churchill. When Nabila took an overdose of pills, Soraya tried unsuccessfully to stop publication.

The two children urged their father to give Soraya something, and *Al-Riyadh*, Saudi Arabia's leading newspaper, weighed in with an editorial criticizing Khashoggi for failing to invest in Saudi Arabia and allowing personal scandal to taint his homeland.

"Isn't the gossip about your personal life damaging to the reputation of the country?" the paper asked.

Without the knowledge of her lawyers, Evans, Khashoggi's general counsel, met secretly with Soraya at Mohamed's home in Salt Lake City, where Khashoggi's son was attending the University of Utah. Khashoggi had maintained all along he would take care of her, but not until he had won.

Evans heard out her complaints and then recommended a settlement to Khashoggi.

The amount remained a secret. When reporters asked Mitchelson about it, he said, "I'm smiling, aren't I?"

The British press latched on to a figure of $100 million, but the true amount was considerably less—$2 million, plus $10,000 a month for life. Given the interest rates at the time, Khashoggi's lawyers figured the total package—which was never revealed—was worth $3 million.

It wasn't the billions she had asked for, but it was enough

to maintain a decent life-style, complete with a London flat and a country home.

Called Five Meadows, the house stands back from a country road in Headley, near Newbury, England. The size of an average suburban home, it is surrounded by a high wall to discourage intruders, but the gate is left open. The lawn near the driveway has become muddied from pickup trucks that park in front of her garage. The home itself has a tile roof and leaded-glass windows. A blond baby-sitter looks after Soraya's two younger children.

As part of the settlement, Soraya Khashoggi had to turn over the manuscript of a book she was writing and refrain from talking to the press about her former husband. Said to be so hot that it had to be kept in a Swiss bank vault, the book so lacked new disclosures that lawyers for both sides yawned when they read it.

A year after the court decision, Soraya married a third time, this time to Arthur Ringwalt Rupley IV, the twenty-two-year-old former boyfriend of actress Britt Ekland. Reputedly the heir to a real estate fortune in Virginia, he had met Soraya eighteen months earlier at a party.

They were married in a two-minute ceremony in the chapel of New York City Municipal Clerk David Dinkins. His deputy, Herb Ryan, fetched a witness out in the hall—the next man waiting to be married.

Rupley told the *Washington Post* that he loves Soraya, then pregnant with her eighth child, for her beauty.

"Looks mean a lot to me," he confided. "For forty-two and eight children, she's absolutely stunning."

In the same interview, he admitted to being a "flighty" person.

"If somebody comes up to me and I find her more exciting than Soraya Khashoggi, well, that's the way it goes. Soraya Khashoggi knows this," he said. "She knows she has to keep me happy."

Less than a year later, the marriage was over, and Soraya Khashoggi was in court again, this time asking that Rupley be jailed for violating a court directive that he stop pestering her with calls.

The father of her eighth child was never revealed.

• • •

In October 1984, Khashoggi flew friends from all over the world to a black-tie party in Vienna for Mohamed Khashoggi. It was his twenty-first birthday, and for the occasion, Khashoggi rented the Auersberg Palace, once the scene of royal concerts played for nobility by Mozart, Beethoven, and Wagner.

To put the guests up, Khashoggi took over most of the Intercontinental Hotel, reserving the top floor for himself.

The guests included Chrysler Chairman Lee A. Iacocca; Robert Mitterrand, the brother of the French president; and dukes and duchesses from all over Europe, including the duchess of Seville, Princess Bridgett of Sweden, and Prince and Princess Von Thurn Und Taxis, two of the continent's richest aristocrats. All of Khashoggi's children were there as well, including Khaled, who was attending Princeton University, and Omar and Hussein, who were going to school in Switzerland.

After receiving a gold rose as a memento of the event, the guests arrived in carriages drawn by white horses, then compared their chestnut-size jewels. The menu included Russian caviar, smoked Norwegian salmon, wild pheasant soup, filet of Dover sole in white wine sauce, Viennese veal with forest mushrooms, omelette surprise, and Viennese pastries, cheese, and fruit.

The Vienna Boys Choir and the cast of *Cats* provided entertainment, followed by a twenty-one-gun salute and fireworks.

Out of one of the carriages pranced Soraya Khashoggi, who sat at the head table. Khashoggi's stunning wife, Lamia, sat at another table.

After Mohamed blew out the candles on a cake shaped like a globe, the guests sang, "He's Got the Whole World in His Hands."

Then Soraya kissed him, followed by Lamia.

To friends, Khashoggi explained his first wife's presence: "She's the mother of my children."

# The Yachts

Those who spend their wealth by night and day, by stealth and openly, verily their reward is with their Lord, and there shall be no fear come upon them, neither shall they grieve.

—*The Koran*

**A**T the height of his divorce battle with Soraya Khashoggi, Khashoggi took delivery of his custom-built, 282-foot yacht, the *Nabila*.

Called by Time-Life's *The Luxury Yachts* the "most opulent modern yacht afloat," it was a movable city with its own discotheque, helicopter and landing pad, operating room for medical emergencies, swimming pool, high speed motorboats, and communications center with forty-five Touch-Tone telephones for placing calls worldwide.

Named for his only daughter, the $70-million vessel was Khashoggi's third yacht. A smaller yacht, the *Khalidia*, usually cruised in the Caribbean. Another yacht, the *Mohamedia*, burned in a French shipyard when a worker was using a blowtorch.

The *Nabila* was Khashoggi's escape. More than his twelve

residences, more than his three commercial-size airplanes, this was where Khashoggi felt at home.

The boat could be found anywhere from the China Seas to the Gulf of Mexico.

"The entire world is our port," the captain of the *Nabila* boasted when queried by a newspaper reporter in Monte Carlo.

But usually, the *Nabila*, with its name in raised gold letters on each side, could be found on the shimmering Mediterranean, where it drew envious glances from industrial tycoons and movie stars and was the locus for Khashoggi's only sport, water skiing, done from behind his $150,000 speedboat.

Decorated in beiges by Roman designer Luigi Sturchio, the 1,800-ton vessel was built at a shipyard owned by Lorenzo and M. B. Benetti in Viareggio, Italy. In July 1980, it was ready to sail.

Borrowed by Hollywood for the James Bond movie *Never Say Never Again*, the yacht has a crew of forty and is capable of speeds up to twenty-one knots generated by its two 3,000-horsepower engines.

Via a communications pod that bounces signals off satellites, Khashoggi can talk or exchange computer data with any of his homes, offices, or Rolls-Royces all over the world. The yacht's bridge is equipped with an auto pilot, three radars, satellite guidance, an Atlas ecosounder, and an aeronautical VHF for communicating with the yacht's own Augusta 109 helicopter and Khashoggi's fleet of airplanes.

The boat has eight staterooms, including two master suites—one for Khashoggi and a smaller one for his daughter.

In addition, there are six guest suites of identical design—each with an entrance hall, boudoir, bedroom with walls of Chinese lacquer, and bathroom of onyx.

Each suite is named for a precious stone and varies in color from lapis lazuli and topaz to emerald and ruby. The suites and staterooms come equipped with a television set that appears and disappears, swivels and rises, at the touch of a button at a bedside console.

Khashoggi's stateroom has mirrored ceilings, abstract art, and controls to open and shut the curtains from his ten-foot-wide bed. Miniature waterfalls enliven the marble bathtubs in several of the bathrooms.

The dining room gleams with a long Chinese lacquered table flanked by sixteen white leather chairs.

The spacious main salon is lighted softly from above and

furnished with suede- and silk-covered couches, the walls draped with Thai wall hangings. The curved bronze bar is, in fact, a sculpture by Gio Pomodoro. A mirrored grand piano was a gift to Lamia Khashoggi from Liberace.

Soft chamois leather is used extensively on wall and ceiling panels—removable to give access to the network of cables and tubes they conceal.

The on-board movie theater has a library of eight hundred films and video tapes. Cocooned in dark leather panels, it's furnished with deeply cushioned chairs, each the size of a sofa.

Poolside on the top deck, which is surrounded by bullet-proof glass, a platform covered with cushions rises hydraulically high above the deck, so Khashoggi and his guests can sunbathe nude in privacy. Khashoggi can get to the pool directly from his bedroom in his own elevator.

The full-size disco features gleaming, gilded bronze flooring and laser light shows and clouds of mist generated by controls operated by the disc jockey. Here, corporate executives rub elbows with stars ranging from Sean Connery and Farrah Fawcett to Koo Stark and Frank Sinatra—along with ever-present glamorous young women.

Most often, it is on the *Nabila* that Khashoggi throws his birthday parties. For his forty-eighth, he picked up two hundred guests at Monte Carlo, then cruised for two hours while his guests ate beluga caviar and sipped Dom Pérignon. At 9 P.M., the boat picked up two hundred more guests at Cannes, including Brooke Shields, David Niven, David Niven, Jr., and Stewart Copeland, the drummer from the Police rock band. His father, former CIA operative Miles Copeland, travels with Khashoggi to weight-loss spas in Germany.

The guests on board the *Nabila* dined on the finest duck, lamb, and venison, served on deck. At 7 A.M., having danced all night, they went home.

The next year, Morgan Fairchild attended a similar party on board the yacht. As a birthday present, Lamia gave her husband a five-inch gold globe. Purchased from Bulgari jewelers in Monte Carlo, it had sapphire seas, diamond continents, and a ruby marking Mecca.

In the summer of 1981, the *Nabila* was cruising the Mediterranean with Hollywood actress Melissa Prophet on board. After stopping at Sardinia, the yacht sailed to Naples, where

Khashoggi heard that U.S. Navy pilots from the U.S.S. *Nimitz* had shot down two Libyan planes over the Mediterranean.

While the yacht was taking on fuel at the dock, some of the *Nimitz* pilots walked over and admired the boat. Hearing they were there, Khashoggi invited the crew on board.

After taking them on a tour, he had his chefs—two French, two Chinese, and two Arabian—whip up dinner. With a gleam in his eye, Khashoggi had the captain quietly haul anchor. Not until the curtains were pulled back after dinner did the four hundred pilots realize they were floating around the *Nimitz.*

"I'm kidnaping all of you and telling your country it can get you back for $1 billion," Khashoggi told the pilots.

"You should have seen their faces. You could tell they didn't kow what was going to happen to them," recalled Melissa Prophet.

The pilots nervously declined his offer to take them to Sardinia for three days and danced away their sorrows in the yacht's mirror-ceilinged discotheque.

Just the night before, they had seen Prophet in *Van Nuys Boulevard*, shown on board the *Nimitz.* One of the officers was so taken with the former Miss California, who recently starred in *Invasion USA*, that he asked Khashoggi for her hand in marriage.

"All summer, we had the most beautiful people on board, but none of them—not Franco Zeffirelli, not any of them—was as much fun as those guys from the *Nimitz*," Prophet said later.

Mireille Griffon picked up the ringing telephone in her luxury apartment on a bluff overlooking the Mediterranean. Beneath her were the twinkling lights of Monaco. It was just before midnight. The voice on the other end didn't need to be identified. It was a voice she knew from countless calls and meetings in the past ten months.

"I'm calling from the ship," the voice said. "Everything is okay. Everyone's very happy. The captain is with the four chicks. He dressed them up with Christian Dior dresses at two thousand francs each."

The voice went on: "Is there still some money that he owes you?"

"Yes, two of my girls weren't paid," Griffon said.

"Okay, I'll tell them to pay you pretty fast," he said.

The caller was Abdo Khawagi, a short Lebanese man who once was secretary and masseur to Adnan Khashoggi and now worked for him as a part-time agent on specific tasks. He was calling from the *Nabila*, moored off the coast of nearby Cannes.

To disguise Khashoggi's identity, Griffon and Khawagi always referred to Khashoggi as "the captain."

Griffon smiled at the irony. Before she met Khawagi, she worked in Monaco at an American stock brokerage firm. Her job was supervising cleaning women at night. Now she still supervised women at night—and was getting rich.

Griffon had a job many would envy: She was madam to the richest man in the world. Khashoggi accounted for 50 percent of her business, and he was paying hundreds of thousands of dollars for her services.

It had all happened so quickly. Ten months before the June 2, 1983, telephone call, she was dining at a chic Monaco restaurant with a friend. They were musing about Prince Rainier's toyland, the thirteen-square-mile principality whose chief reason for existing is the world's most famous gambling casino.

With its white sandy beaches, posh hotels, and picturesque towns, Monaco seemed to have everything—or did it? Perhaps there was something missing, Griffon's friend suggested.

"It needs nice girls," Griffon said.

Griffon was not thinking of schoolgirls or chorus girls. She had in mind escort girls—refined and lovely women able to make good conversation with the rich and famous who came to Monaco to absorb the glamour and gamble at Monte Carlo.

Born in Paris, the daughter of a model and a railroad man, Griffon yearned to be part of that world—to wear diamonds from Cartier and step from a flashy sports car into the Hôtel de Paris or the casino at Monte Carlo.

All her life, she had worked hard. In the north of France, she shoveled coal in the mines at the age of twelve. At various times, she lived with families on farms, earning her keep by making butter and doing other chores. She was sent to a Catholic boarding school. But her mother didn't pay her tuition, so she ended up working for the nuns.

Eventually, Griffon returned to Paris, becoming a salesgirl. She married and had three boys. After divorcing, she moved to Cap d'Ail, a French village that abuts Monaco. There, she tended to attract pretty models as friends. They provided her with glimpses of a life she had only dreamed about.

Slim, with high cheekbones, Griffon could almost have been a model herself. She had long red hair, pretty brown eyes, and an upturned nose. Only her rough hands suggested her impoverished background, and her age—forty-one—made her an unlikely candidate as a fresh-faced cover girl.

Now her liking for model friends and her liking for money began to come together in her head. She saw her chance. Griffon asked one of these friends if she would accept escort assignments from her. The girl agreed, and Griffon found that getting clients was no problem. There were always men who craved attractive company, and she could pay friends to refer them to her. But one of her first clients said it was more than company that he wanted.

"I don't need a green plant," he said.

Madame Mimi, as she came to be called, was happy to meet the need. She called her service the Select Models Agency.

A friend introduced her to Khawagi, who did odd jobs for Khashoggi when needed. For the favor, she paid the friend 5,000 francs.

Khawagi was eager to please his boss, and the two struck a deal: Khawagi would swing Khashoggi's business to her, and he would act as paymaster. This would increase his importance to Khashoggi. From errand boy, he advanced to chief procurer.

Until she met him, Griffon was doing a retail business, servicing mainly Arab clients. With the addition of Khashoggi to her roster, Griffon became a wholesaler with a cash flow that made her dizzy.

She didn't need to be told who Khashoggi was. On the Riviera, a Garden of Eden that stretches like a necklace from Marseille to Menton and includes Nice, Cannes, and Monaco, Khashoggi is a legend. When not in Marbella or some other exotic port, it is here, on the Côte d'Azur, that the *Nabila* often sits like a New York skyscraper in the clear azure waters off Cannes.

This is Khashoggi's playground, with tales constantly bruited about of the parties on board and the stunning girls who always seemed to be arriving on the ship like chocolate-chip cookies being popped into an oven.

It was Khawagi, a man with a high forehead and thinning hair, who did the popping. Like most of the people who worked for Khashoggi, Khawagi had multiple duties. That was the Arab way. An economist who works for a wealthy Arab investor might analyze the stock market, but he might also act as receptionist. He could be summoned to plug in a tape recorder.

When he was employed full-time for Khashoggi, Khawagi administered Khashoggi's daily massage, which he had upon waking. Since that could be at 8 A.M. or 3 P.M., Khawagi always had a lot of free time on his supple hands. Gradually, he assumed other duties as well. As a part-time agent for Khashoggi, he arranged parties on the boat, hired the limousines, and saw to the delivery of the gifts Khashoggi bought on irrepressible spending sprees: He would shell out $60,000 in a one-hour stroll around Cannes.

On his first meeting with Griffon, Khawagi told her of Khashoggi's strange appetites, appetites that had their roots in Khashoggi's upbringing in Saudi Arabia, where women's faces were always veiled.

From his uncle Yussuf Yassin, Khashoggi had learned how women can be obtained without the anxiety of dating. He had no time for it, and no stomach for it.

"Your women are a tillage for you, so come unto your tillage as you wish," said the Koran. Khashoggi took the injunction literally. He was a man of action. He had more important things to do than wait for a woman to decide if she wanted to go to bed.

What's more, Khashoggi learned from Yassin that women could be tools in his business; they create a more glamorous atmosphere and help provide access to those in power.

For Khashoggi, more of a good thing was always better. So, as his wealth grew, his thirst for women became unquenchable. He ordered ten for an evening, sharing them with friends, princes, and business associates and using them himself.

Over time, he became corrupted by his own wealth. The more girls he bought, the less they satisfied him. He always wanted fresh new faces and women who would outdo the previous ones.

It was not a side of him that he actively publicized. In the welter of feature articles about him over the years, the subject of call girls has never been mentioned. In 1985, when producer Robin Leach devoted an entire hour of his syndicated television show, *Lifestyles of the Rich and Famous*, to Khashoggi, the program dwelt on his home in Marbella, the *Nabila*, and the DC-8. It said nothing about call girls. Yet Khashoggi made little effort to conceal his liking for ladies of the night.

Before giving a deposition in an arbitration case against Northrop Corp., Khashoggi trooped into the lobby of the Frankfurter Hof Hotel in Frankfurt, Germany, his bodyguards enter-

ing first. They wore black silk shirts unbuttoned to the navel.
Aides hauled in dozens of pieces of luggage. Then came five
girls whose appearance gave the impression they were not of
the highest moral character. Sitting in the lobby were the three
arbitrators, including James A. Finch, Jr., a former chief justice
of the Missouri Supreme Court. They looked on, aghast.

Certainly, he was not the first man of greatness to have
an unorthodox sex life by Western standards. Hadn't Lord
Byron cavorted with dozens of prostitutes while maintaining
two mistresses on the side? Hadn't Warren G. Harding and
John F. Kennedy been relentless womanizers while married? If
Khashoggi carried it to extremes by demanding eight women
at one time, it was the way he did everything.

He had to surpass everyone else.

By the summer of 1982, Khashoggi was tiring of the women
being supplied to him on the *Nabila.* They were all the same.
They could not make conversation. What's more, they *looked*
like prostitutes. Khashoggi could buy the finest caviar and
champagne the way other people buy cigarettes. Why not the
best females?

The timing was fortuitous. Griffon was just starting her
agency, and her wares were just what a bored potentate de-
sired.

By now, she had left her job supervising cleaning ladies
and was operating full-time out of her Cap d'Ail apartment
on Avenue Savorani.

She recruited girls in bars and discotheques, and her standards were strict. Each girl must be between the ages of eighteen and twenty-four, as classy and elegant as possible, lively,
able to make conversation, and very, very clean. Griffon always
asked them to take off their shoes so she could see their feet.
Then she could tell, *tout de suite*, if they had good hygiene.

Griffon had a knack for choosing girls with just the right
combination of innocence and sexiness. Take Valerie, for instance. Most men would.

Twenty-one, blond, and blue-eyed, Valerie had incredibly
erect posture and breasts. She looked directly at men and smiled
easily. With a peaches-and-cream complexion, she was very
self-contained, very confident, yet had a playful tone to her
voice. She could pass for the knockout, innocent baby-sitter
down the street.

Or Anneli. She was an impressively endowed Swedish girl

with a slim build and ash blond hair that curled down to her breasts. Anneli was sultry and liked to pose in a black bathing suit cut up to her hips. She was enough to make any man forget whatever he was doing and stare.

Griffon dispatched the girls with the help of a beeper. Hearing the tone, a girl called Griffon's apartment for her next assignment. Yet Griffon was not in the business of selling meat. She was selling class, and she wanted everyone to enjoy the experience—her customers, her girls, and, of course, herself. For each customer, she took pains to select the girls she felt were the right ones.

To aid in that pursuit, she printed up "press books" with pictures of each girl. Similar to ones provided by real modeling agencies to their clients, the books each had thirty-five pages. On each page were three photos of the same girl in different poses. Many times, one of the poses was a reproduction of a cover from *Vogue* or European magazines such as *Grazia*, *Guide*, or *Pellicce Moda*.

On each page, Griffon listed the girl's first name. In smaller type, she listed her dimensions and the color of her hair and eyes. Anneli, for example, was listed as being five feet seven and a half inches tall. Her measurements were 35−25−34½. She had blue eyes and blond hair. Another girl, Asi, was five feet nine and a half inches tall. Her dimensions were 34−24−34. Diana's were 36−20−36.

Sometimes, Griffon showed the books to clients, but usually she looked at them herself and selected from them. Like a hostess serving moist pieces of chocolate cake at a birthday party, Griffon delighted in choosing the right slice and bestowing it with a flourish.

As time went on, Khashoggi and Griffon's other clients became even more demanding. Khashoggi would spot a comely playmate in *Playboy* or *Penthouse* and request that Griffon fetch her. Griffon would call the photographer and offer to share the fee if he would put her in touch with the girl.

At least fifteen times, Griffon performed this service, but she began to dread it. Each time, the girl would arrive from the United States, and Griffon would not recognize her. Perhaps the girl was pretty, but not nearly as pretty as in the retouched photos run by the magazines. So Griffon spent two days getting her in shape, tanning her on the beach and redoing her hair.

For her efforts, Griffon was justly rewarded. For a night, she charged 5,000 to 10,000 francs—$500 to $1,000. For a weekend, it was 20,000 to 30,000 francs—$2,000 to $3,000. She kept 40 percent, and the girls could keep any additional presents, which might include jewels, furs, or as much as $600 in cash. The centerfold girls were extra. They cost 150,000 francs, or $15,000, including the cost of their trip.

Having begun with a cadre of twenty girls, Griffon now had a battalion of three hundred working part-time for her. She did not want to tire her girls, so she limited their schedules to one engagement a day. At that pace, simple arithmetic indicates a full-time worker could net more than $100,000 a year, tax-exempt. Then there were the "tips" that could exceed the basic remuneration.

To Griffon, the agency was more than a business. It defined her image. She thought of herself as having surpassed Hernande Grunet, better known as Madame Claude, one of the most celebrated madams in French history.

For thirty years, Madame Claude specialized in providing the best women money could buy for French intelligence officers and chiefs of state. The women were flown on private jets all over the world for a weekend. In 1977, her service came to an end when a French court sentenced Madame Claude to jail and fined her 150,000 francs.

Griffon knew that Madame Claude took a higher cut than she did. She knew she required her girls to share their tips with her. That was not Griffon's way. She felt more like a friend to her girls. She felt responsible for them and gave them lessons in comportment. If the girls were tired, they could take a day off. Every two weeks, Griffon paid to have a doctor examine them.

The title of "brothel mother" did not bother her. Almost as much as she adored her two voluptuous cats, Lilah, a gray colorpoint from Canada, and Casanova, a Persian with champagne fur, Griffon cared about her girls.

Yet her concern didn't interfere with her business sense. When they reached the age of twenty-five, she retired them.

Griffon didn't want the girls to know who Khashoggi was. At first, she called him "the captain." Later, it was "the prince." But Khashoggi himself made no secret of his identity, and the girls soon developed their own nickname for him: *papa gâteau*—sugar daddy.

Much as others might offer chocolates or fruit after a meal, Khashoggi provided the girls to friends, associates, or members of the Saudi royal family. The liaisons were on the yacht, in the planes, in Khashoggi's homes, or in hotels in London, Paris, or Venice. There were baths in champagne and strange couplings—Khashoggi might order a call boy and a call girl to make an emir's evening more intriguing. Griffon always made sure the same call girl and call boy never went on an assignment together more than once. They might ruin everything by falling in love.

Khashoggi himself spent little time with the girls. They were mainly for show. They enhanced his image, giving him an aura of glamour and machismo. They gave him an edge over less glamorous competitors.

In his younger days, Khashoggi was a lion in bed. Now he might spend fifteen minutes with two or three of them in his ten-foot-wide bed. He would massage them and fondle them and play with them. They were a form of amusement, a droll side to Khashoggi such as moved him to list "people" as one of his hobbies in a biographical sketch.

The girls were Khashoggi's dolls, much like the presents he bought each year just before Christmas at a Las Vegas toy store called Wonder World. Wonder World is like a K mart, only bigger. He would go down the aisles, accompanied by the manager and five assistant managers.

"I'll have a dozen of these, and eight of those," he would say. The store trucked the toys out to the airport and loaded them on Khashoggi's Boeing 727 or DC-9, and the toys filled the planes to the gunnels. Like Santas on sleighs, the pilots flew the planes to one of Khashoggi's homes, where the toys were shipped to the children of Saudi princes and of executives of companies that Khashoggi did business with.

Perhaps most of all, Khashoggi craved the women for companionship. For all the glamorous people around him, for all the chiefs of state who dined at his table, Khashoggi was a profoundly lonely man. His wife Lamia had once been part of his entourage of girls, but for all her tanned good looks and intelligence, the Italian beauty could not fully satisfy Khashoggi's longing for company.

When Khashoggi went to Las Vegas to gamble, he kept his executives up until 4 A.M., insisting that they remain while he bet with thousand-dollar chips. It was a duty they abhorred, but they had little choice but to trail after him until they dropped from exhaustion. Then Khashoggi would make calls from his suite to friends or his executives all over the world.

The girls helped fill the void. Khashoggi treated the call girls to dinner and showered them with bracelets and dresses. If they wanted a sniff of cocaine during their romps, someone in Khashoggi's organization could supply it. Khashoggi was gentle with the girls, and they liked him.

At least one of Griffon's girls, Michelle, said she would give her services free for the caviar, the excitement, and the ambiance.

There were many Michelles.

*C'est un monde extraordinaire. C'est trop!* Griffon thought when she heard the girls' tales upon returning from the boat.

"It is too much!"

Roger W. Bencze, a captain in the French police force, thought so, too. A soft-spoken man with short hair, Bencze knew about Khawagi's June 2, 1983, telephone call to Griffon from the boat. He knew that Khashoggi was called "the captain." In fact, he knew almost everything about Griffon's operation.

Almost since its inception, Bencze had been investigating Griffon's modeling agency. For two weeks before the June 2 call, he had been wiretapping her telephone and compiling transcripts. Eventually, he had fifty-six hours of conversations.

Born in Ohio, Bencze had lived in France since his father was transferred to a U.S. military base there. On his discharge from the French navy, he joined the Gendarmerie.

The Gendarmerie has its origins in the eleventh century. Originally charged just with policing members of the military, it gradually assumed power over civilians as well. While it continues to report to the military, the force shares jurisdiction with the national police over crimes ranging from murder and fraud to prostitution and petty theft.

As a captain, Bencze was in charge of a company that extends to Nice, to Monaco, to the Alps, and to the Italian border, which is a fifteen-minute drive from his station. His headquarters were in a pink apartment building across from the bus terminal in Menton, a picturesque fishing village and sometime resort that is less plastic than Nice or Cannes.

Heading toward Italy, the coastline road from Cannes to Monaco hugs the steep hillsides of the Côte d'Azur, offering spectacular but vertiginous views of the sea hundreds of feet below. In the small towns, flat-faced houses painted pink, orange, and pale tangerine warm to the morning sun. At the larger ports, great ships and yachts stand out boldly white against the bright blue water.

There is no border check between the principality of Monaco and its closest French neighbor, Cap d'Ail, where Griffon made her headquarters. But one slows down, anyway. Cap d'Ail is quieter, with its tile-roofed houses perched on hillsides, houses that present daily miracles of resistance to gravity. There are backyard gardens, walls crowding up to the street. If Monaco is a queen, Cap d'Ail is a woman with a run in her stocking.

Farther east is Menton, full of orange trees and old men. At the foot of its main street lies the Mediterranean; at its head, the foothills of the Alps; in the middle, the town gardens and the station of the Menton Gendarmerie where, each morning at 8, the thirty-four-year-old Bencze met with his men. It was during such a meeting that Gean-Louis Duchène first reported hearing of Madame Griffon. Griffon had placed an ad for escort girls. A real cover girl had answered it. At Griffon's apartment in Cap d'Ail, she was told about the Arab princes who were Griffon's clients. The girl did not like the sound of it, and she mentioned it to a friend, who knew Duchène and told him.

Bencze ordered the story checked out. Within a month, he knew he had stumbled upon perhaps the biggest prostitution ring on the Riviera in fifteen years. Hundreds of girls pranced through Griffon's flat at all hours of the day and night. They drove up in sports cars and wore enough jewels to trim a Christmas tree.

Bencze turned the case over to Marceau Marcq, who headed his special investigative unit, telling him to find out how the organization worked, who the girls were, where they lived, the license plate numbers on their cars, and who supplied the clients.

Most of all, he wanted to know who paid for them. Under French law, it is not an offense to be a prostitute or to patronize one. It is an offense to be a *proxénète*—one who makes money off prostitution.

Each day, Bencze's officers recorded the names, addresses, and license plate numbers in black ink in a logbook. By May 1983, Bencze had compiled a list of the girls and had photographs of many of them. He called an assistant to Guy Robert, the government prosecutor. Bencze wanted a wiretap placed on Griffon's telephone line, and a commissioner promptly signed the order.

The telephone company connected Griffon's line to a small box near the floor, from which wires ran up the wall to a bulky Philips tape recorder.

Twenty-four hours a day, officers listened to the spicy conversations on a speaker. When a call began, the tape recorder started. The officers quickly wrote down the substance of the conversation in longhand. Later, the cassette was placed on another tape recorder and transcribed.

The telephone company recorded the telephone numbers that Griffon called, as well as those of the people who called her. These were listed as well in the logbook.

The first conversation heard by the officers took place on May 13, 1983. Almost immediately, the nature of the operation became clear. A customer called to ask for a German-speaking blonde. There was discussion of the price. Then Khawagi returned a call from Griffon. The two were arguing.

Khawagi had offended one of Griffon's girls by offering to pay her 5,000 francs for a weekend. *Bon dieu!*

Quoting the girl, Griffon said, "She said she wouldn't leave her apartment for 5,000 francs."

"Have her call me back and see if she dares speak to me like that!" Khawagi shot back. "Who is the boss?" he asked.

"Who is providing them?" Griffon asked.

In the end, it became apparent who was the boss. Khawagi agreed to pay 20,000 francs—$2,000—for the girl's services.

The demand for the girls came at any hour. Khashoggi had no schedule and the girls had to be supplied on a moment's notice—*tout de suite, tout de suite! Vite, vite, vite, toujours vite.*

As word of the operation spread, people were attracted to Griffon like flies. Her phone was ringing day and night. Yet she dreamed of bigger operations. Perhaps someday she would expand to the United States. She tried to place an ad in an Arab magazine. Her chutzpah knew no bounds.

Now Griffon could not handle all the requests. It was the end of May, when Monte Carlo is besieged by a hundred thousand fans coming for the Grand Prix de Monaco, most celebrated of all European auto racing events and a chance to see and be seen, to flaunt pretty girls, and to try to break the bank at the casino.

Reviewing the wiretap transcripts each day, Bencze decided that it was time to move in. After the race, Griffon was planning a trip to the Netherlands to recruit more girls. He didn't know when she would return.

As his D-Day, Bencze chose June 6. He asked the captains of the Nice, Grasse, and Cannes Gendarmerie to contribute extra men. For the invasion, he had thirty-five officers. Each man was responsible for apprehending a call girl. The arrests would all be made at 8 A.M., so the girls could not call each other and pass along a warning.

On Monday at 7:45 A.M., Bencze called Griffon's apartment to verify that she was in. He asked for a fictitious person.

"Wrong number," Griffon said.

Fifteen minutes later, Bencze knocked on her door. Eight other gendarmes stood behind him, each armed and dressed in the light blue pants, blue jackets, and visored pillbox hats of the Gendarmerie.

"What do you want?" asked Griffon's maid as she answered the door.

"Ask no questions," Bencze said. "I will ask the questions."

Griffon came to the door. "What is the reason for this?" she asked.

"You know pretty well what the reason is," Bencze replied.

"No, I don't. You are going to get in a lot of trouble, little man," she said.

Bencze looked at her impassively.

"Let's begin the search," he said, displaying a search warrant.

In the apartment, the officers found the press books and telephone numbers of the girls and a packet of envelopes containing a total of about 500 francs.

Down to the Menton station in police cars they went, along with more than forty call girls and other suspects from all over the Riviera.

Never had the officers seen so many beautiful girls.

The two-day trial took place in February 1984, before three judges of the Crown Court of Nice, presided over by Jean-Pierre Ferry. In the prisoners' box were Griffon, Khawagi, and nine other defendants, each pleading not guilty.

"I have judged you an intelligent woman," the presiding judge said to Griffon. "It is in your interest to explain yourself completely and not to play at being an innocent."

Griffon said she had no intention of committing an offense.

She was providing a service—putting together worthy young women who needed to work with another consenting adult, Adnan Khashoggi. It was a modern way for young women to earn money and for Khashoggi to please himself. It was merely, she said, "an escort service, which can be defined as offering women who were in the habit of..."

"Prostituting themselves?" the judge prompted.

"No, we rather say to have easy contact with the clients," she said.

"These clients," continued Madame Mimi, "I didn't recruit them. They contacted me, thanks to the Arab grapevine [derisive laughter in the courtroom], and, naturally, they required the prettiest, the most elegant, the most qualified."

Khawagi was equally aggrieved. "My lord," he exclaimed, "one wonders how certain people could invent such horrors on my account!"

The tribunal judges were unmoved. With the exception of one of the eleven defendants, they found each guilty as charged. Griffon got a year and a half in jail, while Khawagi was sentenced to a year in prison.

Griffon never revealed how much money she made. The French tax authorities still would like to know where she put it. But according to prosecutor Guy Robert's reckoning, she grossed $1.2 million in ten months. He figures half of that— more than $500,000—came from Khashoggi.

To the richest man in the world, it was a trifling sum— less than half his annual jet fuel bill.

# FOURTEEN

# The Swiss Bank Vault

And expend in the way of God; and cast not yourselves by your own hands into destruction, but be good-doers; God loves the good-doers.

—*The Koran*

A S Saudi oil revenues plunged to $37 billion in the mid-1980s, Khashoggi had long since diversified into other parts of the world and was only slightly affected by belt-tightening in his homeland.

Typically, he descends on a country with his planes and entourage and meets for several days with the chief of state and his ministers. In one week alone, he met with the chiefs of state of Turkey, Cyprus, Egypt, and the Sudan.

In October 1984, he descended on Canada with a barber, masseur, valet, doctor, chiropractor, financial advisers, singer Paul Anka, Lamia Khashoggi, and other members of the entourage, riding in eleven limousines to meet with Premier William Davis of Ontario and his ministers.

Earlier that year, he sailed the *Nabila* to the Far East and on board played host to seven kings and heads of state. The trip and entertainment cost $1 million, but he concluded a deal between the Philippines and Japan that will give him a profit of $6 million.

In China, he is planning a project in the Shantou Economic Zone in the southeastern part of the country. It will include a railway between Shantou and Guangzhou, a highway and a bridge, a food processing plant, an integrated fishing operation, a textile complex, a motorcycle factory, and residential and office buildings, plus a hotel and possibly a power plant.

Besides starting developments such as this one and selling new and used armaments, Khashoggi arranges bartering deals among countries. By bypassing the monetary system, he caters to the needs of Third World countries whose economies are on the ropes but have commodities to sell.

China may produce primitive marine engines that a country like Indonesia can afford. Indonesia may have bauxite that China needs. Neither country is good at promoting its products. So Khashoggi, the super-connector, arranges a trade that may involve a third or fourth country with other goods to sell as well.

The deals are often complex, involving purchases of bad loans at discounts and employing terminology like margins and credits. They are surrounded by secrecy, lest other countries learn of more favorable terms extended to others. Always, there is a political as well as a profit motive—a way of improving relations between Third World nations and Saudi Arabia through the expedient of trade.

Nowhere is that better illustrated than in Khashoggi's twelve-year involvement in the Sudan.

As the general secretary of the Arab Tourist Union, Salim Issa was in Khartoum in 1973 for the annual meeting of his group when he had an audience with Sudanese President Gaafar Nimeri.

"You don't remember me, do you?" Nimeri asked Issa.

"Mr. President," Issa replied, "if I had met you before, I would have remembered. I never had the honor."

Then Nimeri reminded Issa of a smoke-filled nightclub in Cairo. In the military at the time, Nimeri was sitting alone, while Issa and his friends were laughing it up at another table.

Noticing Nimeri looking forlorn, Issa invited him to sit with his friends.

Nimeri hadn't forgotten the favor. When he saw Issa again,

he asked him to be his counselor. Issa introduced Nimeri to his friend Khashoggi. Thus began an association that helped steer the largest country in Africa toward the West.

When Khashoggi met him, Nimeri had been in power three years, having taken over with communist support in a coup on May 25, 1969.

The muscular, energetic Nimeri was born in Omdurman, where the White and Blue Nile merge as they flow northward toward Egypt. While he wasn't an outstanding student, Nimeri managed to memorize most of the Koran and captain his soccer team at the Hantoub secondary school, an elite British boarding school in the Sudan.

Nimeri got his first taste of politics at the age of sixteen, when he joined a school strike over lagging independence negotiations for the Sudan. A third the size of the U.S., the country was then jointly ruled by the British and Egyptians.

After graduating in 1952 from the Khartoum Military Academy, Nimeri joined the military and became a lieutenant colonel. In 1964, he took part in an overthrow of the military regime of General Ibrahim Abboud but was not asked to join the new government. Instead, he went for a master's degree in military sciences at the U.S. Army Command and General Staff College at Fort Leavenworth, Kansas.

Staging his own coup in 1969 with the help of communist factions, Nimeri broke with the communists once he achieved power. Ideologically, he was drifting when King Faisal approved Khashoggi's plan to court the Sudan, just 150 miles from Saudi Arabia across the Red Sea.

Soon, Khashoggi was commuting to Khartoum on his DC-9 and lending Nimeri his yacht, planes, and homes. Khashoggi told the Sudanese leader that the Sudan could become the breadbasket of the Middle East—all it needed was some money.

Toward that end, Khashoggi got King Faisal to guarantee a $200-million loan to the Sudan. Closed on March 17, 1974, the loan from thirty-three banks was then the largest commercial loan ever made to a developing country. Khashoggi arranged for Nimeri to meet with Faisal personally to discuss other ways of improving the Sudanese economy.

For his efforts, Khashoggi got a $1-million fee—half of 1 percent of the loan amount. But that was only a portion of his remuneration. Some of the loan proceeds were used to buy trucks and other equipment from Khashoggi. And Nimeri gave

Khashoggi's company, Sudan Resources and Management Corp., the right to develop fourteen resources or industries, including cattle ranching and air transportation.

Later, when the Securities and Exchange Commission was looking for Khashoggi, Nimeri made him economic adviser to the Sudan with a diplomatic passport and the rank of ambassador—all with the knowledge of Prince Fahd, then crown prince of Saudi Arabia. But the U.S. government declined to allow him to enter the country without accepting service of the SEC's subpoena.

In early 1979, Khashoggi flew Nimeri to meet with President Carter. On the tail of his plane, the Triad insignia was painted over and replaced with "Democratic Republic of Sudan" on the side.

Carter agreed to sell to the Sudan thirteen F-5 fighter planes, to be paid for largely by Saudi Arabia, and he dispatched State Department officials to look into pumping more aid into the country.

But Khashoggi's dreams for the Sudan never materialized. To run his operations, Khashoggi appointed J. Melrod Thompson, a former Citibank and Continental Illinois National Bank executive who wore round wire-rimmed glasses and stiffly starched white shirts. His experience had been in managing loan portfolios in Chile and in developing merchant banking activities in Japan and Hong Kong. He had no experience in less developed African countries and soon encountered resistance from Sudanese government officials who resented these highly paid Americans, Italians, Brits, and Swiss.

While an elite, educated class in the Sudan wanted progress, most of the population had been living for thousands of years by raising their own food and making their own clothing. Who were these intruders to try to change all that?

Eighteen months after the $200-million loan was made, most of the money had been spent, there was no sign of new industries, and the country was virtually bankrupt. Meanwhile, Nimeri continued to shift ideologically, most recently toward Islamic fundamentalism. In September 1983, he introduced the Islamic *shariah* law which provides for severing limbs for stealing and public floggings for consumption of alcohol. Before television cameras, he smashed bottles of confiscated liquor outside the presidential palace.

The changes incensed a wide segment of the population, from university professors to army officers. The greatest opposition came from the Christians and pagans in the south, which had been on the verge of seceding when Nimeri took over in 1969.

Nimeri hoped oil discoveries in the south would augment the country's meager cash receipts. But a consortium headed by Chevron Corp. stopped building a 940-mile pipeline there after southern opposition forces killed four of its employees.

To pressure Chevron to resume operations, Nimeri signed an agreement with Khashoggi allowing a company jointly owned by Khashoggi and the Sudanese government to acquire any oil assets not then being developed according to contract. In return, Khashoggi put up a $400-million letter of credit to help finance the new company's operations.

Soon, Chevron resumed its operations.

In February 1985, Khashoggi flew to Washington to plead with President Reagan for the release of $180 million in U.S. aid withheld from the Sudan because it was in arrears with the International Monetary Fund. Boasting of Nimeri's anti-communist stance, Khashoggi pointed to the fact that Nimeri had just agreed to airlift seven thousand Ethiopian Jews out of the Sudan to Israel.

When Nimeri met with Reagan himself the following month, the President agreed to release the money and add 225,000 tons of food to help areas stricken by drought. Meanwhile, Khashoggi arranged secret talks between Baha Idriss, Nimeri's adviser, and Ahmad Qaddafi, a cousin of Libyan ruler Muammar Qaddafi. In return for an end to Libya's aid to John Garang, the leader of the southern opposition, Nimeri offered to silence an anti-Qaddafi radio station south of Khartoum.

With food supplies dwindling, Garang stepped up his attacks on the Nimeri government. Saying Nimeri had "dehumanized" the Sudanese by flogging them and severing their limbs, an anti-Nimeri broadcast attacked the Sudanese leader for forming an unholy alliance with Khashoggi.

"Is he not the man who has sold the country to Adnan Khashoggi?" the broadcast said.

On April 6, 1985, while Nimeri was on his way back to the Sudan after seeing President Reagan, Nimeri lost it all. After weathering sixteen years of coups, counterplots, economic chaos, and a threatened civil war, Nimeri was stranded in Egypt while his plane was refueling.

"The government is finished. The people stand united," his

defense minister, General Abdul Rahman al-Dahab, proclaimed on national radio.

On May 24, 1985, the new Sudanese government declared Khashoggi's agreement to develop the country's oil resources null and void.

Although he still believed the agreement would be reinstated, it seemed to be the end of Khashoggi's longest involvement in a developing nation. As billionaire Daniel K. Ludwig found when he tried to develop the Amazon jungle, a country cannot be dragged kicking and screaming into the twentieth century.

Against the gain that he would have realized if the grandiose schemes had paid off, Khashoggi had sunk only about $5 million in development costs into his projects. For all the talk of acquiring millions of acres to feed the starving, he had never really purchased anything of consequence. As in most of his ventures, his role was that of a promoter, not an investor.

It was not the prospect of amassing and managing vast, visible assets that drove him to scamper across the globe in his DC-8. It was the thrill of the hunt that propelled him, the challenge of bringing together people of diverse nationalities, getting them to focus on a need, and working out a deal. After the deal was made, he lost interest.

It was like meeting a woman for the first time and courting her. To Khashoggi, every part of the process was enjoyable—even when she gave him a hard time.

Then he tried not to fall in love with her.

Secondary was the life-style that the deals supported. If it made the late Prince Aly Khan's look humdrum, Khashoggi had no apologies. Early on, he had decided that people are hypocrites. Many would like to live as he does, to be able to go where they want, when they want, as they please. But they don't dare. They are afraid of what others may say.

Khashoggi was not bothered by the whispering. His self-confidence—demonstrated by his massively flowing signature, with its firm underlining—knew no bounds. He enjoyed living well. He had worked hard for it. Why should he deprive himself?

Besides, the lavish parties gave him access, and access meant power. At his fiftieth birthday party, Khashoggi could point to the leader of a Sudanese political party, a man who might someday become president; to the U.S. ambassador to Italy, a man who had the ear of President Reagan; and to many other notables who enhanced his credibility and might someday prove helpful.

"Where there is power, there is money," Khashoggi told his aides.

Never satisfied with his toys, Khashoggi is planning to replace the *Nabila* with a $100-million yacht to be called *Nabila II*—the most expensive yacht ever built.

Four hundred feet in length, it will be about half the length of the *Queen Elizabeth II*, the biggest ocean liner in service. Everything the *Nabila* has, the new yacht will have, plus a second helicopter pad, door handles in 24-carat gold, a Jacuzzi, saunas, and enough security devices, including antiaircraft missiles, to protect *Air Force One*.

After Soraya Khashoggi sued him for divorce, Khashoggi decided to split up his holdings to make them harder to seize.

Previously registering his companies in Liechtenstein, he now moved them to the Cayman Islands, a British Crown Colony 175 miles west of Jamaica. Here, he could shield his assets from the eyes of even his accountants.

After registering Triad Holding Corp. in the Caymans, he placed some of its most valuable assets, including the Salt Lake City properties, in a separate company owned by a Cayman Islands trust. A third Cayman Islands entity, AK Holdings Ltd., owned his personal assets, including his planes, yachts, and boats.

In the Caymans, his holdings were entirely exempt from taxation. Through the trust, he could preserve the choicest assets for his children.

Like the bedouin, Khashoggi folded his tents at the first hint of taxation, as he did when Great Britain insisted on assessing him for $500,000 in taxes in 1983 on the grounds he had a residence in London.

Khashoggi paid, but soon his presence in England faded. Once he had seventy-nine employees there and enough real estate to house the British royal family: a nine-story office building at 6 Princes Gate, where Triad maintained an office; a five-story office building at 34 Upper Brook Street, another Triad office; six apartments at Roebuck House, Stag Place, where he had a flat and offices; and other homes and offices throughout London and the surrounding towns.

By 1985, he had sold nearly all the holdings or closed them down. The exceptions were a small office for Uni-Triad Enterprises, a Triad service company run by longtime employee Mounir Chalaby, next to the Dorchester Hotel, and an interest in Lloyd's of London insurance market.

Despite worldwide publicity naming him as one of the celebrities who suffered a $165-million extraordinary loss reported by the insurance syndicate in 1985, Khashoggi actually made a slight profit on his stake in Lloyd's, thanks to insurance coverage he had purchased to cover unusual losses.

Even when gambling at the roulette tables, Khashoggi always hedged his bets.

When the press or friends asked how much he spends on personal expenses, Khashoggi or his aides always said it was $2 million a month, or $24 million a year. The figures never failed to elicit gasps, but that much only paid for running the boats and planes.

The true amount of his personal expenditures, as disbursed by AK Holdings Ltd., was $120 million a year, including such items as telephone bills, chefs and butlers, parties, gambling, limousines, and fuel. And the $120 million did not include the costs of acquiring his kingdom of homes, yachts, and planes.

Despite his wealth, Khashoggi had cash crunches like other people. For the most part, his assets are not in banks. Jealous businessmen in Saudi Arabia whispered that his balances back home were paltry compared with Ghaith R. Pharaon's or Suliman S. Olayan's.

Instead, Khashoggi's wealth is in real estate and operating companies. These illiquid assets could not be sold readily. It was one reason Khashoggi maintained $25 million in life insurance, sold to him by his friend Robert B. Williams.

Sometimes checks bounced when payments from contracts were late and money was not shifted fast enough among Khashoggi's accounts. After obtaining $50 million from a leasing deal, Khashoggi told his accountants he wanted $30 million immediately for his personal use. The accountants told him the money had already been allocated to pay off other business obligations.

It was incidents like these that fed rumors throughout his career that he was about to go bankrupt. Then, like the bedouin finding an oasis, Khashoggi would make a big hit—a $1-billion barter deal or a new arms sale. Most recently, in the fall of 1985, he got a piece of a $4.3-billion sale of British Tornado combat jets and trainers to Saudi Arabia, sharing the deal with others close to the royal family.

Then he would celebrate, taking a journey through Europe in his own railway car on the restored *Orient Express*, spending a million dollars at the special salons reserved for him at the casinos in Monte Carlo or London, or ordering a *Playboy* centerfold for an evening's enjoyment.

There were those in his organization who wondered what it was all for. Unlike Rockefeller and Carnegie, Khashoggi had no steel mills or refineries to show for his efforts. There was no Howard Hughes Medical Institute or Hughes Aircraft Co. to remind the world that he had lived.

Khashoggi knew that without him, Triad would likely fall apart, the yachts and planes sold and the tinsel and glamour forgotten.

Yet bricks and mortar were not what interested him. What drove him to achieve unimaginable wealth were people and human relations, a desire, as he put it to a friend, to "amalgamate the world."

"Unless you can communicate with other human beings, I don't care how much money you have, you have nothing for the other person," he would say.

Becoming a recluse like Hughes, wasting away in an airless room while aides shoved papers in front of him to sign, would be a useless life.

What Khashoggi needed most was people, and his money bought him that. He figured only two in ten of his friends would still be there if he had no money. But he accepted it all, accepted even the people who stole from him or took kickbacks, because most of all, he feared being isolated like King Midas, counting his gold in an empty room.

It was that same obsession that found expression in creating closer ties between Saudi Arabia and the U.S., in promoting trade among Third World countries, and in secretly helping to negotiate peace in the Middle East.

The efforts began with meetings between Khashoggi and then Israeli Defense Minister Ezer Weizman in 1978. After Shimon Peres became prime minister, Khashoggi met many times in Morocco or other countries with him or with his emissaries.

Publicly, he denied having anything to do with the Israelis, yet already he was secretly selling ammonia and other Israeli goods to Arab countries, using bills of lading supplied by the countries to show they originated in Italy.

Underlying the diplomatic talks was Khashoggi's belief that negotiations cannot be carried out in public view. Chiefs of state who take extreme positions at press conferences are likely to speak in more conciliatory and realistic terms in private.

A trusted intermediary was needed to elicit these views and convey them—a middleman who could see where differing positions might come together and propose alternatives when differences seemed insurmountable.

On the issue of participation in peace talks by the Palestine Liberation Organization, Khashoggi suggested a middle ground: a joint committee of Palestinians and Jordanian representatives who would meet with the Israelis early on to hammer out their differences.

Then, when Israel feared agreeing to the idea without a firm commitment from the other side, Khashoggi met with an emissary of Peres in London and came up with a solution.

"We will put the agreement in writing in a Swiss bank vault. Thereafter, the two sides can be secure in the knowledge that there is a signed document, available to them alone, which either side can retrieve or turn over to the newspapers in case of betrayal," he said.

After the London meeting, he flew to Tunis to meet for eight hours with PLO Chairman Yasser Arafat, then on to see Egyptian President Hosni Mubarak, King Hussein of Jordan, and Robert L. McFarlane, President Reagan's national security adviser, in the White House.

Earlier, on May 17, 1983, he submitted to President Reagan a confidential "yellow paper" outlining the results of his efforts to date. Named for its yellow cover, it was a forty-seven-page printed document that began with an introduction stating that Khashoggi had traveled thousands of miles at his own expense to elicit the views presented.

Analyzing the Reagan plan for peace in the Middle East, Khashoggi pointed out where the parties privately agreed and where they differed with the plan. Public positions to the contrary, for example, he said all the Arab countries recognize that Jerusalem will remain under Israeli control under any settlement agreement.

Then Khashoggi proposed a novel idea for moving the talks ahead. Ever since he sat on the lap of his uncle Yussuf Yassin, the adviser to King Abdul-Aziz, Khashoggi knew that political ends can best be achieved through economic means, that the carrot is more powerful than the stick.

Yet the Reagan plan contained no economic sweeteners, only barren political trade-offs. If I were an Israeli, he thought, why would I want to make peace with the Arabs? To please the Americans? Where was the incentive? Didn't vested interests like the status quo?

In the "yellow paper" and in his talks with Peres, he proposed an economic aid program similar to the 1948 Marshall Plan developed by the U.S. for Europe. Called a Peace Fund, it would provide up to $300 billion in regional economic aid from the U.S., Saudi Arabia, and Kuwait to Israel and any Arab country that signed a peace treaty with it.

Khashoggi got a positive response from Peres, and, after being briefed by Khashoggi, King Fahd discussed the idea with President Reagan when he met with him at the White House on February 11, 1985. Then Khashoggi accompanied Mubarak and Hussein when they saw Reagan separately to discuss Khashoggi's idea for a joint committee of Palestinians and Jordanians.

As in 1966, when Khashoggi accompanied King Faisal to see President Johnson, he stayed behind the scenes. Khashoggi checked into Washington's new Grand Hotel while Mubarak met alone with Reagan. After Hussein met with Reagan, the king relaxed on board Khashoggi's yacht the *Khalidia*, floating off the Virgin Islands. It was there that Hussein got the news that Reagan, in a show of support for Hussein's peace efforts, would ask Congress for $250 million in aid for Jordan.

Meanwhile, Khashoggi kept in touch with former presidents Jimmy Carter and Richard M. Nixon, asking for their views and letting them know how the negotiations were progressing.

Secretly, Khashoggi obtained approval for each move from King Fahd.

It was Khashoggi's own brand of DC-8 diplomacy, made more urgent by reports received from the CIA that the Soviet Union may be willing to give H-bombs small enough to fit in a closet to terrorist groups in the Middle East.

In the first week of November 1985, he met with five chiefs of state in an effort to nudge the talks along.

If negotiations were to fall apart, the Israelis and Arabs could deny that they had privately agreed to any of the terms of a settlement. Yet if peace comes, Khashoggi will have played an important role, according to those familiar with the negotiations.

For the world's richest man, saving the world was the next logical step in his career. As he passed his fiftieth birthday, the effort became a consuming force in his life, something that surpassed even his nation-state of homes, planes, and yachts in importance—a legacy to pass along to his children.

Besides, he knew that peace would mean more business, and his unique access to heads of state in the region would mean he would get his share of it.

Those contacts were enhanced when he secretly helped pass messages among the U.S. government, Arab countries, Israel, and the PLO during the hijacking of a TWA jetliner in Beirut and the Italian cruise ship *Achille Lauro* in 1985.

As he called Peres from his DC-8 for another frank discussion, he was already planning deals with Arab partners between Arab countries and Israel once his proposal for an aid program helped bring peace to the Middle East.

It was the ultimate fix.

# AUTHOR'S NOTE

This book is based on interviews with 139 people with
firsthand information of the subject, and on thousands of
documents in the form of internal memos, letters, telexes,
financial records, and both public and confidential
testimony in legal proceedings.

The interviews ranged from telephone conversations
that elicited key facts to tape-recorded sessions in the
United States, Great Britain, France, and Spain lasting
several days to weeks. The transcripts of these interviews
run to more than 300,000 words.

Khashoggi did not submit to any interviews until the
book was nearly finished and submitted to Warner Books.
The interviews took place in Marbella, Spain, on August 4
and 5, 1985.

So that people would be more forthcoming, nearly
all the interviews were conducted with the understanding
that no information would be attributed directly to the
person interviewed, but that the book might still refer
to him and describe his actions, words, feelings, or
thoughts.

This does not mean that because a person was
interviewed, information about him came from him. Much of

the information in the book came from memos, letters, or testimony, from other parties to a conversation or transaction, or from people in whom the participants confided.

Quotations are derived either from contemporaneous letters, memos, and transcripts or from later reconstructions by participants to conversations, as described above. To present a more readable account, quotations in most cases are not attributed to the documents they may come from. When a conversation was reconstructed by a second party to a conversation, an effort was made to obtain comment from the individual quoted.

Since the book is an independent work, Khashoggi is not responsible for any of the material presented.

While Khashoggi is widely referred to in the press as the world's richest man, there is no way to be certain that no one is richer. Estimates of his wealth—$2 billion to $4 billion—come from reliable sources within his organization. According to these estimates, his net worth exceeds the wealth of the richest Americans listed each year by *Forbes* magazine. But there are no listings of the wealth of other international figures. Even if there were, such estimates are often inconsistent or unreliable because of undisclosed liens or other liabilities, the differing ways of valuing assets, and fluctuations in market values and exchange rates.

Further, personal wealth is often confused with family wealth. Not differentiating between the two, *Forbes* one year listed Gordon Peter Getty as the richest man in America, since he controlled a $4.1-billion family trust. The following year, the money was split up among twenty-four beneficiaries, and *Forbes* estimated his wealth at less than $1 billion. Similarly, in 1985, *Forbes* listed Sam Moore Walton as the richest man in America, with $2.8 billion in stock in Wal-Mart Stores. But the stock, as in the case of Getty's trust, is held by Walton's family members and is not his alone.

Personal wealth also can be confused with national wealth. The sultan of Brunei, for example, is thought by some to be the world's richest man because his kingdom has annual oil revenues of $3 billion, and he built himself a $300-million palace. But the oil revenues are his country's, and the palace is not his but his government's.

Because of the inherent problems, personal spending, while a short-range guide, is in some ways a firmer indicator of wealth because it requires no assumptions or estimates and is more visible. By that standard, Khashoggi's annual personal expenses of $120 million clearly dwarf any other known level of spending.

In the end, in calling him the world's richest man, I relied on the fact that this is Khashoggi's reputation as reflected by the press, and no one else has been reliably identified as having a higher personal net worth.

Publications that were especially helpful include Robert Lacey, *The Kingdom: Arabia and the House of Saud*; David Holden and Richard Johns, *The House of Saud*; D. S. Roberts, *Islam*; James R. Mancham, *Paradise Raped: Life, Love, and Power in the Seychelles*; and *Saudi Arabia*, the monthly newsletter distributed by the Royal Embassy of Saudi Arabia in Washington, D.C.

The names of Saudi princes have been shortened to their more familiar form unless the longer form is needed to distinguish among them. Since English transliterations of Arabic words, names, and places are phonetic, they differ among published works.

*Those interviewed include:*

James E. Akins, Joseph F. Alibrandi, Stuart R. Allen, Willis C. Armstrong, Franklyn R. Atkinson, Joseph A. Ball, Thomas L. Barton, Roger W. Bencze, Richard E. Berendzen, Judah Best, Kenneth J. Bialkin, Jack A. Blum, Joan G. Boros, Irwin M. Borowski, Peter Butcher, M.D., Plato Cacheris, Roy R. Carver, William B. Caswell, Alain Cavro, Jean Bethine Church, Robert G. Clark, Clark M. Clifford, Erle Cocke, Jr., Hillel T. Cohn, Miles Copeland, Richard P. Crane, Jr., and James H. Critchfield.

Also John D. deButts, Gabriel Doumato, Robert H. Eddington, Hermann F. Eilts, Nesta Wyn Ellis, Robert F. Ellsworth, Ralph E. Erickson, Robert Evans, Samuel M. Evans, James Flannery, Ismet Fouad, Joseph E. Fowler, Dennis Frazier, Roy M. Furmark, E. Paul Ganz, F. William Gay, F. Michael Geddes, Brian P. Gettings, Brenda Godwin,

Roger B. Godwin, Samuel Goekjian, George J. Goodheart, Jr., Richard A. Graser, Mireille Griffon, Glen A. Grubbs, Mohamed Habib, Philip C. Hammond, Raymond A. Hare, Max Helzel, Pat M. Holt, Salim Issa, Larry J. Jacobs, Lee S. Jones, and Robert Trent Jones, Jr.

Also Adnan M. Khashoggi, Lamia Khashoggi, Mohamed A. Khashoggi, Michael R. Klein, Max B. Knudson, Yashar Kutay, Jerris Leonard, Karen G. Lerner, Jerome I. Levinson, William I. Lightfoot, Gale Livingston, Harry A. Loebel, Glen R. Lord, Dennis G. Lyons, Morton P. MacLeod, Patricia A. Makin, James R. Manchan, Charles R. McCarthy, Jr., Charles T. McCormick, John R. McDonough, John McIntee, John W. McMahan, Jack L. Melchor, Marvin M. Mitchelson, Edward P. Morgan, Edward K. Moss, Richard D. Nagel, and Camille Nowfel.

Also Robert W. Ogren, John Orsini, Henry P. Oswin, Michael F. Perlis, Karl B. Peterson, Philip A. Phalon, Melissa Prophet, Maxwell M. Rabb, Randall Reagan, Michael Reese, Harold G. Renegar, Harold Rhoden, Charles Riachi, Ambrose M. Richardson, Guy Robert, Kermit Roosevelt, Sr., Kermit Roosevelt, Jr., Charles F. C. Ruff, Brent Rushforth, Dean Rusk, Isa K. Sabbagh, Donald E. Santarelli, David Joseph A. Sarch, Daniel M. Searby, Lawrence J. Semenza, Robert A. Shaheen, Brian W. Shaughnessy, Raja Sidawi, Earl J. Silbert, Ansbert G. Skina, Eve Skina, Jerry Soderstrom, Ronald J. Sorenson, Samyr P. Souki, Stanley Sporkin, Jan Stenbeck, and Philip G. Studarus.

Also Nicholas G. Thacher, Wallace L. Timmeny, Samir Traboulsi, William C. Turner, Charles B. Tyson, Eugene R. Warner, Jacqueline P. M. Williams, Robert B. Williams, Vanessa Williams, Harris L. Wofford, Jr., Elizabeth Woodin, Zeyad A. F. Yaseen, and Daniel G. Zerfas.

*People whose accounts were obtained from depositions, testimony, internal memos, affidavits, or letters include:*

Roy R. Anderson, Thomas C. Barger, Arlie J. Blood, Ben
Collins, James Corcoran, Robert F. Ellsworth, C. Robert
Gates, Manuel G. Gonzalez, David J. Greenslade, Susan
Hadley, Charles R. Heffner, William H. Holcomb, Jr., Thomas
V. Jones, Soraya Khashoggi, Jeffrey C. Kitchen, Lawrence O.
Kitchen, F. W. Lloyd, Geoffrey Parsons, R. Grant Rogan, Neal
J. Sroka, George T. Sterling, Charles B. Thornton, Robert L.
Vader, Sean Walsh, Robert B. Watts, and O. Meredith Wilson.

*Documents relied upon include:*

Internal memos, letters, and reports of Triad Holding Corp.
and its customers, particularly Northrop Corp. and
Lockheed Corp.;

Confidential reports to President Reagan outlining
Khashoggi's role in Middle East peace negotiations;

Wiretap transcripts of the Gendarmerie Nationale in Menton,
France, and confidential records of the public prosecutor
of the Criminal Court of Nice;

Confidential transcripts of testimony and depositions taken
under the auspices of the American Arbitration
Association;

Confidential records of the Triad Foundation;

Public hearings of the Senate Foreign Relations
multinational corporations subcommittee;

Depositions and reports filed in *Triad* v. *Tumpane* in U.S.
District Court for the Northern District of New York,
*Hedenberg* v. *Khashoggi* in Supreme Court of the State of
New York, and *Habib* v. *Raytheon* in U.S. District Court in
Washington;

Memos, letters, and reports obtained under the Freedom of
Information Act from the Securities and Exchange
Commission, Justice Department, Federal Reserve Board,
State Department, Central Intelligence Agency, Defense
Department, and, through the National Archives, the
Watergate Special Prosecution Force.